WALKING THE RED LINE

WALKING THE RED LINE
Israelis in Search of Justice for Palestine

Edited by
Deena Hurwitz

Preface by
Rabbi Marshall T. Meyer

New Society Publishers
Philadelphia, PA ○ Gabriola Island, BC

Published in Cooperation with the Resource Center for Nonviolence

Inquiries regarding requests to reprint all or part of *Walking the Red Line: Israelis in Search of Justice for Palestine* should be addressed to:
New Society Publishers
4527 Springfield Avenue
Philadelphia, PA 19143

ISBN USA 0-86571-232-8 Hardcover
ISBN USA 0-86571-233-6 Paperback
ISBN CAN 1-55092-176-2 Hardcover
ISBN CAN 1-55092-177-0 Paperback

Printed in the United States of America on partially recycled paper by Capital City Press of Montpelier, Vermont.

Cover design by Anita Heckman.
Book design by Martin Kelley.

To order directly from the publisher, add $2.50 to the price for the first copy, 75¢ each additional. Send check or money order to:
New Society Publishers
4527 Springfield Avenue
Philadelphia, PA 19143
In Canada, contact:
New Society Publishers/New Catalyst
PO Box 189
Gabriola Island, BC VOR 1XO

New Society Publishers is a project of the New Society Educational Foundation, a nonprofit, tax-exempt, public foundation in the U.S.A., and of the Catalyst Education Society, a non-profit society in Canada. Opinions expressed in this book do not necessarily represent positions of the New Society Educational Foundation, nor the Catalyst Education Society.

The lines on pages xiv and 3 from "Natural Resources" from *The Dream of A Common Language* by Adrienne Rich, are used with the permission of the author and the publisher, W.W. Norton & Company, Inc. Copyright © 1978 by W.W. Norton & Company, Inc.

Dedication

I would like to dedicate this book in a way that is representative of cycles — of death and life, of struggle and hope, of pain and peace:

To Lil Moed, an American Jew who became a progressive Israeli, and who gave her self up until her death to the Israeli women's movement and the pursuit of a just peace. And also to Ahlam, the newborn first child of Zoughbi and Elaine, may she have as large a heart as her father, as strong a commitment to justice as both her parents, many Israeli and Jewish friends, and her own state of Palestine in which to grow up.

Table of Contents

Acknowledgements

This book owes its conception to David Albert of New Society Publishers, who had the grace to let others carry it forward when the concept was broadened and changed from his original idea. I am grateful to New Society's Barbara Hirshkowitz, who went from a skeptical collective member to an enthusiastic editor, always warm and helpful.

Among the other people whose contribution was indispensable, Bonnie Schell stands out. So much more than a text editor (who volunteered hundreds of hours entering copy into her computer), she became almost as absorbed as I by the material. A neophyte to the issues, she was an essential reader. Her husband, Sid, deserves thanks also, for providing his computer expertise at critical moments.

I am grateful to Roni Ben-Efrat, Daphna Golan, Haggith Gor Ziv, Mikado, and Stanley Cohen for their help in contacting writers, providing information, and critical feedback. In addition to them, thanks is due Joel Beinen, Daniel Boyarin, Barbara Epstein, Ilene Rose Feinman, Scott Kennedy, and Dave Morton, who gave my introduction a thorough and invaluable reading, and above all, Elissa Sampson, who, with her impressive knowledge and good sense, helped shape several drafts. Thanks to Marilyn Neimarck for her assistance with the preface. Maxine Nunn was helpful, as always, with the listing of organizations. Rabbi Myron Kinberg voluntarily translated several articles, for which I am grateful. Thanks too, to Amichai Asael and Anita Heckman for the cover. A word of appreciation is due to the staff of the Resource Center for Nonviolence, who encouraged the project, allowed its incorporation into my work responsibilities and into our fifteenth anniversary commemoration.

Acknowledgement should also be made to those activists who submitted manuscripts that I was unable to include: Gershon Baskin, Latif Dori, Avishai Grossman, Isaac Hasson, Hanan Hever, Avi Pitchon, Rabbi Stanley Ringler, Dalia Sachs, Hannah Safran, Chaim Shur, Toma Sik, and Dov Yermiya.

Rabbi Marshall T. Meyer

Marshall T. Meyer, one of the rabbis for Congregation B'nai Jeshuran in New York City, is an outspoken advocate for social justice, human rights, and peace between Israelis and Palestinians. A resident of Argentina from 1959 to 1984, he was the founder and first rector of the Seminario Rabbinico Latinoamericano in Buenos Aires. Rabbi Meyer became internationally known for his activism on behalf of the disappeared.

Rabbi Meyer's philosophy was deeply influenced by the legendary Rabbi Abraham Joshua Heschel, with whom he studied and worked as private secretary in the late 1950s.

Rabbi Meyer has received numerous honors for his work, including the America-Israeli Civil Liberties Coalition's Louis D. Brandeis Award for efforts to further social justice (1990); Instituto Superior de Estudio Religiosos' Maimonides Prize (Buenos Aires, 1987); New Jewish Agenda's People of the Book Human Rights Award (Los Angeles, 1985); Argentina's highest decoration for a non-citizen: Order of the Liberator San Martin, rank of "Comendador," for efforts in human rights, presented by President Raúl Alfonsín and Minister of Foreign Affairs Dr. Dante Caputo (1984); and the International B'nai B'rith Dor L'Dor Award for outstanding achievements in the service of humanity (1984).

Married to Naomi V. Friedman, Rabbi Meyer has two daughters, a son, and two grandchildren.

Foreword

Rabbi Marshall T. Meyer

Many people will no doubt be disturbed if not angered by some of the material in this book. Some because they will feel that the arguments are not put forcefully enough. Others, because they will feel that the problems raised have not been placed in the correct historical context. Yet, others are all too anxious to call Israelis who want to find a way to peace "traitors."

As a rabbi, I am aware of any number of very serious problems threatening the Jewish people and Judaism today. It is true that we have never been a monolithic people. It is true that we have had periods of bitter conflict between different sects and factions. I would be hard pressed, however, to find a moment when we have been less united than today.

There have always been fanatics and fanaticism in Jewish history, but again, it would be quite difficult to point to a period when we have had more fanaticism than today. We are ideologically, politically, economically, geographically, and religiously divided as much as at any troubled time in our past. All of these problems seriously worry me. I could add any number of other problems: the Jewish birth rate, the changes in the concept of Jewish Unity, the Jewish "class" society, the type of leadership that represents "organized," mainstream Jewish life, the intolerance between different religious currents, the lack of civility that dominates most of Israeli and Diaspora Jewish disputes. But I want to state unequivocally that the single, most serious issue facing the Jewish world today is the issue of the peace process in the Middle East between Israel, the Palestinians, and the surrounding Arab neighbors. There is simply no other problem that so impacts the destiny of the Jewish people as the issue of peace between Israel and her neighbors.

Many issues are inextricably tied into this issue of peace: the nature of Jewish continuity, the quality and very existence of the relationship between Diaspora and Israeli Jewry, the capacity of Israel to absorb the hundreds of thousands of new immigrants and the contingent formidable economic challenges that this inevitably implies, the type of Judaism to be developed in the future. All of this and more will depend upon whether or not Israel will be able to find a just and peaceful *modus vivendi* with the non-Jewish population of the State of Israel.

How Jews behave as an empowered people is the ultimate test of our spiritual legacy. To be merciful children of merciful parents, as the Talmud calls Jews, when one does not have any other alternative to being the persecuted, is perhaps a bit too easy a challenge. How Israel treats her Arab citizens and how Israel will relate ultimately to the West Bank and Gaza will directly affect the moral fiber of our people for generations. *Walking the Red Line* addresses itself to different aspects of this core problem.

I want to state clearly that I am a Zionist. I have been a Zionist all my life. For many of us, Zionism is the legitimate national liberation movement of the Jewish people. The birth and growth of Israel is one of the greatest Jewish achievements since the destruction of the Second Temple. This in no way means that I am opposed to the national liberation movements of any other people, especially the Palestinians. I believe in a two-state solution, as does a significant percentage of the Israeli population. I believe that Israelis and the Palestinians have every right to independent and secure nations. Furthermore, I believe this to be the ultimate solution. I can only pray that this will come to pass before too much more blood is shed. It is because of these beliefs that I think *Walking the Red Line* is a very important volume.

No one can complain that our world is too simple to be challenging. One is tempted to look with nostalgia at those halcyon days when we were all convinced that our globe would simply blow up with one big bang. Wherever one looks, what appeared to be on the mend is out of joint. The fall of Eastern Europe's totalitarian regimes, which for the simple-minded chauvinists of the West means the final victory of unbridled capitalism and free market technology, appears to be a gross over-simplification. Are there any prophets who would presume to tell us just what type of economy will be employed in the twenty-first century?

Those who lived a messianic deliverance when the mightiest military arsenal in the history of the world representing some 450 million people miraculously defeated the armed might of 18 million Iraqis, have begun to question just what kind of battle was fought, over what, and with what results. Even blind nationalists are pained to see television shots of starving and dying Iraqi women and children.

As our cities stand on the brink of racially, religiously, and ethnically motivated violence, those courageous fighters for human rights in the 1960s are beginning to ask themselves just what lasting victories were gained and how far the U.S. really has advanced in achieving a color-blind society of equality and justice. Those for whom the judicial process is and must be the basis of an equitable society, those for whom the demise of the liberals will finally mean "law and order," even they are wondering what the U.S. Supreme Court will do next.

If a Christian, it is altogether possible that one is involved in taking a painful spiritual inventory of just what type of religious message the Moral Majority brought to the United States. Certainly sensitive Muslims are wondering about the lack of a new theological quest capable of a synthesis in some way similar to that which made Islam viable in the Middle Ages. Fundamentalism in its multi-colored garb surely cannot be the answer to the conundrums posed to organized religion in the twenty-first century.

May I suggest that we desperately need the type of essays in this courageous volume. We need many more books of this nature. My only fear is that the majority of readers of this book will be those who are already convinced of the necessity to find a way to peace. Nonetheless, such literature, carefully researched and thought out, is absolutely necessary to help create a generation of Israelis and Arabs capable of speaking with and living in peace with one another.

Israel is not, nor will ever be, located in Scandinavia. Nor will the Arab states ever destroy Israel. Isaac and Ishmael are destined to live together. According to the biblical narrative, they finally met together over their father Abraham's grave, although what they said one to the other is not revealed. Have there not been enough graves of sons and daughters, brothers and sisters, mothers and fathers to merit the encounter in creative dialogue between the sons and daughters of Isaac and Ishmael now? Can either side really believe that there is anything to be gained by more killing, by more hatred?

May this book do its part to initiate that dialogue of which Martin Buber dreamed, not only when he worked for Jewish-Arab peaceful co-existence, but when he dreamed of the type of dialogue that inspired his "I and Thou." The "I" can only become the authentic and fulfilled "I" in the encounter with a "Thou." When there is a complete "I" and a fulfilled "Thou," perhaps we can arrive at a "We." Together, Arabs and Jews have a rendezvous with history that began thousands of years ago. May we meet again soon in the presence of the Eternal Thou.

—New York City
Erev Rosh Hashanah 5752, September 1991.

UNITED NATIONS PARTITION PLAN, 1947
AND UNITED NATIONS ARMISTICE LINES, 1949

My heart is moved by all I cannot save:
so much has been destroyed

I have to cast my lot with those
who age after age, perversely,

with no extraordinary power,
reconstitute the world.

—Adrienne Rich, "Natural Resources"

אל תגידו שלא ידעתם

Al tagidu shelo yadatem.
—*Don't say you didn't know.*

— Women in Black slogan

Deena Hurwitz

Deena Hurwitz has worked on the staff of the Resource Center for Nonviolence since 1980, currently with an emphasis on the Middle East. She received a B.A. in Community Studies from the University of California, Santa Cruz in 1980. She also works part-time with Middle East Witness' Stateside office.

A grade schooler in the 1960s, Deena recalls the excitement of the marches in Washington, D.C., and New York against the Vietnam War and for Earth Day. And, like many in the 1970s, Deena began her "career" as an activist in the anti-nuclear movement. She has helped to organize and participated in numerous nonviolent direct actions, including occasional civil disobedience, in particular focussed on nuclear power and nuclear weapons facilities. She is a nonviolence trainer, preparing individuals to participate in direct actions, and also teaching more long-term leadership training.

Deena first traveled to the Middle East in 1981. She went to Lebanon, Egypt, Israel, the occupied West Bank, Gaza Strip and Golan Heights in a trip that "changed [her] life." Since then, she has traveled to the Middle East almost annually, for the most part leading study delegations to Israel, occupied Palestine, and various Arab countries. She spent 1989 to 1990 on sabbatical in East Jerusalem, helping to establish Middle East Witness in the region, writing articles, newsletters, and urgent action alerts and learning conversational Arabic.

From 1982 to 1989 Deena was active with New Jewish Agenda (NJA) on both the local and national levels; she was cochair of NJA's national Middle East Task Force from 1985 to 1989. She has also served on the North American Coordinating Committee of the UN Non-Governmental Organizations on the Question of Palestine; the Middle East Subcommittee of the American Friends Service Committee, Northern California; the National Middle East Task Force of the Fellowship of Reconciliation; and is a member of the International Jewish Peace Union. In 1987 she attended the Palestine National Council in Algiers, representing New Jewish Agenda.

In addition to a wide range of speaking engagements and published articles, Deena is the coeditor of an oral history of World War II conscientious objectors and war resisters. "Against the Tide: Pacifist Resistance in the Second World War" was published by the War Resisters League as their 1984 Peace Calendar.

Introduction

Deena Hurwitz

> *"A passion to make and make again*
> *where such unmaking reigns."*
>
> —Adrienne Rich, "Natural Resources"

The Israeli occupation is boundaried by the "Green Line," the armistice line drawn in 1949 to separate Israel from Jordan, and now popularly used to demarcate the borders of the occupied West Bank and Gaza Strip from Israel before the 1967 War. Some Israelis, out of respect for national boundaries and opposition to the occupation, refuse to cross the Green Line uninvited — as soldiers, consumers, tourists, or otherwise privileged members of the occupying society. This refusal to collaborate with the apparatus of occupation is sometimes referred to as drawing a "red line." In other words, a red line marks the personal, moral, or psychological limit beyond which one is unwilling to transgress; or conversely, by which one is impelled to action, perhaps consciously, to incur risk. It varies subjectively: for one person the red line may be refusing to participate in a house demolition while serving with the army. For another it may be deciding to leave the country if Ariel Sharon becomes prime minister.

This book is about the ways in which Jewish and Palestinian activists in Israel perceive and approach their red lines. It is by and about those citizens struggling to gain a measure of social responsibility vis-à-vis the fate of the Palestinians, who have been pushed off their land by successive Israeli governments. Reflecting upon some of the historical, ideological, and psychological constraints and the borders of tolerance for dissent in Israel, these essays frame important questions for activists and students of Israeli social change. What motivates Israelis to protest and at what price do they do so?

Under what pressures of social consensus, what challenges and imperatives, do they protest? Is there a shared "red line" for dissent, and if so, what happens to those who cross it? The individual and collective voices of these essays answer such questions.

As in the United States, there are many different kinds of individuals and organizations working for peace, though that may be defined differently by different people. In Israel the spectrum of groups is ultimately drawn in terms of how far groups are willing to go to meet "the other side," and where the red lines get drawn. The primary division along this spectrum has been described as the difference between a movement of principle and a movement of enlightened self-interest. In other words, some in the peace movement are primarily concerned with what is happening to Palestinians, in terms of human and national rights, whereas others are fundamentally concerned with what is happening to Jews, for they see the occupation as causing the disintegration of "a democratic Israel."

Though they are the common terms used, the "peace movement," or "peace camp," as categorical phrases are too broad to be accurate. For many in the U.S., Peace Now is synonymous with the Israeli peace movement because of its emphasis on media-catching mass rallies. As in the U.S. and Western Europe, the peace movement in Israel is not monolithic, and the distinctions between groups tend to reflect some of the tensions in the society at large.

For the purposes of definition, the Israeli peace forces can be roughly divided into two camps along the lines of concern and motivation described above. The mainstream or liberal peace camp, also called the Zionist peace camp, is focused on keeping Israel a Jewish and democratic state. The progressive peace camp, also called the Left, is concerned more with human rights issues.

The mainstream peace camp essentially consists of the non-parliamentary movement Peace Now and the Zionist political parties: Mapam (old socialist), Ratz (the Citizens' Rights Movement-CRM), and Shinui (also known as the center party), along with what are called the Labor party doves. The kibbutz peace movement (related primarily to Mapam) fits largely within this camp too. For the most part it is strongly pro-U.S., perceiving the U.S. to be an "honest broker," a neutral, positive force in the region. This camp has come to the position that the occupation must end because it is a corrupting force in Israel and gives their nation a bad image abroad. They believe some form of "territorial compromise" must be arranged, but don't necessarily support the creation of an independent Palestinian state, nor accept the PLO as the Palestinians' sole legitimate representative.[1]

The most visible groups in the Left or progressive peace camp are women's groups such as the Women and Peace Coalition, Shani, and the Women's Organization for Political Prisoners; human rights organizations, for example the Association of Israeli and Palestinian Physicians for Human Rights, Hamoked/Hotline-Center for the Defense of the Individual, and the Alternative Information Center; selective conscientious objectors, like Yesh Gvul and Oriental Jewish and Palestinian Israeli groups. Also included are the Arab-Jewish political parties: Rakah/Israeli Communist Party, Progressive List for Peace, Arab Democratic Party, and Hadash/the Democratic Socialist Front. This part of the peace camp has been united on the following principles: the occupation must end, an independent Palestinian state must be established alongside Israel, and Israel must negotiate with the PLO. They for the most part support selective refusal, whereas that position is rejected in principle by parts of the mainstream peace camp (excluding the Kibbutz Youth, which voted to support Yesh Gvul and some Ratz members).

Regardless of their ideology, most people will agree that the women's movement in both camps has been the most successful of all within the peace movement. Relating as women first, and secondarily as Israelis or Jews, creates a bridge (however tenuous) not only between the two camps but also across the borders to Palestinian women (who have responded in kind). A different kind of politics emerges, as political and cultural differences become less central. Women have been in the vanguard in making the larger connections between their concerns (e.g., political power and social status) and the systemic issues at hand (e.g., militarism and the occupation—see Yvonne Deutsch's essay).

Whereas the mainstream peace camp is fully Zionist, the Left is mixed. Some groups have members who are Zionist, as well as non-Zionist, or anti-Zionist, though they may ignore the distinctions (e.g., Yesh Gvul). Other groups are more explicitly non-Zionist or anti-Zionist (e.g., Hadash and the Arab Democratic Party). To be sure, some overlap occurs within the two camps (notably parts of Ratz, especially those who are rebelling over the issues of selective refusal, and some Yesh Gvul members) but generally speaking, these issues delineate a useful polarity around which the peace forces can be mapped.

Between the two camps, considerable agreement has been established around the necessity of Israeli withdrawal from the Occupied Territories as a condition for peace. Arguments for ending the occupation have become increasingly familiar in the public sphere. From the perspective of enlightened self-interest, the demographic issue is invoked, though many in the Left consider it to be a racist argument. Assuming that the present status quo is untenable, annexing the West Bank (nearly everyone in Israel agrees that the Gaza Strip is expendable) would require some measure of civil rights for the Palestinian population, which in turn creates the possibility that a non-Jewish majority could eventually vote the Jewish state out of existence. Otherwise, such a scenario raises the spectre of apartheid, with a Jewish minority ruling over a non-Jewish majority which does not enjoy equal rights. This argument, which was favored by elements in the Labor party, has become less important as Soviet Jewish immigration and the continuing economic pressure on Palestinians makes such a demographic shift less likely to occur. There are those who also argue that holding onto the Occupied Territories eats away at democracy in Israel. And, with the government's Iron Fist policies directing the army to handle the Palestinians with punitive force, the pernicious impacts of militarism leave their mark not only on the victim but also on the oppressor. Racism is perhaps the visible tip of an iceberg whose mass contains many oft-delayed and invisible psychological impacts. These may surface in heightened levels of social and domestic violence, as well as denial, passivity, and indifference.[2] As former chief of Israeli Military Intelligence, Yehoshefat Harkabi, has said, "People are as if mesmerized by the dangers of leaving the West Bank, but are blind to the dangers of retaining it."[3]

Economic considerations suggest that maintaining the occupation significantly drains the country's resources, making it even more dependent on outside aid. With recent massive Soviet immigration, the economic arguments for ending the occupation will undoubtedly become more popular as Israel seeks to finance that immigration with U.S. government loans and grants.

In addition, security arguments against the occupation are expertly posed by some former Israeli generals and security advisors. For instance, the Council for Peace and Security makes the case that the West Bank provides absolutely no added measure of security, no real land buffer in an age of SCUD missiles, for example. Moreover, ruling by force over a Palestinian population which has demonstrated its resolve to resist, and which grows increasingly militant with every new generation, actually heightens Israel's insecurity.

Finally, some parts of the peace movement argue that the occupation must end for the pure and basic reason that it systematically violates the national and human rights of the Palestinian people. Moreover, as long as Israel continues to do so, it can't become a legitimate and accepted part of the region, which it presently dominates militarily due to U.S. support.

The peace forces differ over which arguments are the most critical and appropriate. But how and why the occupation should be terminated is not the only area of divergence. At least as important, and not unrelated, are the differing ways Israelis view the history of the overall relationship with the Palestinians through the course of this century, particularly the rights and wrongs of the various wars (including the most recent one). Did Palestinians have legitimate claims prior to 1967 and at the time of the founding of Israel in 1948? Although critical discussions of Zionism, and consideration of its mistakes or transgressions, are almost taboo in the U.S., they are more easily raised and debated in Israel, as reflected in this collection of essays.

And where Zionism constructs certain codes of allegiance, it presents another red line by how far one will go in empathy with, or expressing agreement with, for example, Palestinian perspectives. There are those who believe that the concept of loyalty ultimately draws the line between the peace camps: loyalty to the "Jewish nation" and state, versus loyalty to some universal values, such as human rights, that when consistently applied, might mean aligning with "the enemy" against one's own society.

The Gulf crisis brought out some of the starkest differences among Israelis. Whereas it dealt a serious blow to the peace movement as a whole, the Gulf crisis also illuminated antagonisms between the liberal and left perspectives. It operated like a Rorschach, mirroring basic instincts, prejudices, and motivations. For example, Knesset Member (M.K.) Yossi Sarid reacted angrily against the Palestinians who, by supporting Saddam Hussein, betrayed those Israeli doves like himself who had risked so much in dialoguing with them.[4] Mainstream peace personalities such as Peace Now leader and Labor dove Yael Dayan and novelist Amos Oz, among others, held a press conference after the Gulf War broke out, backing the war and dissociating themselves from the anti-war protests in Europe and the U.S. During the crisis, this part of the peace movement stood publicly with the Israeli political consensus that the threat to the region came not from Israel's ongoing occupation, but from Iraq's. Dayan was quoted by the Jewish Telegraphic Agency as saying, "Sometimes there are wars that are necessary to attain peace.... Peace Now in Israel means War Now."[5]

Eventually, a consensus of sorts emerged among the mainstream peace forces as a result of what left activist and *The Other Israel* editor Adam Keller described as "frustration at the sudden polarization of political sympathies."[6] The mainstream peace camp proceeded with a "twin-track policy," which meant agreeing to disagree with the Palestinians over the Gulf crisis, but to resume talks with them over the question of Palestine.

Several aspects of the mainstream peace camp's response were strongly critiqued by the Left. First of all, the suspension of dialogue with Palestinians — Peace Now's favored strategy — was based on a feeling of having been betrayed, as if the Palestinians should have acted with Israeli interests in mind, or at least more "responsibly" to them. The nuances of the Palestinian position interested few. For instance, the PLO had condemned the Iraqi occupation of Kuwait. And Palestinians felt their options were a choice between supporting the

U.S., defined as Israel's benefactor and the country that had moved thousands of troops into Saudi Arabia to change an Arab problem into an excuse to dominate the region militarily; and supporting Saddam Hussein, a fellow Arab and PLO benefactor, who had attacked another Arab country. Palestinians perceived it as hypocritical that Iraq's occupation of Kuwait would provoke the mobilization of Western troops in one week, whereas "their" occupation has continued for close to a quarter of a century, and is effectively supported by the U.S.

The dialogue itself had been based on what left activist and academic Stanley Cohen has described as "asymmetrical motivations; on the Israeli side, the politics of bad conscience" and enlightened self-interest;[7] and on the Palestinian side, necessity and coming to terms with their oppressor. Adam Keller has described the history of the dialogue process thus:

> Israelis who met with the PLO [in the years before 1988] desperately wanted some kind of statement from the PLO that would recognize (at least implicitly) Israel's right to exist. They needed this, not least in order to justify talking to the PLO.

> This meant that until 1988, the dialogue with the PLO was confined to a small section of the Israeli peace camp [the Left — ed.], while groups like Ratz and Mapam always declared that they were willing to meet with Palestinians from the Occupied Territories, but would talk to the PLO only if it renounced terrorism and recognized Israel. Once the PLO's position changed in 1988, there was a palpable feeling that a watershed had been reached, the major obstacle had been overcome, and everything could now progress more smoothly. The difficulties experienced during the Gulf War may have exposed these hopes as somewhat naive, and when the dialogue is restored (which is already starting to happen), there will probably be a certain wariness, a fear that was not there before: 'We all agree today, but what may happen tomorrow to divide us again?' It may be that this shift is for the better, insofar as it is probably more realistic. [8]

Moreover, Cohen points to a perennial but hidden truth exposed by the Gulf War: with the possible exception of Eastern Europe, the mainstream Israeli peace camp is the only peace movement in the world that is pro-U.S. And so Israeli "doves" were heard condemning the international anti-war movements.[9] While not denying the "real or potential threat to physical existence," Cohen considers Israeli liberals' uncritical stance toward U.S. foreign policy to be "pathological." [10] This uncritical stance strikes a familiar chord to those whose ear is attuned to the unconditional support of many American and European Jews for Israel.

Other parts of the peace movement took a broader view of the Gulf crisis. Prior to the actual war, Yesh Gvul published a statement (September 3, 1990) which condemned the "Israeli right-wing government for its hypocrisy in denouncing Iraq's occupation of Kuwait while exercising the 'iron-fist' of occupation" against Palestinians. The Israeli Council for Israeli-Palestinian Peace took a similar position in an ad in the mainstream daily *Ha'aretz* (August 17, 1990), blaming Israel for driving the Palestinians into Saddam Hussein's arms.

A press conference was convened on February 6, at which a new movement, Dai ("Enough") presented a petition calling for an immediate cease-fire, the withdrawal of Iraqi forces from Kuwait to be followed by the withdrawal of all foreign troops from the Gulf states, and a negotiated end to the Gulf War. Signed by 126 Jewish and Palestinian Israeli peace activists and public figures, the Dai statement called on Israel not to join the war despite Iraqi provocations, as "Israel's entry [would] only aggravate and complicate the achievement of Israeli-Palestinian peace afterwards." The dean of the Israeli Left, Professor (Emeritus) Yeshayahu Liebovitz, maintained that Israel was drawn into this war in the Gulf because of its government's unwillingness to withdraw from the Occupied Territories, and that "continued occupation and oppression of the Palestinians must eventually lead to a full fledged fascist regime inside Israel, and to the unification of the entire Arab world in a war against Israel." [11]

In his address at the same press conference, Major General (Ret.) Matti Peled also criticized the U.S. for its refusal to accept linkage, referring to Saddam Hussein's initial offer to withdraw from Kuwait if Israel withdrew from the Occupied Territories. "Had Bush declared his willingness to convene an international conference after the Iraqi withdrawal from Kuwait, Saddam would have faced the dilemma of either withdrawing or losing his image as the savior of the Palestinians." [12]

Though many describe the Gulf crisis as having split the Israeli peace movement, in truth it was already seriously fractured. The crisis certainly separated the pro-U.S./anti-PLO forces from those favoring a regional solution and opposed to Western imperialism. But the demoralization and fragmentation of the peace movement in the wake of the Gulf War resulted inevitably from fundamental problems previously existing within and among the various groups.

These essays underscore some of the larger contradictions emerging not simply from the Gulf crisis, but from the questions of why and how people dissent in Israel. Working for social change in any country is a frustrating and often lonely road. In Israel it can be especially difficult because the urge to belong has such a harsh genesis. It is like a homing instinct bred by generations of persecution (or finely tuned manipulation of that legacy for political ends or both). In a society that feels itself threatened, whether one agrees that this feeling is rational or not, conformity is a survival tactic. The risks of being put outside the consensus can seem enormous.

As activists, many of the writers find themselves on a collision course with very fundamental aspects of their society. A critical evaluation of the forces involved in maintaining the occupation brings people face to face with the structures and conditions of power and privilege. In Israel the powerful are primarily Jewish Ashkenazi (Jews of European origin), and privilege is firmly rooted in the military. Confronting these structures sometimes leads to questioning the premises upon which they stand: nationalism (i.e., Zionism) and loyalty, militarism, and a national security ideology that promulgates a normalized state of emergency.

In emergency situations, normal conditions of democracy are seen as subservient to national security needs. Most Israelis, including many peace activists, accept that as a necessary evil. In fact, since the founding of the state, Israelis have been told that they were under "emergency" provisos. Israelis have a firm belief in the apparatus of law (their disregard for international law in the case of their occupation notwithstanding). The various laws that were applied in Palestine before 1948, including the British Emergency Defense Regulations (EDR) Act of 1937 and Regulations of 1945, and Ottoman laws, remained in effect when Israel was established. Ironically the British EDR Act, applied equally against the Palestinian uprising of that time and the Jewish underground, became the basis for placing Palestinian Israeli citizens under the direct control of the Israeli Ministry of Defense from 1948 until the military government was finally abolished in 1966. Palestinian Israelis were routinely subject to curfews and, among other things, pass-identification systems. [13]

Thus, a legal basis for social repression exists in Israel, and the occupation, which depends on a veneer of legitimacy, has developed on this foundation. Whether by serving in the army (and lawyers do perform their reserve duty in military courts), patronizing a store with a sign in its window announcing "No Arabs employed here," or accepting the delineation of ethnicity on one's passport or ID card, everyone collaborates in one way or another in this system. This point was stunningly drawn out in an article-cum-diary-entry written by Ari Shavit during his reserve duty as a guard at Ansar II prison in the Gaza Strip.

> When the formation breaks up, when I go to my tower, tower No. 6, I understand that the problem is the division of evil labor. A division that allows evil to be done here without, it would appear, any evil people. The people who voted for Likud are not evil. And the ministers who sit in the government are not evil. They do not bury their fists in the bellies of children. And the Chief of Staff is not evil. He implements what the elected administration obliges him to

implement. And the commander of the detention facility truly is not evil. And all things considered, the interrogators are just doing their job. And it would be impossible to control the territories without their work.

And the jailors for the most part are not evil. And nevertheless, in some surprising way, all these non-evil people together produce a very evil result. Worse than that: the result is really evil. And evil is always more than the sum of its parts. The sum of its implementers.... That is to say: despite our Beetle Bailey appearance, we are evil. Unadorned. Rather, our evil is evil in disguise. A clever evil. That is, it is an evil which apparently happens all by itself. Evil without evil-doers. Without anyone to take responsibility.[14]

Moreover, with society mobilized around what is portrayed as an unremitting need for self-defense, the concept of a "people's army," composed primarily of rotating reservists, has become an expression of democracy and citizenship. In the West, most peace activists and leftists equate the army with an instrument of the state in its most repressive sense. This Israeli democratic impulse obscures the militarism, and propels peace activists onto the army bus to defend the nation and make the army more responsible and moral. It brings out what in Israel is referred to as the 'shoot and cry syndrome,' made famous in a satirical song ("Yorim U Bochim") by rock star Si Himan. Militarism and brutality become acceptable when they are accompanied by remorse on the part of those who nonetheless correctly do their duty.

Not coincidentally, many privileges of Israeli society (e.g., passports, health insurance, welfare benefits, and in some cases, housing) are "earned" through army service. Veterans benefits function at the level of social services in most other countries. As such, these benefits, of course, are inaccessible or available on a very different basis to those who don't serve, such as Palestinian citizens and Jewish conscientious objectors — one clue as to why conscientious objection is not terribly popular. Thus, a "selective resisters" movement like Yesh Gvul draws its strength from the fact that its members are reservists who have proven themselves "on the battlefield." It is important to be beyond reproach in terms of motives. Yesh Gvul makes it clear that their resistance is based on politics, not cowardice. Having earned their place in society, they feel they have a more credible ground from which to criticize it. Peace Now takes this even farther. Founded by officers, not reservists or enlisted men, the movement greatly values rank and status. But, notably, although using the army to maintain the occupation or to advance an offensive rather than defensive war (as in Lebanon) is now a subject of debate, questioning the institution itself is a red line crossed by very few.[15]

Consensus in any society is based on complex historical and socio-political events and competing political and economic trends. The omnipresent psychodynamic of the Holocaust, firmly institutionalized in Israeli society, gives a self-perpetuating force to the national security ideology and its partner, militarism. Despite the occupation, and all that it means, the Israeli people feel themselves victimized. And victims cannot by definition be oppressors. This powerful semantic trap serves to mitigate responsibility, while at the same time making any references to Nazi Germany strictly taboo, and keeping Israelis from drawing conclusions about how the oppressed can also oppress (see Gabi Nitzan-Ginsberg's essay). "While we would like to think that the experience of oppression makes one more sensitive to other people's suffering," American Jewish activist Elissa Sampson has pointed out, "in fact, prior suffering is no guarantee of future morality. Moreover, the empathy factor is greater when we're not involved."[16] Politicians make very effective use of this victim-only psychology, and it weighs in the choice of tactics and timing for activism.

Along with this victim mentality, denial also helps to build and maintain consensus. This functions in the Diaspora Jewish community as in Israel. Denial manifests itself on different levels. For example, it appears in myths about Zionism and the founding of Israel, and in arguments like that made by Joan Peters in her widely debunked polemic (*From Time Immemorial*) that Palestinians didn't exist before 1948. Yet another perspective sees Israeli militarism as purely self-defense ("we have no choice" because "the Arabs hate us"), which functions in its most raw or honest form as demonization of Arabs. It should be noted that the Intifada forced many Israelis (even in the peace movement) to genuinely see Palestinians for the first time. It was also the Intifada that caused parts of the peace movement to declare that they should and would respect national borders, and stay out of the occupied West Bank and Gaza Strip unless expressly invited.

Still another dimension of Israeli social consensus that influences activism is the issue of identity. "Who is a Jew?" and "What is an Israeli?" are questions which have been (and are still) contested legally, culturally, and religiously. Many North Americans use "Jew" and "Israeli" synonymously, although 17 percent of Israelis are not Jewish. In 1986, Mohammed Miari introduced a plank in the Progressive List for Peace platform during their campaign for the Knesset to call Israel "the state of all its peoples," as opposed to "the Jewish state." It was struck down because it leaves out reference to Judaism. [17]

The massive Soviet immigration currently has Israel's chief rabbis up in arms, since the government is granting the right of return to anyone married to or in the family of a Soviet Jew. Since "Jew" in the Soviet Union has been defined by a Soviet identity card, and determined paternally (as opposed to maternally in Israel) without regard to inter-marriage, this means that many who are immigrating are not Jewish, religiously or culturally.

All issues of identity are relevant on various levels: the right of return, or who gets to immigrate, and the social position they acquire once there. Generally speaking, ethnicity frames prejudice in Israel the way race does in the U.S. Religion, of course, supercedes all else; non-Jews are second-class citizens. Palestinian Israelis are lowest on the totem-pole, with Oriental Jews next; European Jews are the dominant group (see essays by Marcello Wechsler, Meir Amor, and Rev. Riah Abu El-Assal).

The connections between social problems in Israel and the Israeli-Palestinian conflict are hotly debated within the Israeli peace movement. Some see the two as inextricably linked, both historically and in terms of any future resolution. Others believe that issues of class, gender, or other social inequities are secondary, and should be dealt with only after the "bigger" or "political" problem is resolved.

Oriental Jews, like women, are increasingly constructing their arguments to show the relationships between the occupation and their social concerns. Understanding the socio-political dynamics of any subgroup and the many social issues at hand requires untangling a complex web of events and motives based, among other things, on the occupation's history, the use of pre-'67 legislation in a post-1990 world, and subtle racism rooted in European superiority — dynamics which affect Palestinian Israelis and Oriental Jews alike. Indeed, just as the pre-'67 emergency legal structure was so easily transposed into the apparatus of occupation, the occupation has forced a reevaluation of the role of Palestinian Israelis.[18]

*   *   *   *   *

Israel prides itself a democracy. One measure of democracy, at least in the West, is the level of dissent it tolerates and how it deals with those who challenge it. Israelis themselves have a phrase which underscores the relatively low personal cost for activism; they call it the "peace movement *deluxe*." It should be clear that this refers to the mass-rally sort of activism. Democracy has a certain elasticity in this regard; it accommodates the challenges — up to a point. Beyond that is a red line, a border between protest and confrontation.[19] Those who cross that line sometimes discover that they are outside "the family," themselves treated as a threat to the national security (see essays by Roni Ben-Efrat and Michel Warschawski). But sometimes by crossing that line, or even by walking along it, they succeed in disturbing the "consensus" enough to begin to effect change.

Besides being Israeli, the contributors to this volume have at least another thing in common: they are trying to derive meaning and a sense of purpose out of the contradictions of their society. They choose to stay and struggle within Israel. There is no great feeling of heroism or righteousness involved. As Michel Warschawski puts it, "When your house is burning, it doesn't take courage to jump; you just do." A sense of necessity transcends the ideological camps.

Despite — indeed, because of — the special relationship between Israel and the U.S., Americans find it difficult to look critically at Israeli policies. By exposing the range of debate in Israel, these essays chip away at the argument that criticism of Israel, or even debating the premises of Zionism, is inherently anti-Semitic. Such discussions need to be part of an active discourse — embracing pluralism and tolerant of difference — in both our countries.

A debate goes on in the U.S. (especially Jewish) and Israeli peace movements about whether pressure from outside, particularly from the U.S., will help shift Israeli right-wing intransigence, or freeze it, causing the government to dig its heels in further. Some question the legitimacy of outside pressure. But the role of the U.S. government in the region is hardly neutral, and certainly not altruistic where Israel is concerned.

Israel receives nearly $4 billion in aid from the U.S. government annually, making it the largest recipient of U.S. foreign and military assistance in the world.[20] As increasing numbers of Israelis are realizing, Israel would very likely be unable to maintain its present course — not to mention its character in the region — without such outside help (see essay by Shmuel Amir). The "fungibility" of aid makes it possible for the Israeli government to continue the occupation and its settlements policy. Both have been condemned by successive U.S. administrations, which, aside from making statements to that effect, have done little to reinforce their opposition on the level of policy.

While the U.S. government expresses a concern for Israeli security, it continues to sell arms to various Arab states at war with Israel. At the same time it encourages Israel by selling it enough arms to be able to maintain its qualitative edge over all the combined Arab forces. Indeed, the role of the U.S. government in proscribing the conflict and driving the opposition in Israel (as at home) cannot be overstated. The problem of arming all sides in the region has been stated. The U.S. helped build Iraq's power as a tool against Iran only to discover it had created a monster with an independent mind. Israel will also take as much U.S. aid as it can get, but balks indignantly whenever its policies are scrutinized from "outside." Bush's "new world order" is ominous not only because it establishes U.S. military predominance in the region (as well as worldwide), but also because its "peaceful" side is equally hegemonic, guaranteed to maintain U.S. interests, which rest with Israel and the West's perceived Arab allies.

The Baker plan for an Arab-Israeli-Palestinian peace conference is insidious; at face value it sounds a whole lot better than the status quo. But U.S. plans for Israeli-Arab peace pay only lip service to the Palestinian question. The best they will offer Palestinians is a form of autonomy; but not national self-determination. A two-state solution will not be in the cards; not without a great deal more pressure — on the U.S. as much as on Israel.

The fact that the Israeli government wishes to dictate who may represent the Palestinians does not make activists in Israel rally in large numbers. The mainstream peace camp is behind the U.S. all the way. But the U.S. peace camp is no better. Aside from Middle East peace groups, the larger peace movement hasn't quite made the transition from outrage at the hubris of U.S. imperialism to the far subtler manipulations of our government's "peace plans." The U.S. peace movement doesn't stand as a model for Israelis. It can hardly claim to be any more effective in illuminating and confronting the core issues and abuses of power in the Israeli-Palestinian conflict.

Insofar as the U.S. supports the status quo in the Israeli government, and rejects a two-state solution, it too should be seen as part of the problem. Thus implicated, the American people on the whole need to understand the issues more fully and in the context of world perspective. Examining the issues of Israeli-Palestinian peace as central to both genuine security for Israel and a just resolution to the conflict is a good start. Unfortunately, until we perceive it in our own self-interests, the conditions and pressures in the region are not likely to make a big impact at home. But the connection — and it is growing in significance — is U.S. aid. Bush's delay of the vote by Congress on the $10 billion housing loan guarantee to Israel in the fall of 1991 implicitly if not explicitly linked U.S. aid to our foreign policy priorities for the first time since Eisenhower threatened Israel with a loss in aid if it did not withdraw from the Suez Canal. This position, which put Bush in direct collision with the Israeli Prime Minister and the Israel lobby, received an 86 percent favorable rating in the U.S. public, according to an ABC poll.

For all those who seek fundamental social change, a new political and social thinking is essential; especially learning a history that differs from the one we were taught in school. This is no less true in the U.S. than in Israel, as 1992 celebrates the five-hundred-year anniversary of Columbus's "discovery of America," bringing "civilization to a savage land."[21] It is important to question and to disturb fundamental myths of legitimacy here at home. Albeit often fleeing persecution in our countries of origin, we North Americans must confront our own history of land expropriation and European cultural imperialism, our denial of rights to the pre-existing civilizations of Native American tribes.

The danger of complacency in the face of injustice is that injustice becomes routine. It loses its sharp edges as it begins to be accommodated by society. Each year that the Israeli occupation continues, it gets increasingly normative; the right-wing drift becomes more entrenched and harder to change.

In the final analysis, the peace movement is critically important to Israel. Regardless of their ideological camp or where they draw their red lines, on various levels these activists confront conformity in an environment that reifies it. They insist on challenging not only the society, but also each other to not get used to the effects of an enduring occupation. Where the official maps intentionally incorporate the Occupied Territories into Israel, the forces for peace and justice reassert the Green Line, insisting that Israeli policies not be invisible.

Israeli activists must struggle to maintain the clearest grasp of reality, to keep their values intact, and to find meaning and a sense of purpose in their daily lives. But they *are* a force for change in Israel today. They continue to greet deception and injustice with truth and hope and the will to change. The dedication of a chapbook of poems, *Peace Talks*, by Shaul Knaz to his activist wife, celebrates this decidedly obstinate hope:

> To Channa,
> who has the strength not to understand
> why THEY don't understand.

—Santa Cruz, California
October 1991

Notes

1. Some Zionists do accept the PLO and support a two-state solution. Feminism tends to be a countervailing force, and the women's groups as a rule are the most progressive, even in the mainstream peace camp. Thus, for example, Reshet (the Women's Peace Net) and some in Peace Now, may be an exception here. They slide both ways depending upon the circumstances and what the U.S. is saying. After the Gulf War, there was marked decrease in mention of the PLO. But Reshet, represented by Yael Dayan, participated in the May 1991 Women's Geneva Conference for Israeli-Palestinian Peace. Women from Israel, Palestine and thirteen other countries produced a consensus document which referred to a two-state solution.

2. Hebrew University professor Stanley Cohen gave a lecture on this subject, "The Psychology and Politics of Denial: The Case of Israeli Liberals," at the

Psychological Barriers to Peace Conference, organized by IMUT, May 24, 1989. His paper was published in Hebrew in *Amirot Al Shtika* (Words on Silence: the Silence of Israeli Society in the Face of the Intifada). Haggith Gor Ziv, ed., ICPME, Tel Aviv, 1989. English translation from the author.

3. Yehoshefat Harkabi, "The Fateful Choices Before Israel," Essays on Strategy and Diplomacy, No. 7, The Keck Center for International Strategic Studies, Claremont McKenna College, Claremont, CA (January 1987): p. 19.

4. M.K. Yossi Sarid (Ratz) published an article in *Ha'aretz* shortly after the Iraqi invasion of Kuwait (8/17/90) entitled, "Let them try to find me," in which he announced that he was breaking off contacts with all Palestinians. His remarks were widely criticized in the Israeli Left.

5. Elissa Sampson, "The Gulf Aftermath: Israeli-Palestinian Peace Prospects," *International Jewish Peace Union/New York Newsletter*, May 10, 1991.

6. "An Interview with Adam Keller: Postwar Prospects for the Israeli Peace Movement," *Peace and Democracy News*, Summer 1991, p. 29.

7. Stanley Cohen, "Justice Under Fire," *Tikkun*, Vol. 6 No. 2, p. 24.

8. Keller, "Postwar Prospects," p. 30

9. Because of the nature of U.S. interests and U.S.- backed governments, many movements for social change are working to remove U.S. controls or domination in their countries. In various parts of the world, the Middle East among them, the U.S. is associated with reactionary and repressive regimes and policies, and anti-U.S. sentiment is growing accordingly. To the extent that Americans don't realize or understand the negative attitudes with which people in such areas perceive us and our government, we are increasingly isolated and out of touch with a reality that will continue to haunt us (e.g., through incidents like hostage-taking, bombs at military installations and other sites, and terrorist actions against Americans abroad). Israel is in a certain way similarly isolated, by virtue of its policies and the occupation.

10. Cohen, "Justice."

11. "Prominent Israelis call for an end to the Gulf War," press release from Dai, February 6, 1991. It should be noted that there were also varying positions concerning the war among U.S. Jewish Middle East peace groups; and they reflect more or less a similar dynamic to the one which distinguishes Israeli peace camps. Most of the U.S. Jewish groups (outside of the mainstream Jewish community) that work on these issues from an essentially Zionist position (e.g., *Tikkun* and the Jewish Peace Lobby) basically supported the troop mobilization and could not unequivocally oppose the war. Others (e.g., New Jewish Agenda) were more outspokenly against the war, but were ambivalent about what to do about it, given the composition of the anti-war movement (in some cases openly anti-Israel, which raises the specter of anti-Zionism and anti-Semitism). Groups on the left (e.g., the International Jewish Peace Union), and pacifists (e.g., the Jewish Peace Fellowship) were clearly against the war and (in the former case at least), full participants in the anti-war movement.

12. Dai statement, op. cit.

13. Adam Keller, "The Arabs, Israel's Unequal Citizens" and "Civilian Control and the Koenig Document," in *Terrible Days, Social Divisions and Political Paradoxes in Israel* (The Netherlands: Cypres Press, 1987). For a thorough treatment of the topic, see Ian Lustick, *Arabs in the Jewish State: Israel's Control of a National Minority* (University of Texas Press, 1980). For an examination of the "legal" basis of occupation, see Raja Shehadeh, *Occupier's Law: Israel and the West Bank*, (Washington, D.C.: Institute for Policy Studies, 1985).

It is interesting to note the parallels, both in substance and time, with the U.S. South in the days of the early civil rights movement. Although the conditions of emergency are certainly quite different in Israel, the practices and taboos of segregation and racism, among other things, are similar. Further analogies can be found in the obstacles social change activists faced in both countries at the time, especially identifying the problems and making their eradication an accepted topic of public discourse.

14. "Ansar Camp Duty Report, 12 Days on the Gaza Beach," by Ari Shavit, *Ha'aretz*, May 3, 1991, translated and published in English by *Al Fajr* Palestinian Weekly, East Jerusalem. The *New York Review of Books* published a slightly different version, "On Gaza Beach," July 18, 1991.

15. The efforts of Adam Keller to be granted conscientious objector status is a case in point. Adam did his three years of military service and served in the reserves for thirteen years. In 1989, at the age of thirty-four, his opposition to the army's measures against the Palestinian population in the Occupied Territories brought him to request an exemption from the army. This took him a step beyond Yesh Gvul, of which he is also a member, which supports selective refusal of service in the Occupied Territories, but accepts alternative assignments within the Green Line. His exemption request was turned down, and he was ordered to present himself for military duty. Upon his refusal, he was sentenced to twenty-eight days imprisonment and taken to Military Prison No. 6 in Atlit. The following statement is from an open letter written by Adam:

> On arrival at the prison, I was ordered to wear a military uniform. I refused that order too. Thereupon, the guards stripped me naked and put the uniform on me. Even my underwear was taken away, on the grounds that it was colorful, and thus in contradiction to prison regulations which permit prisoners to wear only white, army-issue underwear. I did not actively resist the guards when they undressed and dressed me, but after the uniform was put on me, I started a hunger strike in protest. For two weeks I subsisted upon nothing but sugared tea. During this period, a psychiatrist was brought in, who asked numerous questions about my political views and my childhood. A few days later I was informed that the army had decided to exempt me from military service on psychiatric grounds. It seems the army resorted to this means since Israeli law recognizes only the right of women — but not men — to conscientious objection. Altogether I spent three and a half weeks at Military Prison No. 6, mostly in the prison's Isolation Ward, reserved for prisoners considered to be 'troublemakers.'

16. Elissa Sampson, private conversation, New York, July 1991.

17. In fact, in a deal struck for balance between the competing Labor and Likud alignments, both the Progressive List for Peace (PLP) and Meir Kahane's ultra-nationalist Kach party were banned from running by the Knesset Election Committee; the PLP for being anti-Zionist and Kach for being racist. The PLP was reinstated by the Israeli High Court only three weeks before the election; still they managed to seat two Knesset members: Mohammed Miari and Matti Peled. Kach was not reinstated.

18. My appreciation to Elissa Sampson for helping me draw out these points, among others.

19. Michel Warschawski elucidated this in a public discussion in Santa Cruz, July 4, 1991, where he said, speaking of the Israeli peace forces, "Protesting a policy is one thing; confronting and challenging it is another. In the end, our primary allegiance is to each other, not even to Palestinians with whom we share a common political analysis. Until we are able to be disloyal to our tribe, we will not change anything. We will remain a radical minority, no longer fringe [perhaps], but still small."

20. "The Money Tree, US Aid to Israel," reprint from *Middle East Report*, No. 164/5 (May-August 1990):

> In addition to taxpayer dollars, Israel receives some $2.5 billion/year in private US funds: an estimated $1 billion in short- and long-term loans from US commercial banks; some $500 million worth of Israel Bonds sold by a US firm, Development Corporation for Israel, in turn owned by the non-profit American Society for the Resettlement and Rehabilitation of Israel; and about $1 billion in donations from private citizens. Adding these amounts brings the total private and public money flow from the US to Israel to about $6.2 billion/year.... Israel has the highest GNP per capita of all US aid recipients ($6810). In 1991 Israel [was estimated to have received] more *US aid per capita* ($686) than the total *GNP per capita* of many countries, including Egypt ($670), Morocco ($620), and Sudan ($330).

21. Ironically, in the midst of the anti-Muslim and anti-Jewish Inquisition, Columbus set out in 1492 to search for a new and more direct trade route to the Far East, reputedly to circumvent Turkish and Arab middlemen in between.

Haggith Gor Ziv

Haggith Gor Ziv was born in 1953 at Kibbutz Ginnossar, one of the oldest kibbutzim in Israel. Originally from Czechoslovakia, her mother lived through the Holocaust, hidden in a convent part of the time, and living part of the time with forged documents in Budapest. Her maternal grandmother survived Auschwitz, and they emigrated to Israel in 1948. Haggith's father came from a very Zionist family which immigrated to Palestine from Austria in 1936. He was very active in the establishment of the state of Israel, fighting initially with the Jewish Brigade in the British Army, and then with the Haganah Underground. He played an active role in bringing illegal Jewish immigrants into Palestine. He was a career Brigadier Colonel in the Israeli Defense Forces, though he chose to leave the Army to devote himself to his kibbutz. There he had a management position and later became a businessman. In 1959 the family left the kibbutz because they felt it had lost its idealism, and they moved to Beersheva. Haggith's mother pursued a career there in special education.

Haggith spent five years in Los Angeles, from 1972 to 1977, obtaining a B.A. in Judaism from the University of Judaism, and an M.A. in early childhood education from UCLA and the University of Judaism. She currently teaches at the Teacher Training Institute in Tel Aviv, training early childhood educators. She is also Education Coordinator with the Tel Aviv-based International Center for Peace in the Middle East (ICPME) and writes curricula on democracy, coexistence, and peace education. Her curriculum for kindergarten through twelfth grade on the Israeli Declaration of Independence ("My Declaration of Independence," published by ICPME, 1988) was distributed to 250 schools nationwide by the Ministry of Education.

Haggith is active with various peace groups, including Shalom Achshav (Peace Now) and The 21st Year. She edited a book, *Amirot Al Shtika* (*Words on Silence: The Silence of Israeli Society in the Face of the Intifada*), published in Hebrew by the ICPME in 1989. She currently lives in Tel Aviv with her two children.

I, Tel Aviv, 1990

Haggith Gor Ziv

I was a small child during the Eichmann trial.
The sounds of the quarrels at home still ring in my ears.
He, my father, in a condescending voice, "Those Diaspora Jews,
Sheep led to the slaughter."
She, my mother, in a trembling voice, "You don't understand, you
Weren't there."
At night I used to hear her crying.

He gave utterance to hidden anger, frustration and revenge.
She, to the aloneness of flight, the pain of the inscrutable.
When the quarrels intensified and he would loudly declare:
"They should have rebelled, refused to cooperate."
She would ask: "And where were you then? What were you doing?"
"We didn't know," he said, "If we'd known..." he said.
"If you'd known," she would say, "if you'd known how to listen to
the children's fear, the people's pain,
then and now —
you might be a little less right, a little less judging...."
He in his arguments and she in her aloneness.

He conceived of the Holocaust through a suppressed anger at the
weakness, the degradation of dying stripped of self-respect,
Scorning those who didn't resist or fight back.
She wanted him to grasp the shattering, the suffering,
her affliction growing during the Holocaust.

He built a fantasy of a Jewish state,

A state where we would never be weak,
murdered, led to the slaughter.
She in her pain built a dream of a state of peace
where all would be equal and free,
a state of justice.

He thought that if the Jewish people had enemies,
he should react with arms, self-defense, proud death.
He fought in the Jewish Brigade, the British Army,
in Israel's War of Independence, was a colonel in the army.
She thought to form a loving society with no discrimination,
where no one ridicules Jewish children at school.
She wanted a place where her children wouldn't wake up,
hearing in their nightmares soldiers' steps approaching their house.
She came to the country on the "Exodus," went to a kibbutz,
studied education, worked with hospital children
and as a consultant in special education.

Both of them, he and she, believed that a democratic Jewish
state was the answer....

And I, Tel Aviv, 1990,
some of him and some of her,
a lot of second-generation Holocaust dreams
with other children, other soldiers,
I in a country of fear and silence.

I, Tel Aviv, 1990,
some of him and some of her,
shattered myths of the Jewish national state,
strength and power
broken by many small lies of politicians
Golda agitating the border during the War of Attrition,
while oriental youths screamed about ethnic discrimination.
Amiram, my friend, was at the front. He told me:
"When they said on the radio that the Egyptians attacked, they
    were lying, we got a command to open fire...."
Soldier after soldier...
the sanctity of life, a myth.

The Yom Kippur War,
I was in Los Angeles, phone connected to Jerusalem,
The papers said defeat,
we knew before they did how bad things were,
but we didn't tell them, so they wouldn't worry.

They knew before we did that Eitan had been killed
but didn't tell us,
so we wouldn't worry
hiding information to deter the pain,
lie after lie,
funeral after funeral.

It was only later that I learned Sadat tried to initiate peace,
before the war.

The war in Lebanon....

Myth after myth,
the broken debris of my father's myths, a Jewish state,
religious coercion, Jews who have murdered innocent Arabs
pardoned by the president of the Jewish state.
The broken debris of my mother's myths,
discrimination against Sephardi children,
a rubber bullet in the crushed brain of Muhammad Bassam Hamdan,
eight months old,
the demolished home of Diab Assad Smaaneh,
the hand of Avi Sasportas sticking out of the sand.[1]

Tel Aviv, 1990,
some of him and some of her,
trying to get my life in order
to live in Israel, my country,
my language, my landscapes, green borders,
my red lines.

My life in the shadow of the Intifada,
the Palestinian War of Independence, war of stones.
I make contact with Palestinian intellectuals,
through political activism
touch their fantasies, their dreams
of a Palestinian state where they will not be weak,
discriminated against, humiliated.
A state of peace, equality for all and freedom,
a state of justice for which they long.
My life in the shadow of the Intifada,
in face of the plastic bullets, the tear gas, the live bullets,
my life in face of stones.
In the name of my father's dream,
my mother's dream is crushed.

Want to ask him, my father, his opinion of the Jewish strength
that fires at Fatma Abd Al Salaam Abu Hadir,
nurse,
in an ambulance evacuating wounded from the Temple Mount.
Dr. Tarek sustained leg wounds.

Want to ask her about the boy,
M.W.R., twelve and a half,
beaten during an inquest at the Jerusalem Police Headquarters
from three a.m. till ten p.m. stuffed in a sack,
beaten with a stick.
Interrogation.
He confessed like all the rest.

I wonder how he would explain.
"Isolated incidents," he might say,
rejecting the attempts to investigate the complaints.

My father wordless in his grave (Oct. '66, missed the war)
My mother silent, cries.
He in my imagination, she and I
flee from seeing what has become of the fantasy,
theirs and mine.

My life in the shadow of the Intifada,
trying with all my heart to get wise, grow up,
grasp the knowledge of immoral conduct, illegal acts committed
by my army, my police,
to overcome the terrible anger at legends gone.
Reading only parts of the papers, trying to ignore, forget, what
goes on thirty kilometers from here,
trying to keep the sanity I need to send the kids off to school
every morning.
Clutching at activism in the peace movement, in education,
in counter-culture?
Composing curricula on democracy and peace,
warding off the helplessness, the aloneness.

I, Tel Aviv, 1990,
want to live with a clear-sighted grasp of reality,
to look for the truth, non-mythical,
want to keep my values intact, my identity,
my personal Jewish meaning,
want to live without giving up the things I believe in,
some of him and some of her.

Wondering if. If I can live
and how
in a country that breaks bones according to race,
that breaks into homes and terrifies children.
If I can live
and how
in a reality that invades dreams with fears and knives,
demolished homes, deportation, roaring crowds.
If I can
and how
meet the eyes of children who sleep in tents in the rain?

I, Tel Aviv, 1990
live with a definite sense that the pain and the nightmare will
end only in a just solution of equality for them too
a state for them too
that will be like ours
built on fantasies, disappointments and shattered myths.

Note

1. In Israel, "the Arabs don't have names" — Palestinian victims all too often
remain anonymous. Muhammad Bassam Hamdan and Diab Assad
Smaaneh are the names of two victims of the occupation. Israeli victims, on
the other hand, become household names, national tragedies. Avi Sasportas
was a soldier whose disappearance led to a major search, involving
thousands of people. His murdered body was finally discovered, buried in
the sand near Ashkelon.

Rabbi Jeremy Milgrom

Rabbi Jeremy Milgrom is the cofounder and codirector of Clergy for Peace, an Israeli/Palestinian interfaith initiative of Christians, Muslims, and Jews working for justice and peace in the Middle East. He completed his studies at the Hebrew University in Jerusalem and at the Jewish Theological Seminary of America in New York and has served as rabbi of Conservative congregations in Israel. Jeremy has also taught at the Hebrew University and Teachers College. He is a frequent lecturer in Israel and abroad at international conferences, in synagogues and churches, on university campuses, and for activist groups on the subject of Middle East peace work and the potential contribution and real impediments of religion towards it.

He completed three years of active duty, including combat training, in the Israeli army, as well as sixteen years of reserve duty, the last eight of which involved conscientious objection, starting from refusal to serve in the war in Lebanon and ending with refusal to carry a weapon, which finally led to his release from the army. Jeremy has been active as an organizer, spokesman, and draft counselor in Palestinians and Israelis for Nonviolence and Yesh Gvul. Most of the men whose marriages he has performed have been in jail for refusing to serve in Lebanon or the Occupied Territories.

Like many Israeli activists, his primary measure for the integrity and viability of his peace efforts is in the upbringing of his three children, who have been junior participants in Jewish/Arab dialogue Sabbaths and have been at joint volunteer work camps and at countless protest rallies. Jeremy's most rewarding moment in recent memory came when his oldest daughter, Kinneret (whose birth nine years ago set off his conscientious objection), declared that when she reached eighteen, she would not serve in the army.

The Responsibility of Power

Rabbi Jeremy Milgrom

I choose to relate personally to the spiritual costs of the century of struggle between Jews and Palestinians, of which the occupation represents only the most recent, dramatic, and tragic phase. Most of what follows reflects the pain of my own loss of ideological innocence, which has taken place during the last twenty-three years of my life in Israel. I have lived these years within various substrata of Jewish Israeli society: as an alumnus of both B'nai Akiva (the youth movement of religious Zionists, which is closely associated with the National Religious Party — NRP-Mafdal) and secular Jewish Jerusalem's blue-blooded Gymnasia Rehavia (the private high school of the elite); as a soldier in the regular and reserve Israeli Army; as a rabbi and lecturer among educators working to establish a Zionist common denominator between religious and non-observant Israeli Jews; and as an activist in intellectual and activist circles of the Israeli Left. Over the past decade I have spent the major part of my professional life in dialogue and organizing efforts with Palestinians on both sides of the Green Line, and feel that this association has become an indispensable part of my Israeli identity. Finally, as an immigrant who never cut his ties with his community of origin, the American Jewish experience looms large for me—as a source of values (in the past), disappointments (in the present) and a major arena in the hope for ideological and political breakthroughs.

I began composing this article with ambivalence. I feel that advocating the establishment of a separate Palestinian state, the most logical and just resolution of both the occupation and the Israeli-Palestinian conflict in general, would be re-embracing nationalism, and so a step down from aspirations that are more lofty and value-oriented. It has taken me most of these twenty-three years to recognize that Zionism, as a late nineteenth- to early twentieth-century expression of Jewish survival, cannot be the measure or standard of Judaism for me. I wanted therefore to let the *religious* (as opposed to the *national*) side of the Jew speak. But if my nonchalance, if not iconoclasm (and that of many other Israelis) regarding national symbols — the flag, anthem, president, etc. — makes emotional and ideological sense only after my nationalism has been validated, it would seem that my predilections are not the place from which to start when relating to Palestinian national aspirations. In fact, the more I pondered my own experience, the clearer the essential role of national frameworks became.

As a Jew born into civil rights and equal (if not "higher") opportunity in the United States, moving to Israel became an opportunity to escape from the unwillingness of white America to redress its injustices to American Blacks. As a descendant of Russian Jews who reached Ellis Island in the early 1900s, I felt no responsibility for these indelible blots on U.S. history. Still, I was viscerally shaken by the horror of the American racism I encountered when moving from a segregated elementary school to an integrated junior high school. This was my last stop as an American. Physically intimidated and morally overwhelmed by the victims of a society to which my family and I were basically newcomers, I was relieved to leave behind the burden of witnessing that seemingly unsolvable predicament. We made aliyah; we immigrated to Israel.

By experiencing my peoplehood in a way only possible in Israel, I found a way out of that alienation. As an identifying, practicing Jew in a "Jewish state" then barely twenty years old, I had exchanged the marginality of the Jew, the perennial minority in every American framework, for a taste of the responsibility of power. It took me almost ten years to wake up to the fact that Israel, too, neglected its "minorities;" and another decade passed before I realized that this suffering was structural and not incidental — inflicted by the very elements of collective religious/cultural identity I had come here to celebrate.

I am not alone in recognizing the need to see another reality beneath the varnish of our ideologically colored perceptions. In fact, this direction is alive and well in certain circles in Israel (although too often braced with a massive dose of incapacitating cynicism). Yet it is considered outright heresy (*kofer ba'ikar*) in the Diaspora, where myths live an extended lifetime.

We Jews saw ourselves as unique in history, having maintained our existence in exile for two thousand years until the return to our ancestral home was made possible by circumstances and international consent (and guilt feelings). But that didn't change the fact that we were still colonizers. Ideological formulations based on nineteenth-century European nationalism and alliances with imperialist countries found Jews eager to see themselves as the bastion of Western civilization in the "primitive Levant." Add to that nascent Arab and pan-Arab nationalism, and historic Arab (and non-Arab) rejection of the national dimension of Judaism. The resultant mix sealed the enmity between the two peoples and ignited the embers of cultural and religious differences with the fuel of competing nationalisms. The Arabs, particularly the Bedouin, were reminiscent of the nomadic Patriarchs, and there was the romanticism of the Orient. But they were still "natives." Just as God had instructed Abraham to follow Sarah's lead regarding her domestic rival, Hagar, his Egyptian mistress, so too, could we do with them as we saw fit.

A favorite Zionist escape from responsibility is to see the conflict as predestined, primordial, the latest expression of universal anti-Semitic antagonism to the Jew qua Jew (*Esav soneh l'yaakov*). This approach tries to slip the activist, nationalist characteristic of Zionism into a history of passive persecution. Under Ottoman rule, the Jewish community in the land of Israel/Palestine during the pre-Zionist era (before 1880) was largely composed of pilgrims with no national intentions, who generally enjoyed a subservient coexistence with Arabs. National liberation for this community of religious Jews was envisioned as coming through supernatural messianic intervention, prayer, and piety. In fact, an overwhelming majority of the current Jewish population of Israel is here not as Jewish nationalists or their descendants, but arrived as refugees, or the descendants of refugees.

Zionism's basic goal of providing "a national home for the Jews" did not carry with it an explicit or even conscious program vis-à-vis the Arabs. However, the chronic blindness of Zionism to the existence of the Palestinians, epitomized by the famous aphorism "a land without a people for a people without a land," was ominously myopic. During the sixty years of pre-state Zionist activity, Jews and Arabs raced against each other in society building, according to rules set by European powers, while Zionism functioned with short-term pragmatism, without considering the consequences of ignoring its impact on the resident people. The hostile, frequently violent reception accorded them by Palestinians did not engender cooperation but rather set the pattern of unilateral, oblivious action by Jews.

On the positive side, many Jewish activists incorporate the struggle for minority rights in Israel into their Zionism. They see it as an expression of Judaism and a patriotic duty, basic to the survival and moral standing of the state of Israel and its Jewish majority. An example is Ben-Gurion's famous statement that the entire Zionist enterprise isn't worth the tears of a single Arab child.) Thus the chauvinism of the national-religious (NRP) Zionists is ostensibly challenged by a liberal religious nationalism that shares the same goals but emphasizes tolerance of the non-Jew (the *ger* — the stranger), a prominent theme in Jewish heritage. I have generally identified with this tendency, although a number of factors make me feel increasingly uncomfortable here.

On the ideological level, I believe that Zionism must be separated from the state of Israel: Zionism is a matter of concern for Jews and as such, is either the business of the worldwide Jewish community, and not just Jewish Israelis, or the concern of Jews in Israel and therefore should not be imposed upon the non-Jewish citizens of the state. Zionism promotes the communal existence of Jews in the land of Israel (Zion), while the domestic policies of the state of Israel must serve the interests of all its citizens, and its foreign policy reflect its participation in the global family. State policy which tries to produce demographics "favorable to the Jewish people" will inevitably lead to discrimination, for example against non-Jews in Israel, and because it curtails the freedom of Soviet Jewry to emigrate wherever they choose.

Intellectual honesty demands recognizing that the tolerance in the classical texts extends primarily to individual non-Jews, not to a collective people demanding national self-determination and sovereignty. But it is rather in bad taste for immigrants to refer to the original inhabitants of the land as "strangers." There is definitely strong Jewish support for inalienable Palestinian rights and for the vision of genuine coexistence, but it has not been adequately articulated by religious peace activists.

Finally, on the spiritual level, I began to see that I was overloading the ambiguous symbolic language of religion with political urgency. As this struggle came to represent for me a prophetic Judaism, the observance of a holiday or the performance of any religious ritual began to dim in significance. I now realize that the dialectic of my Zionism has driven a stake between me and most Jews. Without community, it is hard to be religious; yet the communion of human rights activism lacks the transcendence of religion. I am challenged to acknowledge my attachment to my people without worshipping its paranoia; to accept my national identity without losing my own self-determination; and most important, to retain a belief in the accessibility of spirituality in wells that have quenched the thirst of people working from all directions.

Like Jonah, whose flight to Tarshish did not save him from the necessity of confronting Nineveh, I know I will never live in a painless, idyllic society free of conflict and grievance. Unraveling the intertwined Palestinian and Israeli national movements, and reconciliation between them, seems so distant that generally concerned people do not see past the immediate political issue of ending the occupation. But beyond the ephemeral headlines and debates, in my efforts to maintain long-range visions of justice and peace, two nightmarish examples of U.S. national and group struggle remain primary to me: the pursuit by American Blacks of civil rights and the tragic history of the Native American people. While drawing these analogies cannot take everything in each situation into account, it provides useful analysis, depressing hindsight, but also hope and energy for seizing critical moments in a reality that is still in formation.

The more frightening of these North American legacies, the genocide of Native Americans, is rather remote, but increasingly accepted as relevant, as the Israeli-Palestinian conflict reaches new depths of savagery during the Intifada. More and more Israelis express themselves in terms of "us or them." The close call suffered by the Jewish people during the Holocaust, far from sensitizing them to the abuse of power in the service of inhumane ideology, has made them obsessed only with their own vulnerability. "Never Again" means "Never Again *to us*"—all threats to Jewish existence must be eliminated, at any cost. This includes, if necessary, even an entire nation of innocent bystanders. Israel's rejection of comparisons with racist South Africa is not as categorical as it once was; the history of unholy alliances with repressive dictatorships makes for a strange empathy with power under siege. The release of the Palestinian people is essential to the resurrection of Judaism, the very goal that Zionism set out to accomplish.

The denial, mostly latent, or at least ambivalent, of Palestinian nationalism, is now the most radical force in Israeli politics. On the religious plane, these forces invoke an apocalyptic pseudo-messianic Judaism with antinomian tendencies or an intolerant tribal ("biblical") religion. Many Israeli expansionists seek to validate the secular aspects of the ideology of Greater Israel by comparing it to the nineteenth-century U.S. doctrine of Manifest Destiny, equating the Jordan River to the Pacific Ocean. However, in a post-imperialist era, world opinion, if not Jewish moral restraints, will it is hoped not allow the genocide of the Palestinian people. That Israel should expect to get away with its subjugation of the Palestinians, as the Russians did with Lithuania and Latvia just before World War II, is anachronistic wishful thinking, particularly in view of the recent melting of the Cold War blocs. The sympathy and guilt accorded to the Jewish people via Israel after the Holocaust has largely dissipated, and the political and economic privileges Israel has enjoyed will not last forever. Diplomatic recognition of Palestinian nationalism is almost ubiquitous and is here to stay, as long as the Palestinian mainstream continues to embrace territorial compromise and mutual recognition and does not force the international community to choose between the two nationalisms.

The Intifada is convincing evidence of the collective Palestinian will to live. The de-stratification of Palestinian society, signs of solidarity both within the territories and among the more assimilated segments of the community abroad, and the pervasive willingness to confront the occupying forces and make the ultimate sacrifice have surely strengthened national identity, even if political dividends have not been forthcoming as yet. The Green Line has been restored to the public consciousness, and most Israeli civilians confine their commercial and recreational lives to the pre-'67 border. However, the Jewish settlements are firmly entrenched, and the physical risks in living in the territories have not deterred new settlers from taking advantage of government incentives to move there. Israeli society relates to the Intifada largely as an inconvenience, and doesn't see the price of occupation as too expensive, emotionally, morally, or militarily. It seems willing to respond to the escalation of violence by Palestinians with more lethal, draconian, and increasingly anarchistic measures of reprisal.

Yet, as the Intifada has indicated that the Palestinian people are surviving occupation, the proper conclusion might be that they survive not *because of* but rather *despite* the Intifada. If the political struggle for self-determination cannot be won at this point, perhaps the most effective long-term strategy would be to maintain the presence on the land at all costs (*sumud* in Arabic). Leaving aside morality, it must be said that the prospect of mass deportation of Palestinians from the West Bank is real enough to demand reconsideration of the sanctioned use of violence, including stone throwing, as part of the Intifada.

It might help to differentiate here between active non-violent struggle and non-violent passivity. Palestinian Israelis (Palestinians who did not flee or were not expelled in 1948 and who have Israeli citizenship) have responded more by accommodating than by resisting their subjugation. They thereby earned a contempt from, among others, Palestinians suffering occupation, which has turned into grudging admiration in circles that have come to see their steadfastness on the land (*sumud*) as no less heroic than the organized confrontation with Israeli authorities of the Palestinians in the Occupied Territories. But I perceive a difference in the two communities through my political and ideological partnerships with them.

The Palestinians I know in the West Bank cities of Bethlehem, Beit Sahour, Ramallah, Batir, Nablus, Hebron (al-Khalil), and so on, are primarily middle-class professionals, academics, and clergy; and have been under Israeli occupation since 1967. The following partial list of "routine" hardships they suffer goes largely unreported in the local and international media. Every one of them has:

— 1. been under round-the-clock curfews for days and weeks on end. In refugee camps like Jabaliya and Jalazoun curfews have lasted for thirty-five days and more, with only a few hours off once a

week to stock up on essential foodstuffs. This pre-dated the Gulf crisis when the curfew lasted the full duration of the war.
— 2. had their houses invaded by soldiers, and many have been choked by tear-gas grenades set off inside their homes.
— 3. either been put in jail themselves and/or members of their immediate family have been jailed, finally to be released without charges.

Virtually every one has been treated with brutality and unnecessary harshness by Israeli "security forces" whose real job is to break the spirit and dignity of the Palestinian people. Yet each of them radiates an amazing spirit of openness, pride, acceptance and lack of bitterness, a deep concern for what Israeli decree may come next but also a confidence in their ability to find Israeli partners who will join them, morally, if not physically, in the struggle.

Despite years of involvement in dialogue, interfaith, and anti-racism organizing in Israel, I haven't been able to celebrate this uplifting feeling with Palestinians of Israeli citizenship. Although I can testify to the presence of elements essential for coexistence—acceptance of the other and willingness for compromise and reconciliation—the underlying feeling I have more and more is that of dealing with a subdued, truly occupied population. The Palestinians in the West Bank and Gaza *know* that it is just a question of time before they will be freed of Israel and are able to choose to relate to me and my fellow Jewish activists when and how they want (as they do now under duress). Palestinians in Israel proper have lost both their birthright and their blessing. Their brethren are in exile, they have lost almost all their lands, they are socio-economically disadvantaged, and they have become a minority in their own homeland.

Marginal to the national ethos, proletarianized and under-represented in the echelons of power, the cause of the Palestinian Israelis is as basic to Israel's survival and moral standing as the eradication of racism, the legacy of two hundred years of slavery, is to the U.S. It has been, however, an almost silent cause for the last forty-three years, overshadowed by Israel's external security problems with the Arab countries and international terror, and since 1967, by issues pertaining to the occupation of the West Bank and Gaza. It is as if there were a pact of neglect, signed by pro-Palestinian activists and Israeli apologists alike, in which the unsqueaky wheel gets neither grease nor even sympathy. Meanwhile the lack of resolution looms as an enormous Pandora's box, undermining and nullifying understanding and progress.

The redress of the injustices suffered by Palestinian Israelis would require the repatriation of the Palestinian refugees, who number between two and three million, the rebuilding of almost four hundred villages destroyed after the war of 1948, and the restoration to

Palestinians of agricultural lands expropriated over the years "for the public good" (i.e., for Jewish farmers). Since these demands would entail a major restructuring of the Israeli society and economy, and could jeopardize the sacrosanct notion of the Jewish majority ("the demographic balance"), they are suppressed and rejected by most Palestinian Israelis as too radical and unattainable. What remains of their national aspirations is the demand for individual civil rights. Whether they will succeed or not depends *ideologically* on Israel's commitment to being a pluralistic Western democracy and not merely a nation-state, and *practically* on a lessening of external security concerns. As long as the state of war with neighboring Arab countries and the Intifada persist, chances for progress are slim indeed. Currently, government surveillance, if not direct control, exists over every area of Palestinian life in Israel. For example, sermons in mosques are recorded, and security clearance must be gained by applicants for teaching positions in elementary schools and for foreign funding of voluntary organizations. This high level of control will continue to be seen as a legitimate exercise of Jewish sovereignty in the interests of "national security."

The average Israeli does not consciously embrace a platform of discrimination against Palestinian citizens of the state; nor is she or he wont to deny the existence of the injustice. The official rationalizations are beginning to be seen as just so much propaganda. But sentiments of coexistence and tolerance are generally couched with the demand that they "behave themselves," and refrain from nationalist statements. For example, problems arose in negotiations between Peace Now and the Committee of (Israeli) Arab Mayors concerning slogans to be used at the "Time for Peace" human chain that stretched across Wadi Ara in the Galilee on January 12, 1991. The demand for an explicit statement of the PLO as the representative of the Palestinian people, a sentiment held unanimously by the mayors, was rejected by Peace Now as too provocative. In these mainstream peace movement circles, issues such as the right of return (*haq al-awdah*) of Palestinian refugees and the restoration of expropriated land are not legitimate topics for discussion. Seen as digressions from the struggle to reverse the currently controversial government occupation policies, these issues have been pushed aside and sealed off by the Israeli consensus. Peace Now tries not to step outside this consensus.

Whereas Peace Now prides itself on its spirit of compromise and sacrifice in promoting the risky idea of territorial concessions for peace, its carefully crafted aura of pragmatism and self-interest negates the softness of empathy and reconciliation, the emotional dimension essential in melting the non-rational resistance to peace found among so many Israelis. The tactical separation of efforts to end the occupation and the "unmentionable" root issues of justice undercuts the universal, spiritual appeal of peace. Thus, ending the occupation is reduced to an issue of partisan politics. As long as the peace is perceived as territorial compromise without a clear demand for justice, it will be suspect in the Jewish public's eye. It seems a twisted logic, perhaps, but Jews would perceive such a peace as a disingenuous camouflage of more radical demands which they, putting themselves in the shoes of Palestinians, imagine they could never suppress.

Much of Israeli society has lost its faith that justice can be attained in the Palestinian-Jewish conflict. Like Nietzsche, it sees morality as the weapon of the weak; in this case, the Palestinians. For Jews, it is (and has been) military might and diplomatic stubbornness that make right and are the only applicable instruments of survival; hence the awful affinity many Israelis feel towards totalitarian regimes that are also fighting for survival. However, despite their obvious preference to look after their own interests in this way, I believe many Israeli Jews are deeply troubled by this alienation from justice and desire reconciliation. They need to see a solution which they can look squarely in the eye, not just in terms of realpolitik, but of Jewish morality and compassion.

There has been a thorough and official whitewash of the injustice done to the Palestinian people and a systematic eradication of Palestinian roots. This erasure is fervently expressed in the transformation of abandoned Arab homes into highly-sought-after real estate and of villages destroyed in 1948 into campsites. Beyond the Green Line in the West Bank too, Canada Park was planted on the site of the village of Emmaus, destroyed in 1967. Formerly Arab streets and neighborhoods are renamed in Hebrew. Yet, amazingly enough, this revisionism meets up with occasional resistance, as evidenced by the popular use of original Palestinian names of neighborhoods, campsites, and mountains. The Palestinian refugee may have been eradicated from the Israeli textbook, but he or she is not an abstraction (as is the Native American for most North Americans). The majority of Israelis have at least a limited relationship with a Palestinian who has a brother or cousin in exile. Such issues are perhaps rarely verbalized in their interactions, and may be treated as incidental, but there is little doubt that they lurk in the background, with surprising doses of frustrated empathy.

Most Jews cannot be blamed for their ignorance of mistaken, generally short-sighted, occasionally deliberately discriminatory policies, and the resulting suffering on both sides. Truth is but one additional casualty in this ongoing conflict; disinformation is a weapon developed and maintained in the laboratory of the propagandists. There is, however, a disturbing cynicism among those who do know; a passivity that ultimately spells a lack of responsibility for redressing the grievances. It is a copping-out that we can no longer afford or tolerate.

My rationale for being in Israel has obviously been transformed through the above process of revelation. My prognosis has certainly been sobered by the continued mistakes and failures of all sides to the conflict, the peacemakers notwithstanding. As a Jew, I am more upset by Jewish failures and feel accountable for them. I understand Israeli intransigence as the product of anger and insecurity due to European anti-Semitism culminating in the Holocaust, which has fueled a desperate energy to survive, which castigates Palestinian interests standing in its way as inferior and illegitimate, if not outright evil. I am constantly stunned by our irrationality when we prefer to accept and prolong a bad situation instead of negotiating for a better one. I see this irrational behavior as inseparable from, a continuation of, the Holocaust. Love has not vanquished over hatred; despite the redistribution of international power, the universal law of the preservation of aggression has only found a new victim.

I still feel, however, that the situation is not irreversible. Our conflict is not ageless. Israel does not carry the burden of an extended oppression of the Palestinians; most of the refugees of 1948 are still alive. Nor is there a legacy of Arab anti-Semitism. From a global perspective, the recent monumental reforms in Eastern Europe and the amelioration of apartheid in South Africa prove the susceptibility of doctrinaire regimes to forces of democratization. I believe that the human spirit will prevail here as well.

Gabi Nitzan-Ginsburg

Gabi Nitzan-Ginsburg was born in Israel in 1964. His parents, both immigrants from Argentina, met in Israel. His mother learned the language very quickly and became a Hebrew teacher. Later she became the principal of the WUJS Ulpan (adults' Hebrew school) in Arad. His father was a third (and last) generation butcher, a chain which began in Russia, flourished in the cannibal realms of Buenos Aires, and died pitifully in Israel, leaving him no choice but to start a new career. Gabi spent an itinerant childhood, in Israel and abroad. From 1967 to 1969 the family lived in Buenos Aires, and in 1971 they moved to Colombia, both moves for his father's work with the Jewish Federation.

Gabi grew up in a very Zionist family; his grandparents' generation was almost completely erased by the Holocaust. Yet, their basic ideology is one of humanism, anti-racism, and anti-nationalism. Gabi writes, "I don't think my mother could write such a sentence as 'There is a similarity between Nazi Germany and Israel.'" I wrote that sentence in the following essay, with tremendous efforts. I hope that my daughter or son will be able to write that sentence in a more steady hand. More than anything, I wish they will have no reason to write such a thing."

At the age of eighteen, Gabi was drafted into the army; it was during the Lebanon War. It was then that he began writing for newspapers. "I called the editor of *Coteret Rashit*," writes Gabi, "which I believed to be the best newspaper in Israel, and told him a few lies about myself (by army laws, soldiers aren't permitted to have anything to do with the media). He knew I was lying, but he figured that was the army's problem." At first he wrote articles under a pseudonym; later he wrote an unsigned column vaguely based on *The New Yorker's* "Talk of the Town." Finally, he completed his army service, and began signing his columns. He started to write a new, more politically oriented column at the same newspaper. Two dominating topics in the column were feminism and the Palestinian problem.

In December 1989, Gabi and a friend founded an organization called Red Light, in an attempt to stop police brutality against Palestinian workers in Israel. The volunteer hotline answered calls every night, from young Palestinians who were beaten, tortured, or abused. Red Light went with them to police stations (to complain against policemen) and to hospitals, to give legal advice. Red Light's sudden exposure of so much brutality created a public lobby against police violence. For the first time, the police found themselves prosecuted in court for beating up Palestinians. After Red Light's first year of activity, there was a clear decline in the statistics of police brutality against Palestinians in the Tel Aviv area, where the main problem existed.

After *Coteret Rashit* was closed, Gabi started working for the daily *Hadashot* ("News"), where he now continues to work.

"Feminist men are still an exotic item in Israel," writes Gabi. "Even women's feminism isn't very legitimate in most Israeli circles. My writing on feminist topics, although consisting of nothing original, received a lot of response. In 1990, I received the annual prize of the Israeli Women's Lobby, for contributing to the raising of the status of women. I have felt a little uncomfortable, because I know that if a woman had written the same articles, she wouldn't get half the attention. On the other hand, this is the best prize I've received since school days, and I don't really mind."

Gabi is married to Aimee Ginsburg, who was born in Cincinnati, grew up in Los Angeles, and moved to Israel at the age of eighteen. Also a journalist, she makes documentary radio programs. They have one dog and one cat.

Living Comfortably with Taboos

Gabi Nitzan-Ginsburg

Every group which oppresses another learns, at some point, that in order to continue the oppression undisturbed, it is necessary to manipulate some strong social taboo, one which is widely adhered to. Violent husbands can cruelly and fearlessly beat their wives; they are protected by the taboo which says that dirty laundry is washed at home, not at police stations. Perverted fathers (or other members of the family) can sexually abuse their children expecting no intervention; they are protected by the taboo that children mustn't speak of sex, and certainly not with strangers. Sadistic commanders and officers in the IDF [Israeli Defense Forces, the Israeli army — ed.] training camps are able to harass and even terrorize young men to the point of suicide (unofficial statistics testify to at least two suicide attempts a week); they are protected by the taboo saying men may not be weak.

We, the Jewish nation living in Israel, have a taboo under whose protection we are able to ignore widely accepted moral codes. Our taboo is so dominant and so awesome that even within the most liberal and tolerant circles it may not be mentioned. It begins with a "sh," it ends with an "ah," and there's an "o" in the middle. [Shoah, or Holocaust–ed.]

The Shoah is not a taboo, of course, when it comes to the Jews-as-victims. Arafat has been explicitly named Hitler by the Israeli Prime Minister. Around here, the equation between the PLO and the Nazis is not only legitimate but actually encouraged. A comparison,

Originally published in *Amirot Al Shtika (Words on Silence)*, edited by Haggith Gor Ziv. Reprinted with permission from the International Center for Peace in the Middle East.

however, if only for the sake of differentiation, between Nazi Germany and post-occupation Israel? Any suggested attempt of linking the Holocaust and our present lives would be the most morbid and monstrous disregard of taboo imaginable.

Why? Why is it allowed to debase the *Shoah* by tenuously comparing Nazism to the Palestinian Liberation Movement, while a more careful and balanced use of the true meaning of the phrase "to remember and not to forget" is forbidden? Battered children, psychologists say, will often grow up to be battering parents; and sexually abused children are potential sexual abusers. Why is it that we are not allowed to ask whether something similar is happening to us?

It is forbidden to ask because such a question will brutally undermine our basic societal axiom: that the Germans, by nature, were loathsome monsters; and the Jews were — and still are, by nature — innocent, good-hearted and harmless sheep. The ultimate, eternal Victim.

Even when the Ultimate Victims violently conquer, blindly exile, kill women and children, loot, burn, oppress, and destroy, they still remain the Victim. It has never been proven otherwise (and will never be provable: that's the beauty of the taboo). They remain righteous, and anyone claiming differently would be at one with the Nazis, the Cossacks, the Inquisitors, and the pharaohs. They remain righteous, their actions may never be questioned. They have suffered so much for so long that they have unlimited credit. The world owes us infinite reparations, many times more than would be possible to repay. Anything we do, therefore, is but a symbolic withdrawal from the enormous world credit account in our name.

In order to break a taboo that has ceased to serve as a defense mechanism and has become lethal, one must use obscenities. That's what children do, as a necessary step towards a healthy sexual maturity. They yell "prick" and "cunt" and speak compulsively of sex, until the barrier that hides the proper perspective from them is broken down. Apparently, we also need an infantile outburst, a sort of anal stage on the way to maturity. Perhaps we need a few idiots who'll claim consistently that Israel of the eighties is *exactly* like Germany of the thirties. That Jews here are just like German Nazis, and that Shamir and Rabin (and not Kahane and Ze'evi) are Hitler and Eichmann. Let them not recoil when we all attempt to defame them, and when we demand their deportation, institutionalization, or at least arrest on charges of public harm. Let the idiots continue their raucous blaspheming, encouraged by our rebukes, until we'll have no choice but to beat them on the one court where our advantage is strongest; where the game played is one of intelligent confrontation, rational and articulate. We will not bury their theory alive. On the contrary, we shall phrase it clearly, drawing out the pros and cons supporting or disputing that theory. We have no reason to fear such a comparison; unless we assume that the pros may outnumber the cons. We have no reason to object to this discussion; unless we believe we really are Nazis.

I don't believe we are Nazis. I have, therefore, no problem with the comparison. It is rather pleasant to discover over and over again, that my prime minister is, indeed, not Hitler. And since I no longer fear encountering my mirrored reflection in brown uniform, I have no problem admitting that for every five, ten, or a hundred — no matter — differences, there is also a streak of similarity. There are similarities between us and Nazi Germany. Clearly, only *some*. Clearly, there are also many differences. Clearly, there are a million "but's." But it's vital for us to be able to say the implicitly crude sentence, the writing of which quickens my pulse and makes my palms sweat: there are lines of similarity between us and the Nazis. Period.

There are lines of similarity between all oppressive nations in the world. The Nazis weren't the first, nor the last (only the most organized). There are similar lines between the French in Algeria, the Afrikaners in South Africa, the whites in Native America, the British in India, the Greeks and the Romans in the ancient land of Israel, the Russians in Afghanistan, and the Germans in the thirties and forties. And yes, there are similar lines between Nazi Germany and ourselves. And yes, it is worrying, very worrying. The lines of similarity between us and all those listed oppressors are worrying. More so when it comes to Nazi Germany, after we have seen there is no absolute human red line, no finite moral border, no preset boiling point, no proven critical-mass. There is only a circumstantial connection between the strength of certain known ingredients and the level of cruelty.

A partial list of these ingredients will include, roughly, the following factors: racism; population's unrest; the presence of a weaker, alienated group; territorial expansionism; megalomania; dehumanization of the victim; an absolute majority of an indifferent, blind, and disinformed population; stirring of paranoia (parallel to the demonization of the victim); elevation of the armed forces to an indisputable status in the national value system; a governmental tolerance towards nationalistic/racist-oriented murder and acts of violence; a fictitious judicial system; suppression or limitation of the right to free speech; and — of course — a cynical and manipulative misuse of hardship, superstitions, and social prejudices. A combination of all these ingredients (and a few unique others) paved the way for the Afrikaners in South Africa, the British in India, the French in Algeria, the whites in eighteenth-century America, and all the rest. The strength of each of these ingredients, as well as the element of time, determined almost mathematically the level of cruelty and hatred achieved by each of these groups.

Now, if we are ready to examine our position on the scale, the bottom of which is occupied by, say, Holland or Denmark or some peace-loving tribe in the jungles of Borneo, and the top of which is reserved for, most likely, Nazi Germany — we have only to find out which ingredients we contain, and to what degree.

Racism? Immeasurable. In its dormant state, it exists in expressions like "chosen people" or "Jewish mind." At its most banal it is personified in "dirty Arab," "Arab labor," and later in "death to the Arabs," and "Arabs into the sea." At its official level it is found in separate laws for Jews and Arabs (the right of return, for example, is obtained by Jews only). In a discussion at the House of Representatives, on whether the honorable Knesset Member actually said, "Every Jew is worth a thousand Arabs," or merely "For each Jew —a thousand Arabs." Racism, reaching its maximal dosage, is manifested in a comprehensive system of racial laws such as the Nuremberg Laws. All levels, excluding the last one, exist in Israel. There are no racial laws. But then, Germany didn't always have them either.

Population's unrest? We have plenty of that. Both economic and political. (The Arab nations' contribution to this unrest is substantial, of course. It is, however, irrelevant: the dosage, at any rate, is high.)

Territorial expansionism? Let's call ours "above average." There are higher ones, but our Declaration of Independence has not left out state borders for nothing.

The presence of a weak, alienated group? Certainly. What's weaker than refugees? What's more alienated than Arabic-speaking Muslims and Christians?

Megalomania? We must at least admit our vast sense of self-worth. Launching satellites, instructing warfare in Zaire and Panama, and exporting computers to Japan, is compelling for us. Being a nation like all nations? Nah, lions don't eat birdfood.

Dehumanization of the victim? The media and Knesset no longer raise an eyebrow on hearing expressions such as "human beasts," "drugged roaches," and "two-legged monsters" [used to describe Palestinians — ed.]. On the other hand, the scientific claim that the Arabs are genetically and physically lower forms of being, is not popular here (although it is customary to regard them as primitives, able to survive in crumbling shacks with open sewers and contaminated drinking water).

A majority of an indifferent population? A year ago, one of the evening papers published a one-question survey: Should we talk with the PLO? Over sixty percent supported the idea, with more or less enthusiasm. A week later, a different paper published another one-question survey: Should the Intifada be dealt with by extreme military measures? Over sixty percent supported the idea, with more or less enthusiasm. The conclusion? The majority of the population is completely indifferent to whatever measures the government takes, as long as there's quiet. An honest government will see this as a mandate for a peaceful solution. Another government could use this passivity murderously.

Stirring of paranoia parallel to demonization of the victim? Both consensus parties, Labor and Likud, have used the "demographic threat" as a primary lever for provoking fears: Those Arabs are multiplying mighty fast, and soon they will be more numerous than we and they will kill us. By striking at them, in fact, we're only protecting ourselves.

Elevation of the army's status? That ingredient is to be found here in almost maximal dosage. We have our reasons, of course. So did the French in Algeria.

Tolerant attitude towards racist/nationalistic violence? Dozens witnessed the murder of a thirteen-year-old girl in Kiffel Charet. One of the shooters, Gadi Ben-Zimra, is well-known. He walks around freely, as does Rabbi Moshe Levinger, as do the Jewish underground[1] members and many others. For a Jew who hath sinned is still a Jew.

Fictitious judicial system? Not even one percent of all Palestinians arrested since the Intifada have been found innocent; not even the one suspected of stone throwing who was 100 percent blind. Thirteen thousand Palestinians have been imprisoned for long periods without trial or any proof of their guilt.

Suppression of free speech? Even death notices are censored in the Palestinian newspapers. Prisoners in Ansar III are forbidden to read books such as *Hamlet* or *Lord of the Rings*. The Al Hakawati Theatre was closed down. The media is often banned from entering the territories. TV censures every slight mention of pro-Palestinian sentiment.

And as for the last ingredient, the cynical and manipulative misuse of hardship and social prejudices — we've elevated these to a form of art. Manipulatively, shamefully, and arbitrarily using the Holocaust. All the other ingredients have been nurtured and bred under the patronage of the *Shoah* taboo.

This isn't about the writing on the wall. This is about the foundations of the wall itself: all the dangerous ingredients are already present, and the dosage is threateningly high. At the moment, the main element keeping us away from topping the cruelty and oppression scale, is the element of time. This is no slight matter. We still have enough time to jump off the train, so that we never reach that despicable, bottomless level. As time passes, more and more Israelis may discern the possible implications, and object firmly. It is fair to deduce that never — never — will we find ourselves in Nazi Germany's heavy boots. But to ensure that this never happens, we must be aware and worried about its possibility. Ignoring it would be a step in the wrong direction.

We therefore don't have to shut the door in the face of our taboo-protected question, "What shall we tell our children twenty years from now?" We no longer have to respond, repulsed, to the question, "What will be our alibi when our children ask us where we were in 1991?" We don't need to outlaw the question, "What separates us from the Nazis?" We must act according to the answers that will satisfy our children's questions. We must sure that our alibi is solid and leaves us off the suspect list. We must bring out more and more differences between us and the Nazis. Then, and only then will we be neither shocked, angry, nor outraged when anybody dares ask, "How are you different from the Nazis?" We will have an excellent answer.

Note

1. "The Jewish Underground" refers to a group of Jewish Israeli terrorists (*Terror Neged Terror*, TNT, Terror Against Terror) whose target was the Palestinian population of the Occupied Territories. Among their victims were two prominent and popularly elected Palestinian mayors, Bassam Shaka'a of Nablus, who lost both his legs when a bomb placed inside his car exploded, and Karim Khalaf of Ramallah, who lost one leg in a similar episode.

A third mayor, Ibrahim Tawil of El Bireh, was saved from a similar fate when he was warned by the army. A non-Jewish Druze sapper who was ordered by his commanding officer to open Tawil's garage door, was blinded when the bomb exploded in his face. Fifteen Jews were indicted in the incidents, including an army major who was charged with providing intelligence information to the settlers concerning the routines of the mayors. TNT was responsible for numerous other acts of terrorism until they were caught in 1984 planting bombs on Palestinian busses in East Jerusalem, timed to go off at rush hour.

Yvonne Deutsch

Yvonne Deutsch was born in Timisoara, Romania on March 8, 1954, perhaps a prophetic sign of her strong identification with the women's movement, which celebrates International Women's Day on March 8th every year. She immigrated to Israel in 1962. Yvonne graduated in 1980 with a B.A. in Hebrew literature and African history, and in 1982 received a B.S. in social work at the Hebrew University in Jerusalem. At present she is enrolled at the Hebrew University and studying for an M.A. in cultural studies with an emphasis on women's issues. Yvonne spent five years working in a mental hospital's halfway house. She now works as a supervisor of student training at the School for Social Work of the Hebrew University.

A peace activist since the late seventies, the failings of her education with respect to Palestinian society first became apparent during Yvonne's army service (1972 to 1974), and grew during her subsequent years at university. There she had her first contact with Palestinians. She was an organizer of the Israeli Committee in Solidarity with Bir Zeit University and the Committee Against the War in Lebanon. She is a current organizer of Women in Black in Jerusalem and among the founders of the Women and Peace Coalition.

Yvonne lives in Jerusalem and shares her life with André Rosenthal, an Israeli lawyer who defends Palestinians' civil liberties and rights. They have two children.

Israeli Women:
From Protest to a Culture of Peace

Yvonne Deutsch

This article is dedicated to the memory of Lil Moed who worked with us in creating feminist peace activity and was a source of inspiration and support to many of us. I wish to express my thanks to Sherna Berger Gluck for her useful remarks and to André Rosenthal for the translation of the article into English.[1]

> It is a natural reaction to hate those who have made us suffer. It is also a natural reaction to inflict pain because one has suffered pain, and to justify it ideologically. In this small land both our peoples are stuck in a fateful embrace. I believe that our finding each other here is potentially for the greater unfolding of life. In order to fulfill this potential, we all need to become more fully human, which, to me means activating our capacity to understand the suffering of others through our own, and to transform pain into healing.[2]
>
> —Dalia Landau

In January 1988, a month after the outbreak of the Intifada, ten women, long-time leftist activists against the occupation and in favor of solidarity with the Palestinian people, organized a women's demonstration against the occupation, dressed in black, in a central Jerusalem square. Within a few weeks additional groups of what is known today as Women in Black organized themselves throughout the country. At the same time in Tel Aviv, a group of feminist and leftist women activists organized slide shows in a central street of the city which showed the army's brutality against the Palestinians in the territories. The exposure to the realities of the occupation was important then, when information still did not flow to the media.[3]

During that year several women's peace groups were established. By the end of the year, after a conference entitled "A Feminist Response to the Occupation," a nation-wide coalition, Women and Peace, was established in order for the women's peace movement to become a meaningful force in Israeli society.[4]

In December 1989, among the "1990 — Time for Peace" activities was a women's conference and peace march from West Jerusalem to East Jerusalem, organized by the Women and Peace Coalition. Led by the extra-parliamentary Left (which mobilizes Ratz and Mapam women), the participants, both Jewish and Palestinian Israelis, Palestinian women from the territories, European and U.S. women, and women from the Palestinian Diaspora, joined together demanding an end to the Israeli occupation of the West Bank and the Gaza Strip, respect for human rights, a two-state solution — Israeli and Palestinian — and calling on the Israeli government to negotiate for peace with the PLO, the Palestinian peoples' representative. These very successful events raised many expectations and hopes for a change in Israeli society. There was a feeling among us in the Women and Peace Coalition that the grassroots would become empowered and eventually develop into a meaningful political movement to pressure the government to find a political solution to the conflict.

During the third year of the Intifada (1990), members of the Women and Peace Coalition and Reshet (Israeli Women's Peace Net, established in May 1989 and grouping Labor and prominent women working within the establishment who did not join the existing coalition) came together to organize with Palestinian women from three women's committees in the territories (the Federation of Palestinian Women's Action Committees; Union of Palestinian Working Women's Committees; Women's Committee for Social Work). They were planning a joint political event that was to take place at the year's end. It was intended as a political breakthrough because it was creating an alternative way of trying to reach a solution to the conflict between the two peoples. Unfortunately, our plans were ruptured by the Gulf crisis. Although we continued to meet, we were unable to mount a jointly sponsored event.

*   *   *   *   *

Zionism and the establishment of Israel as a Jewish state is regarded by many Jews as the political solution to the Jewish problem of suffering from persecution. It became especially urgent after the Holocaust, and Palestine — later Israel — became the homeland of many Jewish refugees. The ideal was to create a new Jew who would be the antithesis of the weak and helpless Jew of the Diaspora. However, in the process of shaping a common national sentiment and identity, the Jewish state did not succeed in merging into the region and becoming an integral part of it. The historical Jewish lack of existential security, combined with the history of the establishment of the state and Arab reaction to it, made Israeli Jews develop, again, a ghetto mentality. We did not succeed in freeing ourselves from the Jewish-outsider-fearful mentality, and no matter how strong we are militarily, we still hold an internal self-image of weakness. Today we are the occupiers and aggressors but we feel as if occupied. This state of mind and psychology of the people, which is very well used by the politicians, makes it difficult to undertake protest activity against Israeli military actions, or the oppression of the Palestinian people, and to hold solidarity actions with the Palestinians.

With the Intifada, one could see a sizable awakening in the scope of protest and solidarity activity and it was no longer the sole realm of marginal avant-garde groups. Women carried out the majority of the activity, be it in "mixed" groups where they had an important organizational role, or in the women's groups. Precedents exist for this political phenomenon of women organizing around concerns for peace — and not only for women's issues. In 1982, a group of feminist women called Women Against the Invasion of Lebanon organized protests against that war. These movements should be seen as part and parcel of a world-wide development of women's activities in pursuit of peace.

We can clearly see the influence of feminist consciousness in the creation of a new and critical definition of militarism. This influence was possible in Israel partly because of an increasing lack of confidence in the army that started after the 1973 war[5] and came to a peak with the war in Lebanon, which was regarded as a war of choice.[6] Since the late seventies and early eighties, we have also witnessed the beginning of a personal and cultural preoccupation with the Holocaust. The breakdown of Israeli heroism made it possible to confront the emotional meaning of having been victims. The emotional aspects of dealing with mourning and loss creates the potential to relinquish the need for compensation. An inconsistency develops between the self-image of a weak and persecuted person on the one hand, and a military power on the other hand. This causes the army, quite apart from its role of defender in a war situation, to take on a further role of compensating for the feelings of helplessness, weakness, and vulnerability. Thus it became a symbol of the Jews' independence, a source of national pride, and also the main means of acquiring status in Israeli society.

So, five years after the creation of the first feminist women's peace group due to the Intifada, a meaningful Israeli women's peace movement was developing. There are many explanations for this phenomenon, but I will mention only two of them. The main reason is to be found in our marginality; in our status as outsiders and the "other" with respect to all that involves the army. This grants us relative freedom to express our views since we are not to be found in the midst of the conflict of the men who "shoot and cry."[7] It certainly also facilitated the development of a relationship with Palestinian women who know that we do not take an active part in suppressing the Palestinian struggle, and that we are involved in peace activities.

Then too, the Intifada clearly uncovered the army's role as an oppressing force and is destroying the false, but still enduring image of the enlightened occupier. It strengthened the Israeli skepticism with respect to the army's morality. It brought to the fore the fact that we can no longer ignore the Palestinian problem. Furthermore, the existing political party system effectively prevents the advancement of women in their ranks to any meaningful position. Therefore, women find venues of political expression which are extra-parliamentary.

*　　　*　　　*　　　*　　　*

Doors and barriers were opened and women of different national, religious, class, professional, and personal identities met and spoke about peace during this time. The meetings were moving and of a special quality and strength. During the Peace March even the skeptics among us were overwhelmed by the power of the experience and the discovery of the unique strength of women when we work together. However, during the mutual process of discovery there were many signs of lack of trust and suspicion.

Our lack of existential security creates a significant barrier in the bringing together of our two peoples, and this was apparent in meetings. Many Jewish women, even among those who protest the occupation, have difficulty feeling solidarity with Palestinian women or with the Palestinian people. They expressed confusion in receiving words of support from Palestinian male laborers, who, returning home from a day's work in Israel, would pass them on the road. They found themselves isolated by their own society, while receiving encouragement from Palestinian society. It is a difficult experience since the main reason for their protest is concern for the quality of the Jewish society. Those same women found it difficult to relate to a Palestinian woman recounting the horror of the deportees, expelled because of political activity. Their initial response was to identify with the official military explanation. "Clearly they did something against the security of the State, otherwise they would not have been deported." It is easier and more immediate to accept and believe an anonymous response which is "ours," rather than believing another woman recounting the story of her deported husband.

Experiencing an increasing loss of faith in the military authorities is a painful process, because as Israelis we are all raised on the myth of the defending and moral army. Women can say that they identify with pacifism and at the same time recount with pride that their son is serving in one of the elite units of the army. To belong to the army means to belong to the people and state. And for many of us, being ex-refugees, or immigrants, it is difficult to begin to cut the umbilical cord with the society. It is complex to discover that our feeling of belonging is no longer as significant as it once was and that perhaps for the building of a different and peaceful future we must seek other sources in which to root that need.

The process of political and feminist consciousness raising is linked to this painful process of questioning existential problems of self-determination, belonging, alienation, womanhood, manhood, the attitude to the army, war, peace, justice, violence, and nationalism. Such questioning of beliefs, values, and identities becomes accessible to women, in varying degrees according to personal security and self-identify, and to age and social class, among other things.

Political activity at a time of crisis of identity and values, combined with actively dealing with those issues on an emotional level, represents the coherence of the political and the personal. We raised in the public consciousness subjects of emotional and political significance, consistent with our belief in the destructive effect of the split between the personal and the political, a split which enables the existence of the evil within us (in the sense used by Hannah Arendt). Aside from raising the questions of women's role in peace-making and the influence of occupation on women's lives, we also raised issues like racism, prejudice, and fear as obstacles to peace. Because of this work, and because we are women, we also must discuss our attitudes towards the army, both on the personal and public levels. This is one of the most difficult subjects to deal with, and we have so far not dared to discuss it publicly.

*　　*　　*　　*　　*

Within this maze and confusion there are among us those who have a vision of creating a *feminist political culture of women* — which begins with the commitment to a *culture of peace*. Such a culture cannot be created in a vacuum. It must have links with those relevant aspects of women's lives which exist largely in the private sphere and the backyard of history. It is our role to explore that culture of women and adjust it to our political and cultural needs, while creating changes according to a feminist critique.

An example can be found in an interpretation of the following story from ancient Jewish literature, written towards the end of the fifth century.

> Rabbi Shimeon Ben Lakish said: God may be likened to a King who had two sons. He became enraged against the first of them, took a stick and thrashed him so that he writhed in agony and died; and the father then began to lament over him. He later became enraged

against the second son, took a stick and thrashed him so that he writhed in agony and died. And the father then exclaimed, 'No longer have I the strength to lament over them, so call for the mourning women and let them lament over them.'[8]

One can see the dichotomy between a man whom anger leads to kill as opposed to the women, who are represented as capable of containing the emotions of loss and the unbearable and traumatic reality. The lament may contain protest, but we do not see here an upheaval of the women in response to the terrible killings.

Women in Black has been the most significant Israeli protest movement since the beginning of the Intifada. In June 1990 there were thirty simultaneous vigils all over the country. The choice (conscious or not) of the black dress can be interpreted in different ways depending on the cultural context. According to the story of Rabbi Shimeon Ben Lakish and also in Western culture, it is connected to mourning and lament.[9] But it must be pointed out that in our case, as Women in Black, we not only mourn over the killings, but we express our anger and protest about the occupation while connecting it to the meaning of violence and killing in concrete, daily life. In creating a feminist political culture with which we can identify, and in transforming the traditional role of the lamenting women to meet our needs and to establish meaning in Israeli culture at the end of the twentieth century, we do not satisfy ourselves with the role of lamenting and containing the pain. We are, rather, seeking ways to influence the grassroots level and the political system as a whole. We do not settle for the social role of lamenting and accepting the madness of killing. We do not relegate women's culture to the backyard of history, and we are struggling for a change in which our world vision will be of political significance in the nation's decision-making.[10]

In the different women's organizations and in the meetings and dialogue which have developed through them, there is a potential for building solidarity and sisterhood among women. Some of us see the occupation and the national conflict as delaying the advancement of the women's struggle in our society. A peaceful political solution becomes a stage along the road to cooperation between Israeli, Palestinian, and Arab women in dealing with the role of women in our societies. We hope that our joint experiences will develop trust among the women of the area and eventually lead to a sense of common gender identity, which will have a significant influence for social change in the region. Today strong national identification on both sides prevents certain very critical issues — like the essence of militarism and armed struggle — from being challenged publicly. If we are to create a women's peace culture, however, it is necessary to discuss these very issues. Otherwise, silence and individualism keep us from working together on women's issues. A political solution to the national conflict is only a step which will free us from the restrictions of this reality. We hope that it will enable Palestinian, Israeli, and Arab women to commit ourselves to non-violence, which is crucial in creating a peace culture.

*   *   *   *   *

Following the crisis in the Gulf and the disappointment of many Israelis at Palestinian support for Saddam Hussein, the Israeli peace movement itself experienced a crisis, and the level of activities dropped. At the same time and also in view of overall feelings of helplessness regarding political developments in Israel in particular and in the Middle East in general, the number of Women in Black vigils grew smaller. Political developments in the area had played a significant role in the development of the relationship between Israeli and Palestinian women. After long months of common political work, we not only failed in organizing a common political event for December 1990, but our relationships also almost reached a dead end. A year after "1990 — Time for Peace," world leaders started a war and we found ourselves prisoners of a conflict that was not ours. The culture of war — or militarism — had its victory over the culture of peace.

During the war, because of the direct threat to Israel, most of the Women in Black found it difficult to continue standing in the open expressing opposition to the occupation. Only in Jerusalem and Tel Aviv, after three weeks, did some of the women return to the vigil. In those days of the war, more than usual, we had to go to the streets with a clear message, not only against this specific war but against all wars, against the principles of war and destruction. And during this period many of us had to spend more time with our small children. We tried to keep our sanity in the microcosms of our family, and protect our children and ourselves from the terrible fear of destruction to which we were exposed day and night through the media. This terrible war was used as a legitimate means to achieve political and economic goals. By the summer of 1991 only eleven weekly vigils continued to stand, and many women were feeling burned out and helpless.

Since the war, the Palestinian people under occupation have been going through new oppressive measures. In effect, the Israeli government has created two large ghettos for the Palestinians, the West Bank and the Gaza Strip. Exit from the territories is now by special permit only; on the whole only those Palestinian workers who are essential to the functioning of the Israeli economy are issued such permits. And the territories have no adequate economic infrastructure to cope with the influx of labor.

The Israeli peace movement, including the women's movement, still has not recovered from its crisis and there is a clear regression in the scope of activities. Our political activity over the past three years has been dedicated to changing attitudes among Israeli women. Now, though we are continuing this focus, some of us think that political change will occur only under international economic and cultural pressure, or sanctions, on Israel. We are also looking for ways to continue our political relationships with Palestinian women. In May 1991 an Israeli, Palestinian, and international women's peace conference was held in Geneva, having been postponed from December 1990. The Women and Peace Coalition worked also on a joint Israeli-Palestinian women's demonstration for the occupation's twenty-fourth anniversary. We are trying to work against the feelings of regression and defeat.

*   *   *   *   *

For the creation of a peace culture within Israeli society we must confront, emotionally and politically, painful basic issues that the Jewish Israeli society tends to repress, and that are connected with the establishment of the Jewish state. The exposure of the truth and learning to deal with it has to be a main issue in creating a culture in touch with the needs of the peoples of the whole region.

Israeli society should be aware of the price Palestinians paid, and are still paying, for the self-determination of the Jews. Palestinians view the establishment of the Jewish state as "the catastrophe of '48." In the process of consciousness-raising, we must realize that because of this historical development, we have the *duty* to create a culture of peace in the region. It is not the choice of "bleeding-heart liberals," but the duty of a people whose self-determination brought destruction and pain upon others.

The creation of Israeli identity, in contrast to the Jewish Diaspora identity as humiliated and helpless, did not succeed in freeing us from our self-image as weak and persecuted. That such an inner image persists while at the same time we develop a militaristic culture and create a sense of belonging, for example, on the basis of army service and a view of the army as a "holy" institution, has been and is a significant danger to our society's mental and social health. Jewish Israelis do not conceive of the army as a necessary evil because of the reality of danger or war, but as an institution with political, social, and economic power. With this power it defines social values and priorities, and forms the main origin of status and a sense of belonging in Israeli society.

In the present political situation, in which even Western societies argue for the value of peace but have not yet chosen to stop their reliance upon weapons, it is difficult for Israelis to put forward a unilateral demand for disarmament and the investment of military resources in social development. In the utopian political view this should be the attitude. It should very clearly be the ideological-cultural demand of women working for peace, social justice, and freedom. But it should be emphasized that women from the so-called "developed" countries have the main responsibility for such a call.

*   *   *   *   *

In the forty-plus years of its existence, Israel has not succeeded in integrating itself in the region. It has created alienation and hate between itself and the Arab peoples, refused to acknowledge their development needs, and allied with a Western world that relies on economic exploitation of the Third World. In creating an alternative feminist culture, we must ally ourselves with the needs of all peoples, in particular with the needs of women in the area in which we live. Israeli feminism makes a grave mistake in relying only on Western feminism, which suits our personal needs for emancipation. We must break our own alienation and ignorance and create links with Arab feminists and Arab women's culture, one often hidden behind the veil. Those of us with a feminist consciousness must strive to create an indigenous feminism which develops from the women's culture existing here, and will be suitable to the needs of women in the Middle East. We must stop turning our backs on our own region, and we must break down the wall of estrangement which hardens the hate toward us. Our loyalty should be to the eastern region in which we are living, and we, the women, must be the bridge between west and east, as between north and south.

Notes

1. The first version of this paper was presented at the Fourth International Interdisciplinary Congress on Women, Hunter College, City University of New York, June 1990.

2. Dalia Landau, quote from an open letter to Bashir Khayri, who was deported by the Israeli authorities in January 1988. *Jerusalem Post*, January 14, 1988.

3. The Israeli government periodically closes off the territories to press coverage, as it did then and did again during the Gulf War until the end of April 1991.

4. The Women and Peace Coalition includes activists from Women in Black, Shani-Israeli Women Against Occupation, Women for Women Political Prisoners-Jerusalem, Peace Quilt project, Tandi Movement of Democratic Israeli Women, Women's International League for Peace and Freedom, Women to Women, Women for Coexistence, and independent women.

5. In 1973 Israel was taken by surprise by the Egyptian and Syrian attack. Confidence in the army's capacity to defend the state was questioned and the myth of the all-capable army was shattered, creating a crisis in Israeli society.

6. In Zionist history, Israel goes to war only when it has no choice because of the Arab states; in this case this dubious apologia could not be used.

7. "Shoot and cry" is an expression which criticizes those who actively participate in the oppression of the Palestinians, yet feel that they have to justify their actions by expressing their personal hardship in doing so: "this hurts me more than it does you." It was popularized in a song by rock singer Si Himan, "Yorim U Bochim."

8. From "Lamentations Rabba," the ancient commentary, or midrash, on the Book of Lamentations from the Bible, which was read and preached on the day of mourning for the fall of the Temple. I was introduced to the story by Galith Hasan-Rokem.

9. Dalia Sachs called my attention to the fact that in some cultures black is a symbol of women's strength.

10. According to anthropological studies, in hunting and gathering societies there existed separate social organizations for men and women, but the men would not conceive of going to war without first receiving the women's explicit agreement.

Marcello Wechsler

Marcello Wechsler was born in Buenos Aires, Argentina in 1955. With a Polish mother and Argentine father of Russian Jewish origin, he came from a family that possessed the cultural and social characteristics of many other Jewish immigrants, laborers whose roots lay in Eastern European Yiddish culture. In the sixties, with the boom in anti-Semitism in Argentina, his parents decided to emigrate to Israel. There, the years of economic crisis drove them, just before the '67 War, to try their luck once again in Argentina.

Back in Argentina, at the age of thirteen, Marcello began an active involvement with one of the socialist Zionist youth movements: Dror, affiliated with the Labor party. In 1973, when he was eighteen years old, he was elected secretary general of Dror. These were boom years for the revolutionary left in Argentina. As a consequence of his political involvement with these radical organizations, he was expelled from the ranks of Dror by its Israeli leaders.

Although this crisis led him to gradually abandon his Zionist ideology, Marcello decided with his mother and younger sisters to return to Israel, for the most part because of the difficult economic situation in Argentina in those years. Back in Israel, the family lived on a kibbutz. The politics of the kibbutz movement with respect to the Arab-Israeli conflict brought Marcello to the conclusion that kibbutz life was impossible for someone from the militant left.

Moving to Tel Aviv, he joined Matzpen, and began a nine-year stint as a solderer in a metallurgy factory. It was there that he began to understand the problems of the Israeli working class, and within that, the specific problems of Oriental Jews. During the Lebanon War, he declared himself a conscientious objector and spent one month in military prison.

Today, Marcello is a member of the editorial committee of *Iton Aher*, a bimonthly journal examining social and political problems in Israel. He is director of the Shahar Youth Movement, which organizes Oriental Jewish youth in poor neighborhoods and development towns to fight for their rights in the high schools. Marcello is one of the founders of Tidua, also known as the "Alternative Popular Institute, Conscientization," dedicated to the political and social education of adults of Oriental origin. Marcello is also a member of the Alternative Information Center collective in Jerusalem.

The Connection between the Question of Peace and the Question of Orientalism in Israel

Marcello Wechsler

No mass political movement in Israel to date has made the connection between the problems of the Israeli-Palestinian conflict and the social questions within Israeli Jewish society. The histories of protest against the occupation and of social protest are entirely separate.

I begin with the premise that the attainment of lasting peace between Israelis and Palestinians is not simply an issue for the elites of society. It is rather a political act which demands the cooperation of the absolute majority of the Jewish and Palestinian populations, which today stand on opposite sides of the political barricade.

Furthermore, the ability to achieve real change in the balance of forces between those who support the oppression of the Palestinian people and those who oppose it requires a basic shift in attitude of the majority of the Israeli population. That is, among the working class and lower white-collar workers, the residents of the poorer neighborhoods and cities, most of whom are Jews of Oriental origin from Asia, Africa, and the Arab countries in the Middle East. Over sixty percent of the Jewish population in Israel is Oriental.

To activists, a deep mystification surrounds the reasons behind the conservative political stand of this majority. This lack of insight is particularly obvious in the predominantly Ashkenazi (Jews of

---

Translated from Hebrew by Judith Green

European origin) peace camp. Only if the characteristics and critical history of the Oriental community is understood can the peace movement hope to successfully communicate with, and ultimately effect a political shift with this sector.

Background of the Oriental Community

Historically, Eastern European Jewry had a number of advantages over Oriental Jews. These advantages also help explain the birth of Zionism within the Eastern European community. The first plus is the territorial continuity among the various communities, and the second is the development of Yiddish culture, a culture parallel to and distinct from gentile culture, and preserved even after the arrival of capitalism. For the most part, Oriental Jewry, as opposed to Ashkenazim, was much more rooted in its indigenous countries, culturally and linguistically. The territorial continuity was also absent, as the communities were far apart from each other, and even on different continents. Zionism, and the autonomous movements (like the non-Zionist, socialist, and labor-oriented Bund), could only have been born and bred under the conditions which existed in Eastern Europe, because only there was the ground ripe for their activities.

The manifestation of anti-Jewishness is another area of difference between the Ashkenazi and Oriental historical experience. In spite of anti-Jewish propaganda in the Arab countries, Jews, in fact, enjoyed a special relationship to the culture for hundreds of years, a relationship which was protected by the laws of Islam concerning the children of the Mosaic Law. Anti-Jewishness grew and changed into a political movement in the Arab countries as a reaction to the successes of the Zionist movement in Palestine and did not flourish previously. In contrast, anti-Semitism was an institutionalized phenomenon in Eastern Europe.

Still another important point of departure was the development of secular Jewish culture in the cities of Eastern Europe, within which Zionism blossomed as a political movement. In the countries of the Middle East, Asia, and Africa, on the other hand, the process of secularization was expressed in the choice between the Arabic culture of the environment and the culture of the colonialists.

The Attitude of the Zionist Movement toward Oriental Jewry

The origins of Zionism as a political movement are distinctly Eastern European. As such, its observations about the Jewish world, its political analyses and visions, touched only upon this European Jewish community. The Arab world, within which the Jewish state was supposed to rise, was foreign to the Zionist leadership, and was considered primitive, dangerous, and hostile. In such a framework, there could be no honorable place for Oriental Jews, since they behaved and spoke like Arabs, and indeed were part of the "Levant."

Thus, Oriental Jewry, for the most part, was de facto excluded from the characteristics of the Zionist movement. It was living proof of the disingenuousness of Zionist ideology (founding myths), which spoke and still speaks of the community of destiny of Jews from all over the world. The question of Oriental Jewish immigration took on urgency for the Zionist movement when the scale of the Holocaust in Europe, the natural region of support and sustenance for the movement, became clear. The destruction of millions of European Jews, and the cutting off of the Jews in Russia, left Zionism with only two serious sources of immigration: the United States and the Arab countries.

The dynamics of the Zionist movement, in the context of conflict with the Arab world and the Palestinian people, demanded then, as now, a strategy of mass immigration of Jews, in order to break the negative demographic balance. In contrast to most colonialist movements, Zionist leaders did not vaunt exploitation of the natives, but rather their replacement by Jewish immigrants. This strategy expressed itself for the first time in the 1930s, especially during the years of the Arab rebellion, as exemplified in the slogan: "Jewish labor and Jewish production."

The potential for Oriental Jewish immigration already existed by that time. Economic scarcity, the reliance of Zionism on religious messages (aliyah — i.e., "redemption," etc.), growing anti-Semitism, and the willingness of Arab rulers to carry out the transfer of these communities, all helped determine the choice of this human reservoir. The Zionist movement disdained no means in actualizing this strategy: agreement with Arab rulers concerning economic dispossession of the communities in exchange for transfer, agreement about acts of provocation (best known are the terrorist actions in the synagogues of Baghdad), assistance given the secret police in the Arab countries by exposing communist activists (again, in Iraq), among other things. The Zionist movement used, and continues to use, the suffering of Jews for its own ends, in the most cynical way. Today, the time has come for the Ethiopian, Argentinian, and Soviet Jews to play this role of pawn.

A Class-Based Oppression

The dynamics of Zionism turned the immigration of the 1950s into a source of cheap Jewish labor for Israel. The reasons for this were many. To begin with, even before the establishment of the state, a de facto ruling class existed, made up of the Zionist leadership, especially the Labor party (Mapai) officials, the Histadrut (national labor union), the fighting bodies (the Haganah and Palmach), the kibbutzim, and the private urban bourgeoisie. This ruling class was mainly Ashkenazi, members of the Second and Third Aliyah (two waves of immigration, respectively: 1904 to 1914 and 1919 to 1923), and those who were native born (*sabra*).

This elite lacked a cheap labor force and soldiers for the national army at the time of the declaration of the state and the expulsion of the Palestinian natives. The Orientals filled this void much more naturally than the Ashkenazi refugees from the Holocaust who immigrated at the same period. Whether because of the cultural similarities, or because of a clear prejudice, or both, the chances of the European immigrants integrating into the ruling class were greater.

Most of the professional Oriental immigrants were unable to fit into the developing capitalist economy in Israel. Small merchants, peddlers, money-lenders, and craftspeople were forced to become simple laborers, without professional qualifications. Even the intellectual class had no place in the ruling establishment. They were foreign to the Israeli manner and story, to the cultural habits, and the tendency to imitate Europe. Writers, actors, lawyers, artists, and musicians lost their livelihood in a single blow. Few succeeded in bringing any property with them. Usually the transfer of the Oriental Jewish communities was effected in return for dispossession of their property by the local government. The wealthy immigrated, as one would expect, to Europe and the United States.

The aim of turning the Orientals into a working class has continued in Israel until now, and it constitutes an integral part of the process of recreating a class structure. With the economic boom which followed the 1967 War, a certain social mobility opened up for the Oriental community in Israel. This was the period of the Oriental "nouveau riche;" businessmen and building contractors, for instance. This phenomenon isn't unique to Israel; in many immigrant communities worldwide, economic growth makes it possible to jump a rung on the social ladder. However, in spite of the mobility of the end of the 1960s and the beginning of the 1970s, the Israeli ruling class remained almost entirely a mosaic of early Ashkenazi settlers and their progeny. Opportunities slowed down with the beginning of the economic crisis ushered in by the October War of 1973 and essentially disappeared during the 1980s.

Cultural Discrimination

One of the most flagrant failures of Zionism is that, after forty years of statehood, a slogan like "the integration of the various immigrations" (*mizoug galouyot*) is not realized in relation to the social conditions of the Orientals. The reigning ideology, as conveyed through public relations and the image of the state, requires oppressing every independent expression of the Oriental communities. Since the state was "a Western bastion" in an Arab region, the identification of the ruling class with the interests of the powers in the area (and hence their culture and ideology), the isolation from and contempt for the Oriental world, naturally gave birth to the desire to wipe out any signs of that tradition in the "new" culture. The means of oppression were varied: distortion of Oriental Jewish history, deliberate exaggeration of the importance of anti-Semitism in Islamic culture, the creation of myths concerning the wide gaps between Jewish and Arab cultures, the characterization of Oriental culture as a sub-culture, a broad use of Eastern European symbols as pan-Israeli symbols (particularly conspicuous in what are called the "songs of the Land of Israel").

A few outstanding examples of discrimination and oppression can be illuminating. The Oriental communities, at least initially upon their arrival in the country, usually preserved their old social customs. In the desire to build a developed, capitalist economy, Zionism as an ideology and political structure made an enormous effort to destroy the pre-capitalist social tradition of the Oriental Jews (the *hamula* or extended family structure). Then too, the Hebrew language was a central tool in the process of Zionist "integration." In order to remove the centrifugal processes of the various ethnic groups, first and family names were changed, and the Oriental accent was eschewed.

In the realm of religion and tradition, the establishment used two parallel approaches to make the Orientals conform. On the one hand, the Mapai (Labor party) establishment worked for speedy secularization by acts of humiliation such as the shaving of sidelocks and the policy of separating parents and children (e.g. rumors of the kidnapping of Yemenite children and bringing children into the framework of Youth Aliyah). On the other hand, the religious establishment was given a green light to activate a play of "Ashkenazation" of the Orientals. This was carried out in the conscription of young Orientals into ultra-orthodox Yeshivot (talmudic schools), and National Religious Party institutions, which produced rabbis and activists who were as far from the Oriental tradition as East is from West.

The ultra-orthodox Orientals were burdened with "difficult commandments:" obliged to wear Eastern European clothing, to learn Yiddish, and especially turned into a religious sect which was completely foreign. In the Arab countries, the religious Jewish population kept the commandments while at the same time living normal lives just like their Arab neighbors, religious and secular together.

The Orientals' experiences of oppression, discrimination, and racism created among them a denial of identity, guilt, and self-hatred. The process of redefinition which the Oriental family went through brought about a crisis in the patriarchal hierarchy and a social deterioration with the absence of any dignified alternative. The fact that ninety-eight percent of Israeli criminal prisoners and the absolute majority of the "poor" drug addicts, prostitutes, and other serious social problems are Orientals, bears witness to the crisis which struck these immigrants and is an indictment against the state of Israel.

Just as the determination that democratic freedoms not be extended beyond the Green Line to the Occupied Territories inevitably endangers and limits those freedoms within Israel itself, so also the discrimination against more than 1.5 million Palestinians cannot be stopped at the Green Line, and will inevitably reinforce the discrimination against Oriental Jews. That is to say, whoever starts with the Arabs ends with the Orientals. Further, just as Zionism cannot truly fight against racism, religious coercion, or the limitation of democratic rights because such confrontations might endanger the exclusively Jewish character of the state so must Zionism also preserve this discrimination against Orientals as a part of its justification against the Arab world and as part of its heavy identification with Western interests in the region. In this sense, every protest of discrimination against Orientals constitutes a threat to the regime and endangers its ability to conscript the Jewish "masses" for its ends.

The Relationship of the Left to the Oriental Question

The attitude of the large majority of activists in the peace movement and the leaders of the Zionist left parties varies between that inherited from the Labor party (Mapai) and the complete denial of the existence of the problem. For most peace activists, the Orientals are a furious mass, with anti-democratic traditions as well as fascist inclinations. For some others, the Orientals are a topic which "one talks about" in an anthropological way: one explains the phenomenon as though it belongs to another continent. There are those who tack on an ideological aspect: with all the importance of the subject, the peace forces "will be at leisure" to deal with it only after a withdrawal from the territories.

The reasons for such attitudes come from the proximity, both historically and politically, of the majority of the peace movement to the Labor party; and on the other hand, because most of these activists and members of left-wing parties come from the middle class of Israeli society. That is to say, there is a class difference between the social makeup of the protest movement and the Oriental majority. This difference does not justify the inability of the peace movement to find the connection between the question of peace and the question of Orientalism, but there is no doubt that "experience determines consciousness."

If the left-wing establishment behaves and thinks like the Mapainiks, it is not surprising that the Oriental masses can't see in it any credible alternative to the government which oppresses and mistreats them. Many dimensions of the Orientals' attitudes are at least instinctively correct. When an Oriental claims that the Left "loves Arabs" and doesn't relate to what is happening in the slums, she or he is pointing to a real phenomenon, even if the explanation is incorrect.

The Israeli Left is used to "talking" with the Palestinians, seeing them as the enemy and a force external to Israeli society. Unlike the Palestinians, the Orientals are part of the society in which the Left is active; they influence its design, and their differences from the "Ashkenazi" Left are a direct threat. The Left is used to sitting with Palestinians, although as foreigners they are "Levantines," but they are still not used to living with "Levantines" in their own home. Behind this behavior is also a rationalization: "First we will make peace with the Arabs, and then we will be free to deal with internal problems." There are dangerous aspects to this conception. First, given that peace is made between social elites, and the Orientals are a herd directed by the elite, it assumes there are no connections to be made between the questions concerning the national conflict and the internal contradictions of the society. Second, it assumes a general acceptance of the Zionist consensus, that is, that all Jews constitute one block against the Arabs.

Some on the Left claim, in order to defend themselves, that in the lower classes, among the Orientals, there rages a storm of anti-Arab racism, anti-democratic notions, and a low level of social conscience; these are adding sin to crime. In this, they are blaming the victims, making them accountable for their situation and consciousness. There is a lack of faith and an arrogance in this expression, as if to say, "That's how they are, so I have nothing to say to them." But the argument is not about facts, rather about how to change the Orientals.

An opposite approach must take into account that problem of consciousness, not to give in to it, but to understand how it is the product of the dominant ideology. This approach also perceives that any radical change in the balance of forces between the Israeli government and the Palestinian national movement must work through the internal contradictions in Israeli society. Indeed, a serious consciousness raising is needed for most of the Jewish population, including but not only within the Oriental working class — we must recognize the historical urgency of throwing off the bonds of Zionism and of solving the Israeli-Palestinian conflict.

The Alternative

The alternative to the direction of the peace movement and a solution to its problems in recruitment is to be found in the Oriental population. Thus a radical change in the general world view of leftist activists is needed. Such a change would include several vital points. First, social slogans used in a casual way cannot substitute for real change in world view and in political action. It is not enough to say "Money to the slums and not to the settlements," which has become a tradition in left-wing demonstrations, without an actual campaign by those peace activists on behalf of the tent residents.

The peace movement's credibility will also rise in the eyes of the Oriental community if and when it breaks away from the Labor party and its satellites and establishes its own autonomy. The recruitment of peace activists in the last elections behind the center-left parties, and the idea that "the struggle against the Right and at its head, the Likud, is the main issue" fatally injured their legitimacy.

The independence of the Orientals from the dominant ideology must come from an autonomous organization in this community, outside the establishment framework. Only by the difficult path of individual experience will this population be able to make the bridge to the questions of the Jewish-Arab conflict. The peace activists should not think of themselves as "missionaries" coming to explain the truth to the Orientals, but as people who are part of their destiny and their struggle.

I am aware that this alternative, its development and growth, often seems like a distant dream, almost unattainable. Nevertheless, however long the path is, we must start down it.

Meir Amor

Meir Amor was born in Israel in 1955, the sixth and youngest in his family. His parents immigrated to Israel from Morocco. For years he "felt uncomfortable whenever asked to give these biographical details, because in Israel being a Moroccan Jew is not considered much of an honor. Like many others who came from Arab lands, my parents were defined as 'the Second Israel.' The 'First Israel' was made up of veteran settlers: those who immigrated from Europe, who became in Israel *Ashkenazim*, the people who contend that they founded an exemplar society in the Levant."

Until the age of eighteen, Meir was raised and educated in a small town in the northern part of Israel, Kiryat Tivo'n. He joined the Israeli Defense Forces (IDF) on October 23, 1973, the day of the announcement of the cease-fire in the October War. Meir left the army six years later as a captain and after being a company commander. During his adult life he witnessed three wars, the Yom Kippur War in 1973, the Litani Campaign in 1978, and the Lebanon War in 1983–1985. In February 1988 he was called up to serve in the reserves in the Occupied Territories to quell the Palestinian Intifada. He refused, and was sentenced to twenty-one days in military jail. In June 1988, Meir toured the U.S. with Peretz Kidron on behalf of Yesh Gvul.

Meir is currently a Ph.D. student of sociology at the University of Toronto, having received his first degree from Tel Aviv University. From 1984 to 1990 he was involved in the creation and growth of the "Israel Committee on Education in Oriental (Mizrachi) Neighborhoods and Development Towns" (HILA in Hebrew).

The Fact of War

Meir Amor

This essay is dedicated to my newborn daughter Tamar Dina Amor. Both my wife Nurit and I hope that she will have a better life than we had in Israel.

In the introduction to the Hebrew translation of two short stories by the late Palestinian author Ghassan Canafani, the Israeli writer Shimon Balas wrote that "one has no better and faithful device than literature to convey and depict the individual's life as part of his group, and one has no better and efficient agent than literature to promote understanding between peoples" (author's translation). Reading Ghassan Canafani's short stories in Hebrew and identifying with the suffering of his Palestinian heroes, says Balas, pulls the rug out from Canafani's major political thesis that there is no possibility for communication between Israelis and Palestinians.[1]

On both sides, Israeli and Palestinian, there have always been people who think, like Canafani, that there is nothing between us but death. This essay is aimed at those who hope, believe, and struggle for a different and peaceful future. I am going to address the Israeli "rejection front" to peace. It is my firm belief that their rejection stems from what I see as the Israeli war structure creating a war culture. That is to say, in Israel today there is a structure of interests which sanctifies and justifies war.

There are two main points to my argument. First, war is not an external and temporary situation, but an intrinsic and permanent feature of the contemporary Israeli society and state. Secondly, political policies aimed at relieving the so-called "internal" social problems and those policies aimed at the "external" environs are related, intertwined, and shaped by a similar economic, political, and cultural process. Thus, in order to understand (let alone change) Israel's politics we have to consider the Israeli social structure, and vice versa.

The political Right in Israel, and the Jewish political Right in the Diaspora, contend that a social structure of war developed in Israel because it was (and is) surrounded by uncompromising Arab enemies and has had to defend itself against their aggression. In contrast, I believe that there were (and continue to be) on the Israeli side concrete reasons and interests contributing to the creation and perpetuation of war. That is not to say that Arab states in general and Palestinian leaders in particular do not share the responsibility for the war business of the Middle East.

The crucial point for those of us who live in and care about the Middle East and its people is: are we going to repeat our parents' history, or are we going to create a different future for the coming generations? The question is will we share Canafani's gloomy existence or will we create an animated reality between us, Israelis and Palestinians? It is not a matter of who's to blame, but rather a question of survival.

I would like to concentrate on the more prosaic causes of the protracted Israeli-Palestinian conflict. My contention is that the roots of the conflict are grounded in a very concrete and palpable base. It is not blind hate between Arabs and Jews or Arabs and Israelis that stirs the boiling cauldron of the Israeli-Palestinian conflict, but the quest for land, labor market opportunities, and political dominance.

The Zionist idea is epitomized in a phrase which claimed to offer the solution to the "Jewish problem" in late nineteenth-century Europe. The phrase was "Bringing a nation with no land (the Jews of Europe) to a land with no nation." This straightforward solution had its devastating drawbacks. One was the deliberate disregard for the Arabs living in Palestine at that time. Another was a refusal to acknowledge the substantial Jewish minority residing in and native to Arab countries.

The idea of Jews creating a Jewish state was a great political breakthrough for Jews in East and Central Europe. Such a state was expected — and not only by Jews — to serve as the vanguard of Western culture and interests in the Middle East. Israel would function as a "rampart" against the barbarism of the East, wrote Theodor Herzl in his famous proposal "The Jewish State" (Der Judenstaat). Herzl offered the proposal as a general plan for the organized (and hopefully supported) evacuation of Jews from the "civilized" nations of Europe.

Palestine thus was seen as a deserted area waiting to be redeemed by a cultural power that would bring the light of progress to a benighted land. European "cultural superiority" provided the moral basis for their "right" to subjugate any native peoples in the pursuit of progress, or more accurately, white dominance and greed. This was the reasoning and the ideological motivation that facilitated European colonialism all over the world. The Zionist movement, as part of the European milieu, shared these conceptions.

Such points represent a distortion of several realities. First of all, at the end of the nineteenth century, Palestine was partly inhabited by Arab peasants and Bedouin. The disregard for these people persists today, reflected in the claims that Palestinians do not exist, that they are refugees, or that "they are not a nation." In fact, the Palestinian people, like the Israeli Jewish people, consolidated and became a nation in the process of struggling over this parcel of land. That is to say, they are both nations because of a specific set of historical circumstances. The Israeli-Palestinian conflict, a struggle that originated eleven decades ago, created the common tie to the land, and shaped the content and form of these two nations. Today, both nations are hard social realities. Israelis and Palestinians are newborn political creatures, each with their distinct history and structure. Palestinians cannot be simply equated to Arabs, and Israelis cannot be reduced and equated to Jews.

A second flaw concerns the way the East European Zionist leadership conceived the Jewish entity itself in the first decades of the twentieth century. The problems of East European Jews were seen as "the problems of all Jews," though they were aware that these communities constituted only part of world Jewry. Before 1948, about 15 percent of the Jewish population in Palestine were Jews from Arab countries. Only after the Holocaust and the creation of Israel did Arab Jews (also called Oriental or Mizrachi Jews) become the focus of significant Zionist agitation intended to promote their immigration to Israel. Today the majority (roughly 65 percent) of Jews in Israel are immigrants (or their offspring) from the Middle East, Asia, and Africa.[2] Most are Arab Jews whose immigration to Israel was not the outcome of a nationalist movement or political conception with Zionist roots. Rather, the establishment of the Jewish state in 1948 had an adverse effect on relations between these Jews and Arabs in the Arab states. This devastating effect, combined with Zionist agitation and some questionable actions, created an atmosphere of emergency and crisis which led to the rapid evacuation of Jews from most of those countries.[3] The significance of Jerusalem as a holy city was a contributing factor that prepared the way, though it had never been sufficient cause (as history teaches us) for mass immigration to Israel.

Arab Jewish immigration to Israel is a neglected research area: too many questions remain open and are waiting to be answered. The well-entrenched and mythical explanation of the religious roots of this immigration is convenient for the dominant and official Israel. But it gives a far from adequate answer to the question of why Arab Jews decided to leave all these countries *en masse* in such a short period and at that specific time. A political and economic analysis of the motives for these "immigrations" on the one hand and of the benevolent process of welcoming them in Israel on the other reveals the cynical use of those immigrants for the purposes of the Israeli government and the Ashkenazi dominant group.[4]

Moreover, the much celebrated "absorption of immigrants in Israel" was actually a disguised form of stripping those new communities of any power or social organization and sense of their cultural identity, in order to facilitate their social subjugation, politically and economically. They could then be settled in "development towns," in order to build a "security belt" on the borders of the young state, at the same time providing the new Israeli economy with the needed cheap and unorganized labor force. One does not need a conspiracy to frame and achieve such goals, only a devoted group of people led by a self-assured political leadership, using its particular goals and ideals as the only criteria for evaluating reality.

These two factors, the dismissal of the Arab inhabitants of the land, and the cynical use of Arab Jews, gave rise to a specific kind of social structure. On the one hand it facilitated the large-scale expropriation of Palestinian land after the 1948 War, on the pretext that they did not exist or were "absentee." Thus the land belongs to the government.[5] In order to legitimize this expropriation of land, the Palestinian Arabs must be kept in a permanent state of invisibility. This goal promises constant and protracted conflict, and therefore the erection of a war machine and structure.[6] The wars that occurred between Israel and the Arab states and the continuous conflict with the Palestinians, are just phases in a long struggle. Since the military buildup serves as the highest imperative to Israel's existence, a society emerged with an economic, social, and cultural structure of war. War has created the Jewish Israeli society in its own image. It is a logical outcome of a hundred years' investment in the project of war.

On the other hand, the subordination of Arab Jews helped boost the economy. They also provided the basis for the economic and political ascendancy of the Ashkenazi Jews, who came just a generation or two before from Europe, and became the dominant group and the ruling elite. The war structure and accompanying cultural suppositions are indispensable ingredients of Ashkenazi dominance.

Such a framework postulated the notion of "Israel as a Western jewel in the Levant" or its corollary, "Israel as the only democracy in the Middle East." More concretely, it is the complete identification of Israeli national interests with the interests of Western countries in the Middle East. Identifying with England and France before 1967 (e.g., the Sinai War of 1956) or with the U.S. since then, isolates and alienates Israel in the Middle East.

These conceptions assigned all inhabitants of the Middle East, Arab Jews included, to a culturally inferior position. Economic vulnerability and cultural suppression of the Arab Jews facilitated the creation of the Mizrachim (Eastern Jews) as an underclass with Ashkenazim as the dominant group.[7] This Mizrachi-Ashkenazi relationship, in terms of class, social prestige, and political power was created and has concrete meaning only in Israel.

The existing structure of social interests produced a culture that by definition sanctifies a permanent condition of conflict. It is a war structure which created a war culture to sustain it. Its interests include the idea of exclusive Jewish control of the land, Western chauvinism, and a military industry in the economic sphere. These together give rise to an overlay of militaristic ideology which itself incorporates Jewish religiosity, claims of Jewish genius, and a replication of Western values. This interlaced network helps explain why any concession to or recognition of the Palestinians is portrayed as a thorough disaster. Any idea of reconciliation or integration in the Middle East and with its peoples is immediately translated as a threat to the hegemony of the Ashkenazim.

Israel can maintain this permanent war situation neither economically nor politically by itself. Today, the war structure dictates a specific set of relations with the U.S., Israel's main political ally and its major supplier of arms and economic aid. The military-economic aid that the United States "bestows upon" Israel deepens its dependence and has a devastating effect on its internal social structure.

American military aid is granted in the form of finished war products produced from U.S. factories. In fact, not a single dollar leaves the U.S. for Israeli coffers. Before its decline, the Soviet Union used to do the same with its Arab client countries. And as the war in the Gulf manifested clearly, other industrialized and economically powerful countries followed the same track. Thus, the Middle East serves as a huge open market for weaponry produced in the plants of the "First" and the "Second World" to wage wars in the "Third World."

American economic aid is given to Israel through loans, for which all citizens of Israel must pay. But only a small portion of the population benefits from such aid. Most of this money ends up sustaining the war economy through salaries for military technicians, engineers, and high-ranking government officials. Despite Israel's emphasis on social democracy, neither the levels of inequality nor the standard of living have improved with more than twenty years of U.S. "support." The reverse has happened; we now have greater social inequality and a huge external debt. For example, the upper 10 percent holds more than 50 percent of the national income and enjoys a high standard of living;[8] whereas the lower 10 percent holds less than 1 percent of the national income and has a standard of living that resembles conditions in most Third World countries. The upper 10 percent is mostly Ashkenazim, whereas the lower consists of Mizrachim and Palestinian citizens of Israel. The standard of living of Palestinians under occupation in the West Bank and Gaza Strip is a more complicated, but related issue.

Through most of the years of its existence, the Israeli government used the Palestinian citizens of Israel as a whip to put down any demands by the Jewish, mainly Mizrachi, working class; by bringing into the job market the unorganized and cheap Palestinian labor force. This was the economic policy in the 1950s and 1960s when the Palestinian citizens of Israel were under military rule. In economic terms, the 1967 War turned the clock back to the Yishuv pre-state conditions. The competition between Palestinians and Mizrachim was renewed on different ground. Since 1970, the implicit policy has been to introduce Palestinians from the Occupied Territories to the Israeli labor market, to both ruin any independent Palestinian economic base and provide greater economic gains for Israeli employers. The accessibility of Palestinian workers contributed to the antagonism between these two groups in the labor market, and has been exploited by employers and politicians alike.[9]

*   *   *   *   *

Mizrachim and Palestinians shared in the past, and share today, a marginal position in Israeli society, that continues to create competition and hostility between the two groups. This competition in the economic sphere is transformed to a mute and subjective inner tension in the cultural dimension and to a showy hostility against Palestinians in the political arena. This helps explain why Mizrachim in general and young Mizrachim in particular, tend to be more right-wing and hawkish. However, these are broad generalizations and convey only part of the story of Mizrachi political behavior. Conventional "wisdom" in Israel explains these trends by emphasizing that Mizrachi culture, traditions, or religiosity prescribe such hawkish attitudes towards Arabs. A short historical overview should be sufficient to demonstrate the shallowness of that argument: Jews lived with Arabs in the Middle East and North Africa for centuries, most of the time much more peacefully than Jews and Christians in Europe. A more concrete explanation of economic interests and aspirations to political dominance would reveal a different story. Moreover, it is noteworthy that none of the ultra-extremist and sometimes racist parties that have existed or currently operate in Israel was ever led by Mizrachim. The leadership of almost all political parties is the exclusive realm of Ashkenazim. Thus we have the main traits of the culture of war.

The war culture impacts the division of labor not only between ethnic and national groups, but between the genders as well. Since war is a male business, women, too, as a social group are relegated to an inferior position in Israeli society. Explicitly or implicitly the rationalization goes as follows: men fight and carry the burden of war, therefore men are the indispensable and vital element in Israeli society. These assumptions are of course false. In fact, women participate in the war effort in a way that goes beyond the actual fighting, though, of course, not in the role of decision-makers. Women carry the burden of war, whether or not they actually participate in combat, because it influences and shapes their lives. Women pay the price of war as widows and single parents after the death of men. They are the ones who care for the wounded and disabled. Women are transformed into a commodity and assigned to the second row in the war culture, thereby also solidifying the privileged role of men. Examining the role of women is significant since it shifts our attention from the short period of time that the noisy war is taking place, to the profound social dimension, and so emphasizes that war is an ongoing social process. Wars continue in "peace" times through their social impact on every sphere of life. In Israel the impact is amplified, because everything is framed by the concept of survival through war.

*   *   *   *   *

Thus I hope it has become clear that the conflict in Israel-Palestine is really between two main groups, Ashkenazim and Palestinians. In order to formulate a message and a project of peace, new actors are required for the scenario. Any peace negotiations that do not include the interests of the majority of Israeli Jews, that is, the Mizrachim, will miss their main target. Just as any other oppressed social group, Mizrachim might change their attitudes toward the conflict if other viable and feasible alternatives are presented. The potential for the formation of an independent political stand on the part of Mizrachim, moving them away from their current status as a right-wing political bloc, makes it imperative that all those involved, and first and foremost Palestinians, examine the dynamics of Jewish Israeli society. This is a legitimate request for involvement and consolidation of a common pathway that stems from a desire for peace.

From the earliest stages of their education, Israeli Jews learn to see war as a nearly objective, preordained reality that is not subject to change. For years, the predominant assumption was that "there is no one to talk to" on the other side, and therefore "nothing to talk about." In 1977 Anwar Sadat changed this formulation — at the expense of the Palestinian people. And the PLO's agreement to dialogue with Israelis and with the Israeli government over a political solution put the final stamp of invalidation on it.

I am a citizen of Israel who is trying to deal with a human problem through human means. The basis for my activity is a belief in the equality of human beings without regard to race, sex, religion, or nationality; and the knowledge that history is the product of human beings. I believe that Jews can live in the Middle East in peace and security. In order to get to peace we Israelis have to change our attitudes toward the East and rebuild our society on different grounds.

There is no logical distinction between the political problems within Jewish Israeli society and those between Israel and the Palestinians, the Arab world, and the world in general. The twisted logic of a zero-sum game is applied in both areas by all people. These rules imply endless war and an ahistorical stand by Jews in the Middle East. Thus, we cannot go on conceiving of war as external to the dynamics of Jewish Israeli society. It is an inherent component of its social, political, and cultural structure.

Wars do not happen as inexorable natural forces; they are made by human beings. In order to be prepared for a six-day war, the war machine must be built and trained for years. The education of young people to see war as inevitable takes effort and many resources.

If war is a human project that harnesses enormous resources and causes untold damage, peace is also a human project. Peace requires courage, steadfastness, and no less worldly wisdom than violent solutions. The efforts needed for peace are also enormous, but the fruits are much greater than the "fruits" of war. Peace, too, has a price. That price is not measured in corpses or graves, but in the simple acknowledgement of the political rights of the Palestinian people. That is to say, their right to self-determination and an independent state alongside Israel. Peace can provide security too, if we strive to build an economic base that will sustain the population of the region and will provide a sound basis for social and cultural development.

The existing structure of war has to be challenged with the idea of peace before a genuine reconciliation will emerge. Just as the war machine was built in a period of a hundred years; we, Israelis and Palestinians, must create a peace project. Peace requires concrete interests, not only idealistic and momentous words. The culture of war needs to be countered with an opposing culture, a culture of peace. The futures of the Palestinian nation and the Jewish Israeli nation are intertwined. We have the right and obligation to create a joint reality of peace. This is the only real option we have for survival, and we must take the risks of making it materialize.

Who are the allies in Israeli society, the ones who can bring peace with Palestinian Arabs?

The allies are the women and men who accept the fact of Israel's existence in the Middle East, as part of the Middle East, with its diverse cultures, histories, peoples, languages, and customs. I am referring to people who have an interest in changing the conditions of their lives; people for whom the culture of war and the resulting social structure has no benefit whatsoever. Mizrachim can play a part in this historic role; the objective conditions exist. What is missing is the subjective desire, and this can be promoted through information and persuasion.

In this last decade of the twentieth century, Israel is a class society dependent on the aid of a superpower to wage war, with a culture that prefers isolation over receptiveness to the world around it. Whatever Israel does, the problem remains the same: Israel is in the Middle East, our neighbors are Arabs, and our partners on the land are Palestinians. The price of rejecting these simple facts is being paid by the two nations in blood and destruction, through inequality and human tragedy. We can change the grounds for Ghassan Canafani's pessimism. It is up to us to create dialogue and a common language between Israelis and Palestinians.

Notes

1. Ghassan Canafani, *Gvarim Bashemesh*, (Jerusalem: Mifras Publishing House, 1978), (Hebrew translation).

2. As of last year, the proportion is undergoing a major change. But the new immigration of Soviet Jews, which for some had been a "White Hope" (see A. Margalit, "Israel's White Hope," *New York Review of Books*, 6/27/91), will not change basic relations between Jewish Israeli ethnic groups, nor will it change dramatically Israel's political relations to the region.

3. Zionist activists (or agents of the Israeli Secret Service, the Mossad) have been accused of bombing the Jewish synagogue in Baghdad, Iraq, as a way of scaring the Jewish community into emigrating (to Israel). On January 14, 1951 a bomb or a hand grenade exploded in the Masu'ada Shem-tov Synagogue, killing four people and injuring about twenty (see T. Segev's *1949 — The First Israelis*, The Dominco Press, Jerusalem (Hebrew), 1984, p. 164 [English edition: Free Press, Collier MacMillan (New York; London) 1986.]). Another example is the well-known "Parasha" (literally, the affair) in Cairo, Egypt. For years, a debate raged in Israel over the question of "Who gave the order?" to set up the bombs which exploded in Cairo. Governments fell, politicians resigned, and we still don't know the answer. No one, as yet, has asked the important question: who gave the order to organize actions like that, and for what purpose. The "Parasha" was actually the creation of official agents of the state of Israel, a Zionist terrorist cell of Jewish youth in Cairo. Their direct mission was to hamper the development of any positive relations between the U.S. and Egypt. The indirect effect, besides the disaster it brought on the people involved, their families, and the entire Jewish communities of these and neighboring countries, such as Morocco, Algeria, Libya and Tunisia, can only be assumed. Both "affairs" are still covered with a veil of secrecy under the cloak of national security. These kind of actions, however, do indicate that the Israeli government was very much involved

in the creation and promotion of the "great immigration wave" of Arab Jews to Israel in the 1950s and the 1960s.

4. D. Bernstein, "Hamabarot Beshnot Hchmishim," in *Mahbarot Lemechkar U'Ibikurt*, no. 5, Haifa (Hebrew), 1980; and S. Swirski and D. Bernstein, "Who worked in what, for whom, and for how much? The economic development of Israel and the ethnic division of labor," in *Mahbarot Lemechkar U'Ibikurt*, no. 4, Haifa, (Hebrew), 1980.

5. C. Keyman, "After the Disaster: The Arabs in the Israeli State 1948-1950," in *Mahbarot Lemechkar U'Ibikurt*, no. 10, Haifa, (Hebrew), 1984.

6. A. Ehrlich. "Israel: Conflict, War and Social Change" in Colin Creighton and Martin Shaw (eds.), *The Sociology of War and Peace*, (London: Macmillan, 1987).

7. *Mizrachim* is the accurate "name" that describes the Arab Jews in Israel in terms not related to geography (*Mizrach* in Hebrew means "East"), but to social content. Mizrachim come to denote a new creation. Out of the *different* Jewish groups coming from the Middle East, Africa, and Asia who were grouped together by the absorption process, a new group emerged that has, to a large extent, the same *Israeli* history; the same economic and political position: *the Jewish working class*; and last but not least, a similar future. Mizrachim is an identity used by members of this group in referring to themselves in private discussions. There are two other terms: *Sephardi Jews* and *Edot Ha'mizrach*. The former refers to the common root in Spain five centuries ago, and thus is devoid of any current political content. The latter is a catch-all phrase invented by Ashkenazi ideology to convey a sense of plurality on the side of Jews from the East (Mizrach) as opposed to the cultural unity of the Jews from Europe.

8. E. Alexander, "An Alternative Economic Plan," *Iton Aher*, no. 15-16 (March 1991), pp. 14-17 (Hebrew).

9. Gershon Shafir, *Land and Labor in the Making of the Israeli Nationalism*, (Cambridge University Press, 1989); and "The Meeting of Eastern Europe and Yemen: 'Idealistic Workers' and 'Natural Workers' in Early Zionist Settlement in Palestine," in *Ethnic and Racial Studies*, vol. 13, no. 2 (April 1990). Today, the presence of the new Soviet immigrants is already influencing relations between the different social groups in Israel. Now the new immigrants are vulnerable, unorganized, in desperate need of jobs, and thus a new cheap labor force. All these factors put them at the mercy of the government's absorption policy, called "free market." Hence the current noisy cry to kick Palestinian workers out of Israel. The Mizrachi working class, experienced from earlier waves of Soviet immigrants who advanced above them (and sometimes at their expense), have voiced complaints against the massive immigration from the very beginning.

Ishai Menuchin

Ishai Menuchin was born in Rehovot, Israel, in 1958. On graduation from high school, he was conscripted for military service; he served with the paratroop brigade, where he achieved the rank of lieutenant. Upon discharge from the army, he registered at the Hebrew University where he studied philosophy and psychology. He has recently completed his masters degree in cognitive psychology. Ishai is married with two children.

Ishai long showed an interest in politics, but became active during the Lebanon War when he joined Peace Now and, subsequently, Yesh Gvul. When posted for reserve service with the Israeli forces in Lebanon in 1983, he refused to report for duty and was sentenced to a term in military prison. Since that time, he has played a central role in Yesh Gvul, as a leading activist and spokesman for the movement.

In 1985, Ishai edited (in conjunction with his wife Dina Menuchin) an anthology in Hebrew entitled *Gvul Hatziyut (The Limits of Obedience)*. Its contributors include Noam Chomsky, Michael Waltzer, Richard Popkin, and Joseph Raz, as well as prominent Israeli thinkers. In 1990 he edited a second anthology entitled *Al Democratiya ve'Tziyut*, 1990 (On Democracy and Obedience) with contributions from, among others, Amos Oz, Haim Cohn, and Professor Yeshayahu Liebovitz. Both anthologies consider the underlying ideas which inspired Yesh Gvul.

Occupation, Protest, and Selective Refusal

Ishai Menuchin

Present-day Israel is a country dominated and overshadowed by occupation. In the immediate aftermath of the 1967 War, occupation was a military fact; today, occupation is the underlying mental state of Israeli society. Occupation has become the main concept, and the main motivating force; it is an essential component of Israeli self-identification. Occupation doesn't merely dominate Israeli society: occupation is built into the very foundations and structure of this society. It is a cornerstone of society — as graphically illustrated by the fact that each successive election brings additional support to the right-wing parties. Reinforcing trends which predate it, occupation has made Israelis more nationalistic and less democratic.

Prior to the Palestinian Intifada, the average Israeli perceived the Occupied Territories as an integral part of their homeland; a pleasantly exotic region featuring cheap markets and good Mideastern cooking; and principally, a source of cheap labor. They gave little or no thought to beatings, mass arrests, demolition of houses, deportations, or unarmed demonstrators shot down by armed troops. Of those who became aware of such unpleasant deeds, a majority brushed them aside as matters arising from the overall confrontation between Israel and the Arab world; or, alternately, comforted themselves with the bland reassurance that "such is the way of the world." Although the

The author wishes to acknowledge the assistance of his friend and colleague Peretz Kidron in the composition of this paper.

Intifada has made the Occupied Territories somewhat less accessible, it has not notably affected those perceptions.

Without doubt, the Israeli government bears direct responsibility for its immoral and reckless policies. But some of that responsibility is shared by the large portion of the people who give those policies their full support, and no less, by those citizens who, while disapproving of those policies, do nothing to resist them. Sharing equally in the repression and exploitation of the Palestinians, full-fledged supporters and faint-hearted critics are thus partners in responsibility for the present dismal state of affairs.

The passage of the years has, however, made growing numbers of Israelis weary of an increasingly repressive occupation. The more clear-minded have realized that they must campaign against the Israeli occupation and support the Palestinian right of self-determination, which is the key to a political solution of the Israeli-Palestinian conflict. The best-known groups that have started doing this work are Peace Now, Women in Black, and Yesh Gvul. Peace Now is a broadly based organization that focuses on efforts to mobilize public opinion for a political solution to the conflict. Women in Black have drawn widespread attention with their regular weekly anti-occupation protests, which take the form of vigils at central locations throughout Israel. Yesh Gvul, of which I am a member, focuses on direct action against the occupation, with a particular stress on support for soldiers who refuse to take part in the oppression of the Palestinians.

For a closer consideration of Yesh Gvul, it is useful to elaborate upon the name as a clue to the group's character. In literal translation, Yesh Gvul means, "There is a border" — a reference to Israel's pre-1967 border. But in everyday conversation, the phrase is an idiom denoting: "There is a limit!" — meaning there's a limit to what we are willing to do, whether as citizens or as soldiers.

This self-imposed limitation is highly important in view of the unique social status of the Israeli army (the IDF). For society at large, the army represents the power of national unity in the face of external enemies. Until recent years, there was virtual unanimity as to the defensive (and therefore "just") nature of the various military conflicts in which Israel had engaged.

The army plays a prominent role in the biography of every Israeli. Every eighteen-year-old Israeli male is required to give three years of compulsory military service; every female does two years. Conscripts are trained and prepared for prolonged reserve service, which men render in annual spells for an additional thirty years; women do little or no reserve duty.

For the young Israeli, enlistment at eighteen coincides with leaving home for the first time, and the first encounter with adult self-sufficiency. Military service is a rite of passage and a token of maturity.

Before the establishment of Israel in 1948, the Jewish community lacked the legal power to enforce conscription; nevertheless, powerful social pressure made voluntary enrollment well-nigh universal. To this day, such social endorsement remains strong, giving military service an extraordinary measure of social sanctity.

Backed up by such powerful social, historical, and ideological bonding, the broad embrace of military service has given rise to a consensus that the IDF is a "people's army" and "stands above politics." Israelis have consequently developed a "blind spot" which renders them incapable of grasping the political role of the army as a tool of the ruling establishment.

As far back as 1967, from the very onset of Israel's occupation of the West Bank and the Gaza Strip, there were Israelis who objected to the occupation and to the immoral policies attendant upon it. Still, due to the prevalent myth of the "non-political army," almost no one went so far as to criticize the use of the IDF as a political tool in maintaining occupation. Few and far between were the individuals who actively refused to take part in the repressive assignments that go along with service in an army of occupation.

This is the background from which Yesh Gvul emerged in 1982, at the time of the Lebanon invasion. Prior to the invasion, a group of reservists had been meeting to consider a refusal to serve in the Occupied Territories. But when the IDF thrust into Lebanon, the ongoing campaign took preference. Members of the group initiated a petition addressed to the defense minister, with signatories requesting to take no part in the Lebanon War. As a new movement intent on avoiding the errors of its predecessors, Yesh Gvul tried to focus its efforts on direct action against the war. After many years of protests, pickets, demonstrations, and petitions, none of which had made any impact on official policy, Yesh Gvul strategy instituted a new tradition of direct action—with dramatic results. The original petition ultimately acquired the signatures of over twenty-five hundred reservists. Many of these, when posted to service in Lebanon, refused to report for duty there, and no less than 160 were jailed in military prisons.

Elevating their act of personal refusal into an overt protest aimed at rallying public opinion against the Lebanon invasion, members of Yesh Gvul sought to shock Israeli society out of its lethargy by challenging the sacred myths which placed the army and military service at the very pinnacle of civic duty. Beyond any doubt, the refusers violated a deep-rooted social taboo; accordingly, the emergence of Yesh Gvul, and the group's support for refusal, evoked violent political crossfire. The refusal to obey "legitimate" orders was widely perceived as a challenge to hitherto unquestioned values. Even active critics of the Lebanon campaign denounced the refusal movement and its supporters.

But the government was exploiting the army for immoral political purposes, and it was against these purposes — and not against the army as such — that Yesh Gvul directed its protest in the form of refusal of service. This distinction — a protest against the political exploitation of the army and not against the army itself — achieved a surprisingly broad measure of public acceptance and even approval. Many objective observers credit Yesh Gvul with a major contribution to ending the Lebanon War.[1]

After the Israeli withdrawal from Lebanon in 1985, members of Yesh Gvul decided to channel their activities back into protests against the government's policy of occupation and annexation in the Occupied Territories. This decision reflects the assessment prevalent in Yesh Gvul that the Lebanon War, as well as the nationalist and racist views which increasingly hold sway in Israeli society, are a direct consequence of occupation. In a sharp departure from the strategy adopted during the Lebanon campaign, the group's protests are not confined exclusively to the politicians who manipulate the army for their own ideological ends. The campaign is now directed equally against the IDF as an army of occupation. We in Yesh Gvul regard occupation, in itself, as immoral by definition, even without its "unavoidable" consequences: the beatings, the tear-gassings, the deportations, the demolitions of homes, and the shooting of unarmed demonstrators.

When the Palestinian Uprising erupted in the Occupied Territories in December of 1987, Yesh Gvul sponsored a collective declaration by reservists which stated:

> The Palestinian people is in revolt against Israeli occupation. Over 20 years of occupation and repression have not checked the Palestinian struggle for national liberation. The uprising in the Occupied Territories, and its brutal suppression by IDF forces, graphically illustrate the terrible price of occupation and the absence of a political solution.
>
> As IDF reservists, we declare that we can no longer bear the burden of shared responsibility for this moral and political depravation.
>
> We hereby proclaim that we shall refuse to take part in suppressing the uprising and insurrection in the Occupied Territories.[2]

Going much further than the Lebanon petition, whose signatories merely *requested* not to be posted to duty in that country, this declaration was a far stronger political statement, because it was a clear personal *commitment* on the part of each signatory to refuse participation in the ongoing campaign of repression. In spite of its militancy, this declaration has to date been signed by over two thousand reservists, including numerous officers up to the rank of major. Since the onset of the uprising, over 150 soldiers have received prison sentences for refusing to serve in the Occupied Territories.[3]

Organized refusal is a powerful political act because it exerts pressure at a sensitive point of national security. By undermining conventional military discipline, it poses a constant threat to the army hierarchy. By rendering the army as a whole less pliant to the will of the political establishment, it reduces its effectiveness as a political tool.

The army is indispensable in maintaining and perpetuating the occupation. When the politicians discover that the armed forces are being progressively undermined and eroded by the occupation and the policing role it imposes, we hope that they will curb the increasingly violent repression of the Palestinian population, leaving the politicians with no choice other than pursuit of a political solution.

We are convinced that there is no military solution to the Israeli-Palestinian conflict. We are equally convinced that occupation will ultimately lead Israel to a dead end. In spite of the destructive course followed by politicians on both sides, we look forward to a peaceful solution whereby the Palestinians will achieve their legitimate national rights.

Yesh Gvul does not support conscientious objection, nor an outright refusal to render military service. Although respecting conscientious objectors (COs) for their convictions, we do not share them; our standpoint calls for "selective refusal" of orders or duties we consider morally or politically unacceptable.

We draw this distinction on the assumption that geopolitical constraints will require Israel to maintain an army for the foreseeable future. We assume further that, like any other army, the IDF will require its chain of command and discipline. We accordingly support universal military service, and expect military personnel to obey legitimate orders. We are, however, convinced that every soldier must clearly define his "red lines" beyond which he cannot and will not go — that point where the orders he receives or the laws he is required to follow are so immoral that he has the right — or even, the obligation — to disobey them.

Compliance with the law of the land is a vital element in the interaction between the individual and the society in which he or she lives. But treading the path of convention and conforming with accepted prejudice can induce most citizens to a blind, unquestioning obedience frequently interpreted as a value unto itself. History is replete with examples of such knee-jerk obedience and its horrifying consequences.

Selective refusal of military service is a form of nonviolent civil disobedience, in total accord with democratic principle. Yesh Gvul fosters selective refusal, whereby a soldier willingly discharges his normal duties, but refuses to take any part in assignments designed to promote or perpetuate occupation and repression. Selective refusal actively rejects immoral acts, even when they masquerade under the cloak of legality, whether civilian or military. In place of the prima facie obligation to the law and obedience thereto, selective refusal reflects a primary commitment to basic democratic values — a commitment which entails respect exclusively for laws of a democratic nature, and a concomitant refusal to obey laws which are undemocratic or antidemocratic.

Such a code of values and behavior reflects a new manner of belonging to society; a social partnership which, not resting content with formal acts such as periodic entry into a polling booth, also undertakes personal responsibility for the acts committed by the society to which one adheres. In a democratic society, it is the solemn civic duty of each and every citizen — including soldiers, who are citizens-in-uniform — to refuse to participate in acts which are, by their very nature and purpose, antidemocratic.

—June 5, 1991
the 24th anniversary of the occupation

Notes

1. Addressing an officers' convention in 1986, Brig. General Moshe Levy, then commander-in-chief of the Israeli Defense Forces, conceded that the decision of defense minister Moshe Arens to commence the withdrawal from Lebanon had been influenced by the refusal movement. (*Monitin*, March 1990).

2. Statement presented by 160 reserve soldiers at Yesh Gvul press conference at Beit Agron in Jerusalem, January 1, 1988.

3. The actual number of refusals is much higher, probably running into thousands. However, the army has adopted a sophisticated policy of containment whereby most refuseniks are not prosecuted in spite of their insubordination. Instead, they are accommodated with alternative postings to duties not offensive to their consciences. The army's gain is a drastic reduction in the statistics of refusal, and military spokespeople regularly dismiss the refusal movement as "a marginal phenomenon."

Michel "Mikado" Warschawski

Michel "Mikado" Warschawski was born in 1949 in France to an orthodox Jewish family. His father was Chief Rabbi of Strasbourg, and a member of the French partisans during the Second World War.

Mikado immigrated to Jerusalem in 1966 in order to study at a Talmudic school. In 1968, while studying at the Hebrew University there, he joined the anti-Zionist organization Matzpen, in which he continues to be active today, as editor of its Hebrew magazine of the same name. He was one of the founders of the Committee in Solidarity with Bir Zeit University (1981), and Yesh Gvul (1982). Mikado was jailed three times for refusing to serve in Lebanon and in the Occupied Territories.

Mikado is a cofounder and the Director of the Alternative Information Center. In addition to his work with the Center, Mikado is a journalist with various European newspapers and magazines. He is married to Lea Tsemel, a renowned human rights attorney and is the father of three children.

The Long March towards Israeli-Palestinian Cooperation

Michel (Mikado) Warschawski

On the seventh of November, 1989, as director of the Alternative Information Center, I was sentenced by the Jerusalem District Court to thirty months (twenty months imprisonment and ten months suspended) for "giving printing services to a forbidden association." Specifically, the sentence was for helping publish a pamphlet about Shabak [The Israeli Security Services, equivalent of the CIA — ed.] interrogations, for the use of activists in the Popular Front for the Liberation of Palestine (PFLP — a Marxist PLO faction, headed by George Habash) in the Occupied Territories. The High Court subsequently reduced the sentence to twenty months, eight of which were to be served in prison. These I served, with a third off for good behavior, in Ma'asiyahu Prison.

Unprecedented in its severity, this sentence only appeared to have anything to do with "forbidden printing." Its primary objective was to warn and deter the progressive forces in Israel from working too closely with Palestinians and from any kind of cooperation with them. The implied message: there needs to be a border separating Israelis and Palestinians, and one must not get too close to this border if he or she wants to enjoy the relative freedom which Israeli democracy allows its

---

Translated from Hebrew by Maxine Kaufman Nunn

Incorporated into this essay are excerpts from the speech I delivered at the solidarity meeting held at the Kol Haneshema Synagogue in West Jerusalem a few days after my sentencing.

Jewish citizens. The Alternative Information Center [see Appendix — ed.] consciously chose to stand on the border and to create a framework of cooperation and of Israeli-Palestinian encounter and therefore must be punished, with a penalty which would deter others.

Many of those present here do not share my political course, nor my degree of proximity to the border. In spite of this, my verdict is directed at you who are approaching the border and acting to create a new quality of relationship between Israelis and Palestinians. The verdict is directed at you as a warning sign: Beware of the Border!

*   *   *   *   *

We were few in number when, in 1968, we went scurrying all over the West Bank in search of Palestinians who shared our opinions or who were at least willing to talk with us. I am proud that the political organization to which I have belonged for twenty-two years, Matzpen, was always the first to open the way for Israeli-Palestinian cooperation. [Matzpen, the Revolutionary Communist League, and formerly the Israeli Socialist Organization, is a Jewish-Arab anti-Zionist organization that was famous in the 1960s and first half of the 1970s for being the only group in Israel to oppose the occupation and defend Palestinian rights. Matzpen supports the idea of a democratic bi-national state. — ed.] Our comrade Khalil Tu'mee was the first Israeli citizen — in this case a Palestinian Israeli — imprisoned after the beginning of the occupation because he tried, on behalf of our organization, to find ways to make contacts and to talk with Palestinians from the Occupied Territories. He was sentenced in 1968 to eighteen months in prison for meeting with Tayseer Kuba, the chair of the Students' Association in the West Bank.

We remained few when we sat with Palestinian activists in European capitals and on U.S. campuses and talked about dialogue and cooperation. This search for Palestinian partners came to us almost naturally; for our political schooling, we had not drawn on the Zionist ethos, but rather on the example of left activists from all over the world, consciously and intentionally cutting ourselves off from Zionism and its values. We rejected Zionism, and Zionism in turn cast us out from the world of sanity and legitimacy. It was precisely the leftists among them who distinguished themselves at witch-hunting, mostly in a manner comparable to the efforts of Herzl Rosenblum (then editor-in-chief of *Yediot Aharonot*, and a most extreme right-wing editorialist).[1] It is no wonder that we looked for friends and partners not only outside the Israeli consensus, but also outside the nationality which had expelled us from its ranks.

Despite this, we still bore the marks of the Zionist education and atmosphere in which we had been raised, and in 1969, when Naif Hawatmeh approached Matzpen directly with the aim of initiating dialogue, he encountered a cool response. Naif Hawatmeh was at the head of a left-wing split in the PFLP at the time, and started the Democratic Front for the Liberation of Palestine (DFLP). In articles and interviews in various newspapers, including *Le Monde*, he made an appeal to Matzpen for Jewish-Arab cooperation against Zionism and Arab reaction, and for a socialist Middle East. We also placed various conditions in the way of such a dialogue. In our defense, the issue of contact with Palestinian organizations was so important to us that it was the background for the splits in Matzpen; in the wake of this all-encompassing political clarification process, all factions of Matzpen almost completely abandoned their original arrogant attitude toward these dialogues.

Even after this we were still a small minority when, in the mid-1970s, we initiated contacts with Palestinian activists in the Occupied

The Border

Michel (Mikado) Warschawski

Excerpt from Michel Warschawski's speech at the solidarity meeting in his honor held November 12, 1989 at Kol Haneshema synagogue in West Jerusalem. Reprinted with permission from News from Within (November 23, 1989).

I would like to dedicate the time available to me to one concept, a concept that appeared again and again throughout my trial and also occupies a central place in the court's decision, namely the concept of "the border" — I coined this term myself, and only later did my judges begin making use of it. And indeed, the concept of "border" is a key to understanding the trial, to understanding both the defendant and the decision of the court.

There is the border that I refuse to cross. The Lebanon border, for example, which, along with my friends from Yesh Gvul, I refused to cross three times. Twice I sat in jail for refusing to cross this border. This border, like the refusal to serve in the heart of the Palestinian population in the Occupied

Territories, especially in universities and intellectual circles. We were also the first to meet Said Hammami (the PLO representative in London in the 1970s) and Issam Sartawi (the initiator of the first formal PLO/Fatah-Israeli meetings), long ago before it was fashionable, and many years before the Knesset even dreamed of legislating the Amendment to the Prevention of Terror Ordinance.[2]

In the middle of the 1970s we were the first to make connections with the students in Bir Zeit University in the West Bank town of Ramallah, so frequently subjected to army harassment. Thus we paved the way for the Committee in Solidarity with Bir Zeit University, a number of years later. In the Bir Zeit Committee, we were among the first to push for broadening the solidarity toward the refugee camps as well, and we made Dheisheh Refugee Camp the focus for Israeli-Palestinian cooperation.

Territories, I openly, and not sneakily, refuse to cross. I refuse with readiness to face the consequences and to pay the price, since the refusal to cross this border and participate in an immoral war or to take part in oppression — this kind of refusal is a political expression that is done publicly.

Another border was erected in my trial as well, when I was required to give the name of the person who gave me the booklet for typesetting. I clarified for my judges that I can't cross this border and that I'm ready to pay the price for it. There is no connection between this refusal and the nature of the person whose name I will not give: there is no difference if he is a friend or an enemy, a person in danger or a person who doesn't have anything to be afraid of. We are talking here about an imperative category that I was brought up with in my father's home and that is related to the joint values of my religious education and my socialist viewpoint. My refusal to cross this border served the court as a way to prove my lack of innocence and shut people's eyes.

The law is also a border, that divides the permitted from the prohibited. Along with my comrades in the struggle, I chose to respect this border. I am not an underground fighter, as was my father, who fought with weapon in hand against the Nazis. I'm also not a suitcase carrier, as were many of my best friends in France who endangered their liberty while materially assisting the Algerian liberation fighters. Many of them paid quite a heavy price for it. They chose to disobey the law; I, not.

The first attempt to initiate cooperation between Israeli and Palestinian university students took place in 1978, and a year later there was a joint initiative by Israeli and Palestinian activists to organize solidarity with the heroic hunger strike of the Palestinian political prisoners at Nafha Prison. On those two occasions, it was impossible to involve even Jewish activists of the Israeli Communist Party, not to mention those of the Zionist Left.

The establishment of the Committee against Jewish Settlement in Hebron and later, the Committee for Solidarity with Bir Zeit University, marked the beginnings of a change in Israeli-Palestinian relations. For the first time, activists who did not belong to the declared anti-Zionist Left began to meet with Palestinian activists and to coordinate political initiatives with them. For the first time this taboo was breached, even if only on the fringes of what later came to be called

---

Together with my comrades I chose to keep to the existing law, however defective it might be. My choices come out of an evaluation that the existing regime ensures us — the Jews among us — a large degree of freedom and democratic rights, and the possibility, however flawed, to mobilize around a political viewpoint that calls for fundamental change of this regime. In the implicit contract between me and the state, I am interested in keeping my part, that is to say, respecting the limits of the law. There is more to it than a simple pragmatic attitude. I believe we need to maintain the relatively democratic infrastructure, and try to widen it rather than exchange it for a regime that suppresses any liberties.

However, within the borders of the law, I chose to be precisely *on the border*, and to relate to my freedom with complete seriousness, and not with quotation marks. The fundamental assumption that stands behind a democratic regime is that everything that is not prohibited explicitly is considered *galat kosher* (strictly proper). This is the difference between democracy and totalitarianism. If people don't know how to keep their rights, they forsake them to the arbitrariness of their rulers who turn them into prohibitions or additional limitations on their liberties. On the issue of rights, the abandonment of a stronghold always brings its occupation by the opposite side. Therefore, rights shouldn't be abandoned — they should be fought for with your teeth. In Jerusalem, we have been doing this by struggling for the right to

the Israeli peace camp. This chapter in the saga of Israeli-Palestinian relations too, was not without "conditions," and some of us have not yet forgotten the Palestinian flags which were removed from the central auditorium of Bethlehem University in order not to offend the overly fastidious sensibilities of the activists from the Israeli Communist party, the Israeli Socialist Left (Shasi) and the Left of Sheli.[3]

* * * * *

The rising of the PLO's international star, alongside the decline of the Israeli solidarity movement in the wake of the Lebanon War, resulted in a shift in relations with the Palestinians. Contacts with activists in the Occupied Territories gradually gave way to showy meetings with PLO representatives abroad. The more hugging Arafat in front of TV cameras became "in," the more the days of volunteer

demonstrate. We have stretched the border more and more; we were ready to be detained, we appealed to the courts, we were put on trial, but we didn't give up our rights, and we have thus achieved rights that in other places in the country are still considered impermissible. By stretching the line of the border we enlarge our rights; by staying far from it, we limit our rights. Therefore I refuse to stand far from the border, in a safe place in the middle. And I reject the position that says, "It's not clear whether or not it's permitted, therefore it's not worth getting mixed up with the law." My judges turned to me with arguments that I stood too close to the border of the law. I am sorry, but only on the border of the law can we widen our rights and examine our freedom.

And there is another border, maybe the most significant for me: the border that separates the two peoples of this land, between Israel and Palestine. This is a border of friction, of war, of confrontation; but this border is also the meeting place of the two peoples, and therefore you ought to stand on it so as to extend your hand in return for the one extended to you.

I have never stood for an Israeli-Palestinian peace that would only be a kind of cease-fire, a kind of "leave me alone and I will leave you in peace." This is not desirable and doesn't have any prospects. An Israeli-Palestinian peace can only be a peace of cooperation and togetherness, or won't be at all. And we should begin building the "togetherness" today — in dialogues, in cooperation, in solidarity. All these are work in Dheisheh and sit-down strikes at Bir Zeit became "out," especially since the former came with airline tickets paid for by various international bodies. Those were the days of the first National Unity Government and Yitzhak Rabin's Iron Fist Policy [a hardening of military measures against the population under occupation — ed.], the days of splits within the PLO — the darkest days of the Palestinian struggle against the occupation. Those were the days when the Palestinians were more than ever in need of the active solidarity of the Israeli peace forces.

This challenge was taken up by a small handful of Israeli activists, mainly from the anti-Zionist Left, who founded, in conjunction with Palestinian activists, the Committee Confronting the Iron Fist.

In the middle of the eighties we established, together with Faisal Husseini, the first framework for joint struggle against the occupation

---

impossible to do from a safe place in the middle of the national consensus, nor from the center of the Israeli Left. You build the Israeli-Palestinian partnership on the border, and only on the border.

If I've contributed even a little to the subject of Israeli-Palestinian peace, it was because of this standing on the border, and through taking the first steps on the way to Israeli-Palestinian dialogue and cooperation. I refuse to be the border guard. My will is to continue to be the one who breaks through the fences of hate and the walls of separation. I apologize for the analogy, but I see myself as a member of the breakthrough unit that sometimes must lie on the fence, and over whose backs the pioneering force passes, widening the gap in the fence, to pave the way for the larger attacking force. The casualty rate in the breakthrough unit is rather high, but this is their role.

I'm not one of those who think that judges receive orders from the political system or the Shin Bet [the internal, domestic intelligence agency —ed.]. However, I have no doubt that they absorb in their regular meeting with the system the values and norms that that system is interested in introducing. And they broadcast it further in their court decisions. One of the values that the political system feels it must inevitably establish today as part and parcel of its policy is that any Palestinian as such ought to be considered a terrorist. Not only the PLO, and not only this and other organizations, but every girl that

— The Committee Confronting the Iron Fist — and in the same spirit, the Alternative Information Center was established in 1984, as a joint framework for Israeli and Palestinian activists.

What was innovative about the Committee Confronting the Iron Fist was that it was the first body that united Israeli and Palestinian activists who continued to be active within their individual frameworks—some in what remained of the Israeli protest movement, and the others in Palestinian national bodies. Because of the vacuum which existed at that time on both sides of the Green Line, the activities of the Committee had an impact far out of proportion to its numerical strength. But the principal contribution of the Committee Confronting the Iron Fist was neither the media coverage it gained in the course of its two years of vigils, nor the many publications it produced and press conferences it held. It was, rather, the opportunity it gave to Israelis

demonstrates and every youngster who . throws a stone. Therefore, the blood of every Palestinian youngster in the Territories is free for the taking, and shooting them with an aim to kill is allowed. Through this, they are determined to strengthen the separating power of the border between Israelis and Palestinians, and to stop any process that blurs the border and proves that Palestinians can be partners to a dialogue and to the struggle for peace.

Didn't the prosecutor in the trial of [maverick peace activist] Abie Nathan state that "citizens who have unauthorized contacts and talks with the enemy hurt the security of the state . . . because they bring about the de-demonization of Arafat"? The crime is de-demonization — relating to any Palestinian as an image of God, and not as a monster. And this is precisely the choice that the court has made, and behind it is the entire establishment that sets the choice for every one of you: You either accept the policy of refusal, keep your distance from the border, and so contribute, even if passively, to turning every Palestinian child into a monster, a demon; or you continue on your way, the way of Abie Nathan, the way of the Rumanian and Hungarian accused, and my way, and search for ways of dialogue as close as possible to the border of confrontation, which is also the border of peace.

and Palestinians to learn, through working together directly, about the conditions under which the activists on the other side worked, the limitations and singularities of each of the two political realities. And especially, it provided the opportunity for combining this learning with united action, without requiring that either side subordinate its needs or principles to the tactical requirements of the other.

It must be clearly understood that the Israelis who worked on the Committee Confronting the Iron Fist saw themselves neither as Palestinians nor as "the Palestinians' Jews," but rather as an integral part of their own people, aiming to awaken its most aware elements to the struggle against the occupation. They never suggested equivalence or symmetry between them and the Palestinians. People like Faisal Husseini (the most prominent activist in the Occupied Territories) and Jibril Rajoub (one of the leaders of the Palestinian political prisoners) represented not only an occupied and oppressed nation, but also a mass movement expressing the will of its people and the policies of its leaders.[4] In contrast, the Israelis represented only themselves — and (a hint of) the possibility of a future mass movement against the occupation within the ranks of the occupying nation. This difference is not trivial. It requires the highest degree of humility on the part of the Israelis, lest the occupier/occupied relationship be duplicated within the movement itself. To the credit of the Palestinian activists, it must be emphasized that they never demanded recognition of this asymmetry, and even showed extreme sensitivity to the needs of the Israeli side. In order for the relationship to be based on truth, the Israeli activists had to express at least their awareness of this asymmetry—of the fact that the two realities of which we spoke had never been and could never be symmetrical.

None of these things could have been done from the center — from the heart of Israeli society and its consensus. They could be done only from the border and on the border. Only there was it possible to meet, talk, and act jointly. Therefore I have always refused to stay in the warm bosom of the consensus. And in 1968 I had already chosen my place on the border — on this side of the border, as part of my society, but as close as possible to the other side.

Precisely because we were acting as Israelis, and not simply as members of the human race, we had to understand and remember that the Israeli-Palestinian relationship which Israeli peace activists wanted to build on a firm base of egalitarianism and mutual respect, was in and of itself a relationship of rape. To transform a relationship of rape into one of mutual respect requires first of all an awareness of the character of the initial connection and the implications which arise from it as long as this character is retained, even if we, as individuals or as "a righteous minority in Sodom," are prepared to do whatever is necessary in order to put an end to the violent character of the relationship. To ignore the nature of the present relationship between the two peoples is not simply in bad taste, it reproduces, as we said, relations of dependency and oppression.

Not only the Zionist Left, but also the leaders of the Israeli Communist party related negatively to the efforts of the Committee Confronting the Iron Fist in which they saw, without justification, kowtowing by Israelis to the "Palestinian Right" (Faisal Husseini). But whereas the former were preoccupied with (critical) support of Rabin, and the latter with conferences abroad and hugs with Yasser Arafat, the activists of the Committee Confronting the Iron Fist were preparing the ground for a new pattern of relations between the Palestinian National Movement and the Israeli peace camp and were making a significant contribution to the shaping of new forms of struggle, which would find full expression with the outbreak of the Uprising.

The Palestinian Uprising brought about a qualitative change in the behavior patterns of part of the progressive Israeli public towards the Palestinian public and their leadership. After two decades of almost completely ignoring the men and women who lived some ten minutes from Kfar Saba or two minutes from Café Ta'amon, the Mecca of Jerusalem's bohemian Left, a change took place whose significance must not be underrated. When I say "ignoring," I need to be specific. The Palestinian had existed as a "problem" or as a miserable victim; not as a person with control over his or her fate, with opinions and the ability to make decisions, initiate actions or struggles. It felt something like a relationship with a slightly retarded child whom you might pity or sometimes be angry with, but who is nonetheless a bother. They were willing to discuss the child's future with his or her guardians — but guardians whom the progressive Israelis themselves had decided upon: sometimes the Hashemite uncle and sometimes more distant family members, sitting on the Security Council or at an international conference. Progressive Israelis took a big step when they agreed to see the PLO as the guardian. At least this was a guardian whom the inhabitants of the Occupied Territories chose for themselves, and not one appointed by others.

But the Intifada brought about a drastic change in the behavior of Israelis — including those in the wider peace movement — towards the inhabitants of the Occupied Territories. The great interest expressed in the visits to hot spots of the Intifada, which Dai Lakibush organized from the first weeks of the Uprising, was the first sign Israelis would abandon the policy of completely ignoring the Palestinians, and of a new thirst to see, hear, and get to know them. Later on, more political meetings with activists began and parallel to them, coordination and cooperation between many groups. The Beita Committee and the residents of Beita[5], Women for Women Political Prisoners, and women's organizations in the West Bank as well as the families of the prisoners, and Hal'a Hakibush and activists in Gaza Strip refugee camps, are but a few examples.

Despite the fact that those most enthusiastic about this Israeli-Palestinian encounter were activists from the center of the peace camp — and not those from its more radical wing, some of whom already had experience with this sort of meeting, and others of whom saw in it a "loss of Israeli identity" or "philanthropic activity" — the leaders of the socialist Zionist camp, from Peace Now, Ratz, and Mapam, stood apart with a disgusted expression on their faces. "It is not our job to kiss Palestinians," they said. That is, until U.S. policy towards the PLO changed. Then these same movement leaders began scurrying around East Jerusalem like drugged mice — and sent their rank and file to demonstrate in the Occupied Territories.

The crowning achievement of Israeli-Palestinian cooperation was the peace demonstration organized in December 1989 at the initiative of the European peace movements, in coordination with Peace Now and the Palestinian national leadership in the Occupied Territories. What two years previously had been seen (even) by the radical wing of the peace camp as activity bordering on treason, when pursued by the Committee Confronting the Iron Fist, was adopted almost down to the last detail by Peace Now — the same initiators, the same Palestinian partners, nearly the same slogans. The power of the Intifada had shaken up the borders between the permissible, the desirable, and the forbidden, as perceived by the Israeli public in general and the wider peace camp in particular. The anti-Zionist activists rejoiced; the narrow path which they had laboriously carved out had become a broad, paved highway along which marched, hand in hand, tens of thousands of Palestinians and Israelis.

My greatest comfort is that one can already see the pioneering force behind us and alongside us. They are not yet the battalions of the peace camp, but there are definitely hundreds who are crossing the fence. In a variety of different ways they are creating a new fabric of relationships between Israel and Palestine: from diplomatic talks to joint activities, from the meetings launched by the doves of the Labor movement with representatives of "the PLO inside" to Women For Women Political Prisoners, on through to the Beita Committee, Beit Sahour Committee, the solidarity visits of Dai Lakibush, the food convoys of Hal'a Hakibush, and more and more.

At the same time, the spokespersons of the Zionist Left began holding more and more frequent meetings with Palestinian public figures in the Occupied Territories. These contacts certainly were not labeled as solidarity, but rather as a sort of negotiations: "between enemies," of course.

Every Israeli has the right to see every Palestinian as an enemy by virtue of his or her being Palestinian, and there is nothing wrong with negotiating with the enemy. Yet negotiations are held between official representatives or official or semi-official agents or mediators. The encounter between Knesset members from the Zionist Left and the official spokespersons of the Palestinian population of the Occupied Territories was based on glaring asymmetry. Whereas Palestinian leaders Faisal Husseini, Radwan Abu Ayyash, and Zahira Kamal represent their people, lead their struggle, and are able to make meaningful contributions to the shaping of representative positions, Israelis Elazar Granot, Tsali Reshef, Ya'el Dayan, and Yossi Sarid represent only a minority — even if important and respected — of the Israeli population, and it is not within their power to express, at this moment, the official policy of the State of Israel or to contribute to its fashioning.

Here is the place to bring up a criticism of the Palestinian leaders in the Occupied Territories. Their honest yearning for an Israeli-Palestinian alliance, and their enthusiastic and justified desire to find dialogue-partners within the broad Israeli public, has resulted in an almost tragic misunderstanding of their relations with the Zionist Left. Whereas the Palestinians were ready for a love affair or even a Catholic wedding, the primary allegiance of the Zionist Left was to their own tribe. Before their contacts with the Palestinians even started, the Sarids and Granots solemnly swore that they would never desert their common home, and that their connection with the Palestinians not only was not based on love, but that its objective was solely to improve the situation of the common home. Whereas the Palestinian leaders have never set any preconditions for meeting Israelis, and viewed the very willingness of the Israelis to relate to them as dialogue-partners as an achievement, the Israelis saw their connection with the Palestinians as a favor they were doing them, and thus expected concessions from the other side. This is a gross reproduction of the occupier/occupied relationship, where the former are convinced that they are doing the latter a favor by the simple fact of sitting down with them, take pains to make this clear before each meeting, and demand a suitable payment as well.

What is more, the Israelis have the sole right to set the agenda of the meetings and to decide what subjects the Palestinian side may not bring up, or even mention (i.e., the refugee question, the Palestinian right of return, Jewish immigration). The Gulf crisis made the magnitude of the gap in expectations between the two sides in the Israeli-Palestinian dialogue and the ambivalence underlying such encounters all the more apparent. When the Palestinian side expressed its support for Iraq, Yossi Sarid and his associates reacted with "Let them come looking for me." That is to say, when the Palestinians their solidarity with the Arab camp and announce this recanting publicly, their Israeli partners will agree to restart the dialogue, but only under more stringent conditions. Later, Sarid changed his approached and published another article, this one entitled "Don't come looking for me." That is to say, there is no redress for what the Palestinians dared to do; there is no forgiveness for someone on the Palestinian side who dared to defend a position different from that chosen by the Israelis.

The Israeli dialogue-partners have the right to advocate any opinion at all; by contrast, Palestinians have to submit their views for censorship by the Israelis, who will decide whether these positions are a pretext for ending the connection. And worst of all, the Israelis solemnly declare their primary allegiance to their own families, take responsibility for all of the wrongdoings of the members and heads of their families; and at the very same time forbid their Palestinian partners to make reference to family ties or to show affection for their nephews, nieces, and cousins. Israeli patriotism and unswerving loyalty to the oppressive, occupying IDF, yes! Pan-Arab solidarity, absolutely not! And as if that's not enough, the Palestinians are asked every morning and evening to condemn and deplore every act that is unacceptable to the broad Israeli public, and if the condemnation isn't heard with satisfactory clarity, they are banished from the table in shame.

The Israeli partners to such dialogues always took pains to make it clear that these were "encounters between enemies" but on the condition that the enemy consistently uphold the positions of the Israeli dialogue-partner, with no right to his or her own independent positions, motivations, or feelings. By contrast, it seemed natural to the Israeli leftist to hug a rightist any time he or she wanted and to emphasize their common interests, and it also seemed natural that the Palestinians should understand and identify with these acts. In other words, the Zionist leftist meets the Palestinian as an enemy, but expects to be treated as a lover.

At one of the meetings abroad between Zionists and Palestinians, some of the Israeli peace activists were grumbling about a Palestinian representative's lack of cordiality. This came after an ultimatum by the Israeli side, demanding that the (Palestinian) refugee question not be mentioned. The response of one Palestinian-American intellectual to the Israelis' dissatisfaction was apt: "To meet with you is just fine. But also to love you? Don't exaggerate!" However, that Palestinian intellectual hadn't yet plumbed the depths of the soul of those who call themselves rational Zionists. They like to both shoot and to cry; they emphasize that they are enemies and behave accordingly; and nevertheless, they want to be loved. They behave like landlords, but want to be treated like guests, and in the best oriental tradition of course.

*   *   *   *   *

I must confess here that I have a good feeling; the message of the court will not be absorbed, and the deterrent won't work, because for many thousands in our society, this border has become an anachronism, and the equation that says a Palestinian is equal to terror is ridiculous. Thousands of you have crossed the border of fear and confrontation, some through meetings, some through organizing material solidarity on the humanitarian level, and some on the political level. And our small opening in the fence has become a paved road, and the day is not far off when it will become a wide, international highway.

Much remains to be done before massive Israeli-Palestinian solidarity is created, but the border has been breached. And with all the criticism I've made here — of the difficulties the Israeli side has in overcoming their arrogance as sons and daughters of the occupying nation, and of the naiveté of the Palestinian activists, children of an oppressed people — we have reached the point of no return. Perhaps some of the leaders of the moderate Zionist camp will be scared off by the price — the price of final separation from the warm bosom of the consensus. But for thousands of others, it is becoming increasingly clear that this is the only alternative to the "circle of blood" and the real danger of a second Masada.[6]

Notes

1. At that time the editor-in-chief of *Haolam Hazeh*, Uri Avneri, published an article in his newspaper comparing a spokesperson of Matzpen, who was defending the right of the Palestinians to self-determination while on a U.S. tour, to Lord "HaHa" (the nickname of a British aristocrat who collaborated with the Nazis). Progressive writer Amos Keinan in *Yediot Aharonot* was also accusing Matzpen members of being not only traitors, but cowards too, because they were not brave enough to place bombs against Jews!

2. Said Hammami developed very good contacts with Matzpen activists, until his assassination in 1978. Issam Sartawi initially arranged meetings with the anti-Zionist Left, later with the Israeli Council for Israeli-Palestinian Peace led by Uri Avneri and Matti Peled. In 1977, Sartawi and three Israeli anti-Zionists (including myself) signed, in Paris, the first joint Israeli-Palestinian official statement. Sartawi was assassinated too, in 1983. It is assumed that Abu Nidal was responsible for both assassinations.

3. The Israeli Socialist Left (Shasi), which later joined the Democratic Front for Peace and Equality led by the Israeli Communist party, was a "New Left" type of organization, mainly active in universities. It is small but still active. Sheli was a left Zionist party composed of people who split off from Mapam, *Haolam Hazeh* activists, radical students, a few Oriental Jews, and a handful of Palestinians. They participated twice in elections to the Knesset, and got up to three M.K.s (Knesset Members). In the late 1970s Sheli split into a right

wing and a left wing, the right wing fusing with Shulamit Aloni's Citizen Rights Movement (Ratz), the left wing being the main component of the Jewish wing of the Progressive List for Peace.

4. Jibril Rajoub, one of the leaders of the Palestinian political prisoners, was released in the prisoner exchange in 1985, and deported in 1988.

5. Beita is a village in the northern West Bank, where in 1988 a settler girl was shot by the settler "guard" accompanying her hiking group when Palestinian villagers threw stones at them. Fifteen houses were demolished as a result, two Palestinians were also shot and killed by the same guard, the sister of one of the Palestinian victims was arrested, and six villagers were deported.

6. At the time of the Jewish revolt against Roman rule, in A.D. 73, Jewish Zealots barricaded themselves in the desert fortress of Masada. Refusing to compromise in any way, or to surrender, nearly one thousand men, women and children held out for three years, until the Romans finally breached the fortress. Rather than submit to capture and enslavement, the Jews committed mass suicide. This dramatic event in Jewish history is regarded by some as part of the Jews' legacy of fortitude, and evidence of religious "devotion." The Jewish Zealots are admired and Masada is a revered symbol especially among ultranationalist Jewish settlers fighting to hold onto the West Bank. One the other hand, Masada is also conjured up by people concerned over the propensity of Israeli leaders to allow messianic or political fervor to overwhelm common sense in political judgement with respect to the occupation.

Daphna Golan

Daphna Golan was born in Haifa, and grew up in Beersheva. She spent four years in Berkeley, California (1984-1988), and was a cofounder of Friends of Yesh Gvul in the U.S. She received her Ph.D. in African studies from the Hebrew University and spent a year in South Africa doing field research.

Daphna currently teaches South African history at the Hebrew University and is coordinator of the African unit at the Truman Institute for the Advancement of Peace. She has been research director of B'Tselem, the Israeli Information Center for Human Rights in the Occupied Territories, since its founding in 1989.

Daphna is an active member of The 21st Year — Against the Occupation. Together with twenty-six others in this group she was arrested in May 1989 while demonstrating in the West Bank against house demolitions. They were charged with entering a closed military zone. She is married and has two children. As part of her work for B'Tselem she has written extensively on human rights violations in the Occupied Territories. Her reports include *Banned Books and Authors* (B'Tselem, 1989), *The Military Judicial System in the West Bank* (B'Tselem, 1989, updated 1990), a report written with Yuval Ginbar, *Human Rights in the Territories during the Gulf War* (B'Tselem 1991), and a report written with Stanley Cohen, *The Interrogation of Palestinians during the Intifada — Ill-treatment, "Moderate Physical Pressure" or Torture?* (B'Tselem, 1991).

Letter to Deena

Daphna Golan

Dear Deena,

Now that you are about to leave, I feel like writing you this letter of explanation, to end a long and somewhat contentious argument we had for the first few months of your stay here. In the beginning, you kept asking me why we don't do more, and I tried explaining. Gradually, our discussions became more and more annoying. You brought me books about nonviolence and civil disobedience, and you gave advice about new strategies for our struggle. I listened, and I was not sure myself why these discussions with you were so difficult for me. After six months, you stopped asking me, "Why don't you do more?" and I stopped looking for the answer, as if we both knew our friendship is too important.

This letter is not an apology. There are two contradictory reasons why I don't apologize. First, I don't think *we* should apologize to *you* — *we* meaning Israelis on the Left, and *you* meaning concerned Americans, even Jewish Americans. Second, an apology usually means asking forgiveness; but in our case there is really no excuse for not doing more. Let me say a few words about the first, before trying to explain, not justify, why we do not do more, why we don't become more radical, why we are as powerless as we are now.

When I think about our relationship with concerned people from the United States, I almost taste the cookie which comes with the coffee at the outdoor café of the American Colony Hotel in East Jerusalem. *You* pay for the too expensive coffee. *We* go home (now a little frightened that our car will be stoned on the way) feeling guilty, frustrated for not having had important plans to tell you about. No, our consumer boycott of settlers' products has not increased. No, the house meetings we organized are still only between academics, Ashkenazi Jews, and the Bir Zeit lecturers. Yes, the last seminar we organized for youth drew only twenty youngsters. Yes, we knew all their parents anyway.

I don't think we should apologize to you. Not because this is a struggle that only Palestinians and Israelis should wage together. On the contrary, especially because I do believe this is your struggle as much as it is ours and that human rights issues have no borders, I think that not only we, but you too, are to be blamed for not doing enough. This witnessing position you have taken is a far too easy one. Fact-finding tours, witnessing delegations, short stays in refugee camps: these steps are no longer sufficient. Have you finished the work back home? Did you do anything serious to convince your Congresspeople to make aid to Israel conditional?

I almost made up my mind not to cooperate with well-meaning U.S. visitors anymore when I met, at the same Friday demonstration of Women in Black, two women, a filmmaker and an anthropologist, both researching "Israeli women in the peace movement," who had each interviewed me for long hours. Both of them were not wearing black. If you are not willing to wear black at this moment, you are not standing with me.

I know you are not all the same.

Remember the night ride in January of 1989 on the bus to Tel Aviv? It took me so long to convince you that we can, just once, go to Tel Aviv, sit in a pub and pretend that life goes on as usual. I think you agreed in the end to come with me by pretending that you were on an anthropological tour to see how Israelis (who are not politically involved) really live. It was winter, and dark very early. The radio was loud with the news as it always is in Israel, and we were screaming at each other. You were talking about [my husband] Amotz's refusal to serve in the Occupied Territories as not enough, saying that these days people should refuse altogether to serve in the Israeli army. I said that Yesh Gvul people oppose this position, and they stress, for good reason in my mind, the fact that all of them have served in the army, but refuse to take part in oppressing the Palestinian people. You could be right, and it is my Zionist education which blinds my eyes when I say that Israel does need an army. But I do want you to understand where my position comes from. And I want to try and explain why total refusal in a context of nonviolence or nonviolent civil disobedience is such an alienated concept for us, and why partial or selective refusal is our chosen way (apart from my fear of staying at home with two kids while my husband is in jail for months).

Why don't we do more, or why is there no serious civil disobedience movement in Israel now? There are many parts to the answer. I think the main reason, though, is that our lives are too comfortable, and we are not really ready to risk too much. Not only in Tel Aviv does life go on as usual. Even we in Jerusalem still live very comfortably. We can still find enough friends who think the way we do not to feel totally isolated. We are not kicked out of our jobs. Those of us in academia (and many of us are), are still invited to conferences around the world, go on sabbatical, and host foreign academics here. We can pretend, while sitting on the faculty club's balcony, taking in the magnificent view of old Jerusalem, that things will be okay, or that there is very little we can change anyway. It is this comfort that causes us to not want to risk too much. It is indeed dreadful to think that only when we are no longer able to go to the cinema or to cafés, either because we will be afraid of bombs planted by Palestinians or of attacks by right-wing extremists, only then will we perhaps do what we should have done for years.

There may be some factors inherent to this conflict which are confusing and paralyzing. The contradiction between a Jewish and a democratic state is extremely hard to resolve for those of us who are second generation to Holocaust survivors, children of immigrants, or immigrants ourselves. There are ideological factors which affect Israeli peace circles, but I would much rather tell you about what affected my personal choice. The first year of the Intifada was the year of hope. Many new Israeli movements were created in support of the Palestinians' struggle to end the occupation. In the covenant of a new group, The 21st Year, there was a call for refusal to take part in the occupation. The idea was that we can no longer *say* we oppose the occupation; we should *do* something against it, even if it entails paying a personal price. At that time the price was not a great personal cost: we boycotted products produced by settlers, or refused to travel or let our children travel to the territories unless invited by Palestinians. It was the extension of Yesh Gvul ideas, and many women who found little room in Yesh Gvul became active in the new movement.

It was in the second year of the Intifada that we realized the struggle was still long and we should really look for new strategies. We started talking about civil disobedience. House demolitions are so obviously immoral and cruel; they are such a clear case of collective punishment that we all agreed we should act against them. We thought if we couldn't stop them, at least we could make the soldiers driving the bulldozers or setting the dynamite think about what they were doing. We chose to act against the destruction of the house of the Daud family in Qalqilya where a boy, fifteen years old, lived with his family of twelve members. He was charged with torching an empty parked car, and his house was to be demolished even before he stood trial.

Usually a house is demolished within twenty-four hours of the court's decision. It was Monday, and we started making phone calls to our well-organized network. We discovered, however, that only three of us could come. People did not say they were afraid; but if they had really been ready to go to jail for months, missing that day of work could not have made such a big difference.

So we had to rethink our strategies, realizing that risking imprisonment was too high a price for people to pay. We changed the original plan. First, we moved the act to Friday. It's a more convenient day, and luckily the house was still standing. We decided, then, to forget our training, and our plans for civil disobedience, and simply go there, and pay a visit to the family whose house was to be demolished.

But the army, probably informed about our previous plans and unaware of the changes, declared — illegally — the area a closed military zone. We entered and found ourselves in jail for five days. It was almost fun — nineteen women in a crowded cell talking politics and giving lectures. In another cell were eight men.

There was debate about our line of defense in the trial. Most of us wanted to win the case, be acquitted, and forget the whole thing. There were two women who wanted to use the trial to make a strong political statement about the illegitimacy of the Israeli legal system and our refusal to be judged according to invalid laws. And obviously, to be imprisoned. I fought with all my heart. I said then that I did not think there was any point in playing heroes when we didn't have any followers; that we would be marginalized and lose all the support we had; that we and the Israeli peace movement were not ready for that, and most important, I said *I am not ready* to pay this price. Gali was just over two years old and I was pregnant again. Five days in prison were enough for me to understand that this was not a way I could choose now. I had never left Gali before for more than a day and a half. This might seem crazy, but I just couldn't leave her. The first night without her was the night in the tent city we built in front of Ansar III.[1] Later, I interviewed a Palestinian lawyer for my work in B'Tselem [the Israeli Information Center for Human Rights in the Occupied Territories] who was in Ansar while we were demonstrating. He told me his wife was pregnant when he was detained. He was released two days before she gave birth. Still, for me, disappearing for five days without saying goodbye was very hard. I know it is a very small price to pay for a just and important struggle. But, I could not think of six months without Gali, certainly not while I was pregnant again.

In the end, we were a group of twenty-seven, most of whom did not want to go to jail. I suggested that those radicals who did want to make a point and go to jail, had many other opportunities to do so since houses were still being demolished, children killed, and detainees held without trial for months on end. But no act of civil disobedience has taken place since. There were no more talks about breaking the law or obstructing the demolition of homes with our bodies. Or, those of us who continued to talk never did anything. No one was really ready to pay that high a price.

You know Deena, I hope you are right. I hope that there are other strategies we have not thought about. I know we need radical measures to take us out of our paralyzed situation, our feeling of hopelessness and failure; yet steps that we, middle class, parents, people who still live too comfortably, will be able to adopt. Because, you see, you are right. A total refusal is the only morally and politically sound form of participation in Israeli society during the occupation. This is something we can write or say. It is not something we can, or are ready right now to do.

Note

1. Ansar III is an Israeli detention prison for Palestinian political prisoners in the Negev Desert. It consists of large tents, exposed to the elements. B'Tselem statistics for the month of May 1991 showed the population of Ansar III to be 6,049: 710 administrative detainees (who can be held for up to six months without charges, and that hold-order can be renewed), 3,582 prisoners already sentenced, and 1,757 awaiting trial. Being within the Green Line, prisoners must be taken across international borders to reach Ansar III. For this reason, among others, the detention facility has been denounced as contravening international law.

Reverend Riah Abu El-Assal

The Reverend Canon Riah Abu El-Assal was born in Nazareth, Galilee District in 1937, the second of eight children in a family with long roots in the city. His name, "Abu El-Assal" (Father of Honey); is derived from the family's traditional business, honey production and marketing. His childhood was a typical one for Palestinians. The family, vacationing in Lebanon in 1948, were denied the right to return to their home in Nazareth, and were designated refugees. Their property was turned over to the Custodian of Absentee Property (an Israeli government office). At his father's request, he returned illegally to Nazareth in 1949, walking across the border with others. Reverend Riah spent the years 1949 to 1953 living with his aunt in Nazareth. In 1953 his mother, brother, and four sisters returned, also illegally. Their expulsion was threatened but never carried out. On Christmas Eve in 1958 his father legally returned home, due to the recognition that his pre-1948 departure occurred while in association with a British firm, Iraq Petroleum Co.

From 1960 to 1964, Reverend Riah attended Bishop's College in Calcutta, and the United Theological College in Bangalore, with a concentration on Islamic studies. He was ordained a priest in the Episcopal church in 1966. He attended Bosey Institute near Geneva in 1972, and American University and Near East School of Theology in Beirut from 1974 to 1975, where he was an M.A. candidate in Islamics. The completion of his thesis was interrupted by the outbreak of the Lebanese Civil War.

In 1967, Reverend Riah was appointed Vicar of Christ Evangelical Episcopal Church in Nazareth, a post he has been holding to this day. Among his many ministry related achievements, he was elected chairman in 1972 of the Evangelical Episcopal Council in Israel and served until 1975 when the post was discontinued by restructuring in the establishment of the new Diocese of Jerusalem. In 1978, Reverend Riah was named Canon of St. George's Anglican Cathedral in Jerusalem. As a non-resident, he was allotted the seat of Damascus. In 1989 he was made Archdeacon in the Jerusalem Diocese.

He is chair and a founder of Al-Sawt (The Voice), a publishing house whose purpose is to deepen Palestinians' consciousness of their roots. Since 1983, he has been director of St. Margaret's Home for the Handicapped and other ancillary programs operated under the auspices of Christ Church.

Reverend Riah also has an illustrious career in sociopolitical activities beginning in the late 1960s. He was one of the founders of the Nazareth Democratic Front, and won a seat in the 1975 municipal elections. In 1976, he cofounded the Committee for the Defense of Arab Land, the group responsible for the first Land Day Strike on March 30, 1976. He has been involved in the drafting of World Council of Churches (WCC) Middle East statements, and in the Human Rights Advisory of the WCC Commission on International Affairs.

In 1981, he participated in the formation of the Progressive Movement in Nazareth, serving on the executive committee. As an outgrowth of this, in 1984 he went on to help establish a new Arab-Jewish political party, the Progressive List for Peace (PLP). He was the number three candidate on their list for Knesset twice, in 1984 and 1988 (the PLP won two seats in 1984 and one in 1988). In 1985 he was elected secretary general of the PLP.

Reverend Riah participated in a six-person Israeli delegation, three Jewish and three Arab, who met with PLO Chairman Yasser Arafat in Tunis in 1985. He returned to Tunis in 1986, and was subsequently banned from travel abroad (though no charges were laid) for twelve months. This travel ban was renewed repeatedly without formal charges for a total of three and a half years (until January 1990). No explanation was given as to its imposition or lifting. Reverend Riah has traveled and spoken extensively around the world, before and since his travel ban.

Interview with Reverend Canon Riah Abu El-Assal

by Deena Hurwitz

Deena Hurwitz (DH): What is your preferred way of identifying yourself?

Reverend Riah Abu El-Assal (RA): I normally describe myself as an Arab Palestinian Christian citizen of the state of Israel. I know it's quite difficult for people to understand a person like me with four identities. I didn't choose it, but I gladly accept it.

DH: Does any one of these stand as a priority?

RA: The 'Palestinian' surfaces these days more than the 'Arab,' the 'Christian,' or the 'Israeli.' Perhaps this is due to the pressures surrounding the Palestinian. Also, it is an attempt to react to the anti-Palestinian attitude inside Israel and in much of the Western countries, especially because of the way the Palestinian position has been described in relation to the Gulf crisis. Besides, Arab, Christian, and Israeli are greatly misunderstood and may mean different things to different communities in the world. Arab equals Moslem in the mind of the Westerner. Christian may mean Italian, Greek, American, or English, and Israeli is understood to mean Jewish. And I am none of these. I am an Arab, but not a Muslim. I am Christian but also an Arab Palestinian; and I am an Israeli citizen but not a Jew.

DH: As an Israeli citizen, a Palestinian from inside the Green Line, how do you relate to Palestinian nationalism, and what is your identity as an Israeli citizen?

RA: In the first place, I am a Palestinian. My nationality was described as 'Palestinian' in the 1950s by the state of Israel, and they continue to attempt to ignore the fact that there is a Palestinian identity.

'Palestinian' has been the only term which was a trouble for so long. So, I am part and parcel of the Palestinian people. Their hopes are my hopes as an individual; their pains are my pains.

We are not talking about details of the solutions for the future, we are talking about the reality. The reality of my being is that I am a member of the Palestinian people. This relationship is a sacred one; no one can deny me the right to be myself. I don't attempt to deny people the right to be themselves, to belong where they believe they belong. This is where my national feelings and affiliations and belonging stem from. It does not mean that I, being who I am, agree with everything my people do or say. Certainly within the Palestinian camp there are factions and groups with different opinions.

Perhaps in the days to come both communities will find a way to a just and lasting solution. The Palestinian Israeli will become a new phenomenon. But every time I say I come from Israel I get asked, "When were you converted?" They think I'm a convert from Judaism. I try to tell them not all Israelis are Jewish. It's got nothing to do with the political reality. To be honest, I always said,"Israel is a reality as much as the Palestinian people, and their rights are a reality." I never think by ignoring a reality you bring closer the solution to your problem.

DH: This issue of dual identity always gets raised in terms of allegiance not to Israel but to the Palestinians and other Arabs in the region. Are Palestinian Israelis clamoring to change the nature of the state of Israel? What is it you recognize when you recognize Israel?

RA: I recognize the state of Israel which has been recognized by the United Nations. Israel is the state of its citizens, not the state only of the Jewish people. It's the state of the Jewish people *plus* the minority which is composed of Arab Palestinians. This is the reality about Israel.

Israel is in bad need of being liberated. It's not an independent state; it's not an independent community. It's a community haunted with fear, and it should be liberated from its nightmares, from its past history. They can't keep living in the past; they need also to project to a better future. If they continue to say that the Palestinians have a greater allegiance to the Palestinian people than to the state of Israel, they need also to say why this is the case. Though, in fact, this is not true. In the last elections, 50 percent of the Arab Palestinians voted for the Jewish parties; not even for the so-called Arab parties.

Through all the discrimination against them, Israel made the Palestinians what they have become. If the Israelis treated the Palestinians with equality; if they had given them the same dignity they've given their own people, if they had given them the same trust they've given to their own people, Palestinians would have responded with the same measures. But the Palestinian is suspected, he or she is always screened, always taken at airports and stripped naked for security checkups—I'm talking about the Palestinians from inside Israel, carrying Israeli passports, having the right to vote, become members of parliament. When those people are ill-treated, when their land is taken, when they are discriminated against in their right to pursue higher education, in their right to keep their jobs rather than fear that they will lose them to the newcomers from the Soviet Union — what do you expect?

How would you expect the Jewish community in Germany or the U.S. would react against a policy of discrimination? Certainly with more mistrust and a greater allegiance to those people who might give them hope for better days or a better life. When Palestinian Israelis demonstrate and express solidarity with the Palestinian people, they make it clear to the whole world that there is a red line. Most Palestinians inside Israel are ready to support the Palestinian people in their struggle for an independent state side by side with Israel. The greatest majority of the Palestinian minority inside Israel — citizens of the state of Israel — would choose to be part of the state of Israel, even when there should come about a state for Palestinians alongside it on Palestinian soil. We will choose to stay.

Israel must invest, positively speaking, in the life and the experience of the minority that lives within itself. Palestinian Israelis can become a bridge. I doubt whether Israel can find a better bridge than the people whom I represent. We are unique as no other group in the world is. Especially the Palestinian Israeli Christians. As Arabs, if we are allowed, if we are not suspected, if we are encouraged, we can speak to the Arab leaders. The Arab regimes are hostile, in fact, not to me as a Palestinian as much as to the government of Israel. But because I'm an Israeli citizen I'm not allowed to speak to them. If I should speak to them, then I'm suspected of collaborating with them. The same is true with Palestinians: I can speak to the Palestinian people, but now the law forbids talking to any official in the Palestinian camp, which is very serious. All doors are closed, whereas all those doors for dialogue should be wide open.

The only way left to me is as a Christian. I can speak to the Christian communities in the world, and we're trying our best to involve the Christian community so that it can become an instrument of peace between the conflicting parties in the Middle East. As an Israeli, if I am accepted as an equal citizen, I can relate to the Jewish people in the world as well as in Israel in a way that I may help to reshape public opinion inside Israel. But when they speak of me as a Palestinian who is not to be trusted, then public opinion in the Jewish sector will not listen to me. So it's not a question of allegiance. It's playing a role imposed on you.

DH: Say more about the experience of Palestinian Israelis as second-class citizens. I know there's been increasing harassment against Palestinian citizens of Israel recently, and specifically with the economic pressures that are happening now with the transfer of jobs to incoming Soviet immigrants.

RA: The Palestinians inside Israel have suffered as no other group of the Palestinian people. Some Palestinians who found themselves refugees had the whole Arab world before them. We had nowhere to go. We were not accepted for many, many years by either party. The Jews suspected us, the Arabs outside what became Israel viewed those who remained inside Israel as collaborators. There were attempts to deny our identity. They referred to us as religious groupings: as Christians or Muslims, others as Bedouins or Druze, and others as Circassians. At most they speak of us as Arabs and Christians, and they attempt to de-Arabize the Christians. It has failed, but the attempts continue. Even today they continue to refer to us as religious communities.

The Arab nation discovered us only after 1967. We were regarded, by virtue of having remained on the land, as the only group of Palestinians that won the very battle that was lost by the majority of Palestinians. And now Israel knows that we, the Palestinians inside Israel, have won a battle without a war by remaining on the land. That's why Israel enacted as many as thirty-eight laws to deprive us of our land. All that is left of the land that we had in 1948 is 3 percent; and even this 3 percent is threatened now. They're trying to expand some of the Jewish towns and cities with the attempt to "Judaize" the Galilee, for example. And they have announced new expropriations.

We've lost our land, and by losing our land we've lost part of the means of our living. As long as our hands were needed, and they had no one to do these jobs: cleaning roads, working at filling stations, and waiting at restaurant tables, they welcomed the Arab labor. With the newcomers, especially from the Soviet Union and the Ethiopian Falashas, perhaps they will find people who are ready to do the menial jobs that the Arabs were assigned. There's a real fear; in Nazareth alone we have more than 25 percent unemployed. This means four thousand families are suffering because the sole supporter of the family is without work.

And there is a greater fear that the more immigrants come from the Soviet Union, the greater the danger of losing one's job. Because the Arab is always last to be employed and first to be fired. This question of unemployment in the Arab sector is very serious: drugs and alcohol and robberies, and God knows what. When people get hungry, they're ready to take bread from anywhere and with different means.

The same labels that were used against the Jews in the world, now the Jews are using them against the Arabs. The term they use in

Hebrew is *ha'aravim m'lochlahim*, "dirty Arabs." I have heard it a hundred times: "this is Arab work," which means not perfect, not complete, not good.

DH: You spoke about the unique position of the Palestinian Christian community, as an Arab Palestinian Christian. Say more about this role that Palestinian Israelis can play in moving your government towards ending the occupation, and perhaps specifically about your efforts with the Progressive List for Peace.

RA: I am of the opinion that there is no hope for Palestinians inside Israel if we accept what may be in the mind of some, that is, a ghetto mentality, an Arab political party, and the like. One of the important events in the life of the people of Israel, and of the Palestinian minority, was this whole idea of an Arab-Jewish party. I speak of it as important, though not great, because it's unfortunate we were not able to penetrate and receive greater support. But it was a little beginning, and many great things in the world had little beginnings.

It was not a party in fact, it was a list. We called it the PLP — Progressive *List* for Peace — where Christians, Jews, agnostics even, Muslims, all could be with their own religious faith, practices, and so on. But we had one common ground: the cause of peace and the question of equality, and we linked the two together. Our struggle was basically for the equality of the Palestinian inside Israel, because we believed that if she or he would receive equality she or he would become a better contributor to the cause of peace in the Middle East, in the world.

Secondly, we believe there is a way to end the hostilities in the Middle East, by Israel recognizing the right of the others to be, while challenging the others to recognize the right of Israel to be. And I think we have contributed in this regard through our visits to Tunis to meet with Chairman Arafat as an Arab-Jewish delegation of equal numbers; and again when we encouraged him to promote dialogue. But Israel enacted this law [the Prevention of Terror Ordinance] against meeting with any officials from the Palestinian community.

The PLP aimed to tell the Israeli community, both Arab and Jew, that there is a way of co-living on the principle of equality. Numbers mattered very little; the Jewish partners were quite few compared with the votes we received from the Arab sector. But the responsibility, the supervision of the work, even the finances and privileges, were divided fifty-fifty. We tried to be an example. The only hope for both Jews and Palestinians in Israel is joint parties, otherwise we're heading toward segregation, and segregation in no way helps either group. It will bring greater mistrust.

I believe in the joint effort of an Arab-Jewish political struggle, even if it doesn't end in a political party, whereby there will be a real living dialogue between the two groups, with attempts to change for the better public opinion in both sectors, but basically in the sector of the Jewish majority. Because even if the Arabs should unite one day, and should be powerful enough to fight Israel, I don't think we will end up having any peace or security in the area.

We always quote the examples of Algiers and Vietnam, and we say that it's not so much the strength of the Viet Cong that won the battle for the Vietnamese, as much as the change of public opinion in the United States. The same was true for Algiers. The Algerians were strong and they were committed to their cause; they sacrificed a million martyrs. But they didn't win the battle. It was not the weakness of France as much as the power of a French people that had changed its opinion on the Algerian-French relationship. They started seeing what was happening in Algiers as something which made them ashamed of this era in their history. So they effected a change in public opinion which managed to change the decision of the government. That's how Algiers got its independence.

Today Israel is strong. But I think the Palestinians are even stronger in their commitment. And I continue to pray that our people do not resort to any means that would make it easy for Israelis to use the other means they have. I want the Palestinians to continue in their nonviolent reaction, in their Intifada, until the day comes when the Israeli people — the folk, the grassroot communities — start seeing the dangers surrounding the Jewish faith, Jewish values, and Judaism. And they should challenge the government to stop humiliating others and encourage it to take the necessary steps to implement all the principles that make for a just and lasting peace, whereby the Jew would see in the Palestinian a neighbor and kin in fact, someone with whom they can live and reshape the history of this area.

DH: You stressed the importance of public opinion in France and Vietnam. What specifically are Palestinian Israelis doing to target, change or form public opinion in Israel? Do you think it's both Jewish and Arab public opinion that requires change?

RA: There is a need to change public opinion among a little group inside the Palestinian Israeli minority about the possibility of co-living, not only coexistence, between Arabs and Jews. There are some who say "Palestine for Palestinians," "Israel is the work of the imperialists," such slogans. But the solution is changing public opinion in the Jewish sector, not only in Israel, but the Jewish community in the world.

For example, twenty-five years ago you would hear people calling to throw the Jews into the sea. This is not accepted anymore. On the contrary it is condemned and denounced inside and outside Israel. By the mainstream Palestinians, this is denounced as being fatal not for the Jews but for the Palestinians. There is an attempt to present the Palestinian image at its best. It's not an attempt, it's the reality. Some people have played with our destiny by being what they've been; they distorted our image, created of us a bunch of terrorists, which is not the case; this is not the Palestinian community.

The dramatic step that Arafat and the Palestine National Council took by accepting the reality of the state of Israel in itself has helped many in the world to view the Palestinian in a different way. There is what I would describe as a *Pax Palestinenza* — a strategy of peace in the Palestinian camp which is very much lacking in the Jewish camp. There is a strategy of war in Israel; there is no strategy of peace. And when the Israelis are confronted with the strategy of peace, because of their history in the world — not their history with the Palestinians — they are suspicious; they say, "This is just another tactic, the Palestinians don't mean it." That's why, even though the Palestinians were the first to ask the Iraqis to withdraw from Kuwait and negotiate with the Kuwaitis, the Israelis were the first to say, "We told you, these wretched Palestinians, they're no good."

Meanwhile the Palestinians managed to win a battle in the world. I was under a travel ban for four years, and now that I'm allowed to travel I've been to a lot of places, from the Far East to the States, and Europe in between. And I can tell that there's been a change in attitude. It is much easier for me as a Palestinian to speak to people, to address audiences, than twenty or twenty-five years ago. More groups in the world are ready to listen to our side of the story, and to believe, and work for bringing a greater awareness to the plight of the Palestinians. Twenty years ago this was not the case; whatever Israel did was justified.

I was in Europe when the massacre at Al Aqsa happened, and I read from Christian as well as Jewish writers condemnation of such an act. Such a thing you would not have dreamt of some twenty years ago, not from a Jew. In fact, I read comments or letters to the editor, challenging a Jewish writer, "How dare you speak in such a manner when Israel is surrounded by enemies? How can you condemn the act of Israel?" But this Jew stood by what he said because he believed that what Israel did on that day did not harm the Palestinians. He said, "You killed twenty people, but you harmed the cause of Judaism, the cause of Israel in the world." That's what I'm trying to tell people. What Israel is doing to me is no longer harmful to the Palestinians. The Palestinians seem to be ready to die for their cause.

There's a change in Palestinian attitudes vis-à-vis Israel, accepting it as a reality, accepting [UN resolutions] 242 and 338. I think Palestinians are now viewed as people able to defend their cause without being irresponsible, not even in their words. I used to tell people we had a good cause but we had bad advocates. Now we have both a good cause and good advocates.

For many years people would talk about fascist Israel; now they've stopped talking about it that way. They say, "In Israel there are people

— the Kahanes, Moledet, Tsomet, and so forth." But they speak of the possibility of coexistence; the recent attempts in Tira in the Triangle and Sahnin in the Galilee, to bring Jews and Arabs together to express the need to strengthen Arab-Jewish relationships. Thousands of people were there. Now there are as many as twenty-five to thirty thousand people in Wadi Ara ready to demonstrate in support of co-living, not only coexistence. So there is something new.

DH: You have the double misfortune, or the double privilege, of being a minority as a Christian as well. Would you speak about the special role that Christians could play or the special problems that Christians face in trying to push your government to change its policies?

RA: What comes to mind first: a little fear, that if things remain as they are, the mere presence of the Palestinian Christian minority inside Israel and Palestine will come to an end. There will cease to be a Christian community in the land where the Christian faith was born. People are leaving; and they are greatly discouraged from staying. People are looking for new opportunities for work, caught in between the two groups or new phenomena of fundamentalism, Islamic and Jewish. Christians in the West seem to be ignorant of the presence of such a community, of its identity, of its history, of its struggle over the last two thousand years to keep the faith.

But for those of us who remain here, we have been called in a very special way to be a bridge of understanding, to bridge the gap, as it were. For many, many years to be active in the so-called sociopolitical life of the community was viewed as something not nice, even evil. And those who were active in the sociopolitical life of the community were labeled as "red" and "black" and God knows what. Now the church seems to be wide awake in the country. Everybody from patriarch to bishops to clergy has become aware of one fact: that we can't stand idle, we can't stand watching things happen as if it's none of our business. Many discovered that part of the mission of the church is to be an instrument of peace in the world; to work for justice, stand for truth, struggle for equality; and help protect God's image in each and every person, irrespective of their religious background. We are no longer called to have only schools or hospitals; we need to be involved in the cause of peace and justice and equality.

I know how I was labeled. At one time they resolved against me in my own church. "This is political activity; you need to choose. If you accept to be there, you are not part of the church, and if you're in the church you're not part of the whole." I can't be one time clergy and another time be the way they describe it — a political person. I strongly believe that my faith helped me, encouraged me to take the position I've taken on these issues.

God in Christ was reconciling the world to himself, and we were entrusted with the task of reconciliation. As People of the Church we ought to be involved in the task of reconciling those in conflict. If we as church people cannot become a bridge of understanding, of building up trust, of reconciling the people, or recognizing the two, then what message do we have if we believe that God sent Jesus Christ into the world so that God may reconcile the world to himself?

DH: How do you identify with or relate to liberation theology?

RA: I try to reread the New Testament, especially the Gospels, and can imagine easily how Jesus shared those proverbs. They were from real life, he didn't invent them. As for what happened here: for many years I applauded David for killing Goliath. They used to tell us that Goliath was a member of the Philistine community, and David was a man who was close to the heart of God. As a little kid in Sunday school I thought David was great; he was one of my heroes. Until 1967, when I tried to read the news of that day, and I noticed that the late [Gamal Abdel] Nasser is viewed as Goliath, and the late Moshe Dayan is viewed as David.

That put an end to it. I mean, the hero that was is now the enemy. And I started asking, on whose side am I fighting? Is Moshe Dayan the David I knew in the Bible? And Nasser the same as Goliath? Strangely enough, after the Intifada began, people asked my comments on the Intifada and the use of stones. I told them, we Palestinians are very good at learning from the Jews. We learned the art of throwing stones from David. But there is a little difference. Whereas David cut the head of the old Goliath, listen to what a Palestinian boy says. He says, "Once I hit the Israeli Goliath, I will not allow myself to cut his head. I will wake him up and tell him, 'With these stones, let us build a home for both of us.'"

When you speak of liberation theology, what comes to mind is being liberated from stereotypes, from views that hinder one's faith. I can't view God as bloodthirsty. I see God as the God of justice, the God of peace, of love. I'd like to always pray to the God who sent his angels.

In these days there has been a great misuse and abuse of the Bible, both Old and New Testaments, for ends that have nothing to do with one's theology or life. Preaching the burning of Lebanon as preceding the second coming of Christ in my understanding as a Christian is not only foolish, it's a very serious mistake. The Lebanese might reconcile now, and Lebanon will not be completely burned the way that prophecy spoke of. And if Lebanon should flourish again, then who's deceiving whom? Is it God deceiving the nations or those evangelicals deceiving the rest of the world? So we started rereading our Bible in a manner where we looked to find the God of justice. I'm a supporter of this new trend of thinking, and there is much to relate to from both camps. Certainly some say this has a political background. Well, we can't avoid the question of politics. You break your fast with the question of politics; you dine, sleep, and wake up with politics. It's the reality of the situation that imposes itself on one's understanding of the Bible.

DH: You know perhaps Mark Ellis's book, *Towards a Jewish Theology of Liberation*? He wrote, "Can the Jewish people in Israel, indeed around the world, be liberated without the liberation of the Palestinian people?" He also wrote of "a theology of liberation that sees solidarity as the essence of what it means to be Jewish and Christian." And what does solidarity with the Jews or with Israeli Jews mean? If security is the principal obstacle always drummed out, how can Palestinian Israelis help remove that fear of insecurity?

RA: I fully agree with Mark Ellis; they can't be liberated without the liberation of the Palestinian people. That's why I began by saying that the Jews need to be liberated; but the Palestinians also need to be liberated.

If I were to speak of solidarity with the Jews in their search, desire, request for security, it is by making them believe that their security lies in the security and peace of the others. By reconciling with the others. I don't see the security of the state of Israel in an extra valley or mountain or river. I don't see it in secure borders; the only secure borders are reconciled neighbors. The closest neighbors for Israel are the Palestinians. We have suffered as much as they have suffered. I keep saying this.

The Jews proved themselves to be hard working; they're noted for their contribution to the history of humankind in many fields. The Palestinians are doing a similar act now. Perhaps being baptized in fire, the Palestinians have been purified, and it has cost them a lot. We are no longer ready to die for a cause; we are really desiring to live for a cause. And they said it to the international community, loud enough for Israel to hear. We're ready to live together; let's give it a try.

Israel keeps talking about finding peaceful solutions for Middle Eastern problems. They have to take the first step. And the first step is to reconcile with the Palestinians. Once Israel finds its way to the Palestinians, they will find that the Palestinians are prepared now to sit down and negotiate; they will find that they are ready for dialogue. It took forty years for the Palestinians to believe that this is the best way to find a solution. Now when they are prepared, Israel says no. For Israel to find its way to the Arab nations in the Middle East, even to the one billion Moslems, they need this very little bridge called the Palestinian.

But the Israeli government, I'm afraid, does not have a strategy for peace. If Israel has a strategy for peace, let them spell it out. I, as an Israeli citizen, should be given the opportunity to know it. Because if their peace means the annihilation of the other, it is not a strategy for peace, it is a strategy for war. They will never have any peace except the peace of death. They should know this; others have attempted to do the same with them.

I challenge the Israelis to talk to the Germans who witnessed the massacres of Jews in Nazi Germany. You can tell how ruined are those lives, even those who had nothing to do with it, but perhaps they were just not able to defend a Jewish person. And the future generations of this country will see this in those who are doing similar acts of humiliating, oppressing, killing, and shooting others here. Those youngsters being sent into the Occupied Territories, what memories will they have ten, twenty years from now when they start having children and grandchildren? They will live all those nightmares for the rest of their lives.

Peace is the only answer, and as a Palestinian, I am not prepared to stand with my own people if the Palestinian peace should be at the expense of Israel. I offer my formula with humility and pride, which has been quoted a hundred times in many ways, at many levels. The peace and safety of Israel depends on the peace and safety of Palestinians, and the peace and safety of the Palestinian depends on the peace and safety of the Israeli Jew. Together we can become the hope of the hopeless.

Yehezkel Landau

Yehezkel Landau was born in 1949 in Santiago, Chile, to Austrian Jewish refugee parents. He grew up in the United States, where he was active in anti-Vietnam War activities and the Jewish Peace Fellowship. He graduated magna cum laude in social relations from Harvard University in 1971. Afterwards he attended Harvard Divinity School, where he received a masters in theological studies in 1976, specializing in psychology and theology and in Jewish-Christian relations.

Yehezkel moved to Israel in 1978 and attended the Jerusalem Academy of Jewish Studies from 1978 to 1980. For the following two years, he served as program coordinator for the Israel Interfaith Association in Jerusalem. In 1982 he became executive director of Oz veShalom-Netivot Shalom (Strength and Peace-Paths of Peace), the religious peace movement in Israel, a position he maintained until very recently. He continues to be among the leading activists of that organization. Yehezkel joined Oz veShalom "in part out of pain over how religiously observant Jews were portrayed in the media (often as violent extremists), feeling the need to work for peace from a Jewish-traditional foundation."

Since 1981, Yehezkel has been a lecturer on Judaism and interfaith relations at several Christian institutions in Israel, including the Tantur Ecumenical Institute, St. George's Anglican College, the Sisters of Sion International Study Program, the Swedish Theological Institute, and at Nes Ammim village in the Galilee.

His various articles have appeared in such publications as the *Jerusalem Post, Sojourners, Christianity & Crisis, IFOR Report,* the *Other Side, New Outlook,* and the *Christian Century,* among others. He has recently edited a book, *Voices From Jerusalem: Jews and Christians Reflect on the Holy Land* (Ramsey, NJ: Paulist Press/Stimulus Books, 1991). Yehezkel received the 1990 Harvard Divinity School Katzenstein Award, presented to a distinguished alumnus.

Blessing Both Jew and Palestinian: A Religious Zionist View

Yehezkel Landau

Since the eruption of the Intifada, the Palestinians have passed through an agonizing time of nation building, testing their collective fortitude and self-discipline, and suffering an anguishing toll in human lives — mostly young lives. For we Israelis the uprising has been a time of trauma and testing, a time evoking instinctive defensiveness coupled with soul-searching. We Israelis wrestle with two fears: fear of the enemy without, and fear of unleashed anger, brutality, racism, and chauvinism within. Our repression will not break the Palestinians. They will grow stronger and more resolute. Who, if not Jews, ought to understand that?

Our soldiers are fighting against the inevitable — namely, freedom and sovereignty for the Palestinians in a state of their own. If we do not accommodate Palestinian nationalism in a two-state compromise arrangement — ideally, in a three-state confederation that includes Jordan — then the Palestinians will grow even more militant and uncompromising, reverting to their earlier rejectionism, and secular or Islamic extremists will depose PLO Chairman Yasser Arafat.

I am active in the religious peace movement Oz veShalom, "Strength and Peace," a name taken from the last verse of Psalm 29: "May the Lord give strength [*oz*] to His people! May the Lord bless His people with peace [*shalom*]!" This strength is an inner, spiritual kind — the kind that the Palestinians are now displaying. It enabled us Jews to survive for over three millennia, even though we usually lacked political and military power, *koach*.

We in Oz veShalom are not pacifists. We serve proudly in the Israel Defense Forces — as do those soldiers who choose, out of conscience, to sit in a military prison rather than serve in the West Bank and the Gaza Strip today. Our religious heritage, not just our history of persecution, teaches us to appreciate the moral blessing and burden that come with the capacity to defend ourselves against aggression. The true test of Torah comes after the assumption of power, when there is a sovereign Jewish head of state to whom Jewish prophets and sages can direct ethical challenges. For too long Jews were the persecuted, prophetic minority under Christian and Muslim rulers. Now we are the rulers, asking God to bestow on us the *oz*, the spiritual strength and courage, needed to take the risks and make the sacrifices required to achieve a just peace.

As religious Jews, we believe that our people's return to Zion is part of the process of global redemption prophesied by Isaiah: "Zion shall be redeemed through justice, and those who return to her through righteousness" (1:27). It pains us that only Israelis on the secular left echo our sacred prophetic tradition, the ethical heart of Torah, while those in the religiously observant communities are either silent on issues of justice, peace, and human rights, or worse, have actively perverted Judaism into chauvinism, territorialism, and pseudo-messianism.

For the religious settler movement Gush Emunim, "Bloc of the Faithful," the idea of "justice" means that God will restore to Israel all the land lost to the Romans and later conquerors over the past two thousand years. The members of Gush Emunim fail to appreciate that their ideology mirrors the common Palestinian belief that "justice" means that the Palestinians will be restored to the houses and fields and orchards they lost some forty years ago. Israel should acknowledge the right of return or compensation to Palestinian refugees; we have to acknowledge also that if the Palestinians had accepted the 1947 UN partition plan, which the Palestine National Council approved in November, 1988, in Algiers, all the wars, all the expulsions and all the subsequent suffering might have been avoided, and we would today be enjoying peaceful coexistence in two neighboring states. (This observation is not meant as a moral indictment. The Palestinians saw their refusal to partition the land as justified because they were considering the quantitative demographic imbalance in 1947, without according Jews in exile, including Holocaust survivors, the qualitative, reciprocal, national right to come home and exercise self-determination in Palestine-Israel. It is not a question of retrospective blame or recrimination, but of *both* peoples' taking responsibility and demonstrating repentence for self-interested choices made over the years.) We need to challenge our compatriots on both sides who cling to exclusive notions of justice, for that clinging is the greatest obstacle to peace.

Gush Emunim interprets *shalom* to mean either the acquiescence of the Palestinians to perpetual Jewish rule or some postapocalyptic tranquillity which the Messiah will bestow but which imposes no peacemaking obligations today. For Jews, both religious and secular, the golden rule must govern Jewish rule. If we Israelis can claim the right to self-determination and statehood, then we must honor the Palestinians' same right, so long as neither threatens the other's right. Gush Emunim denies the Palestinians their right out of a dogmatic belief that only the Jewish people are heirs to the promised land. These Jews forget that the covenantal promise linking the Jewish people forever to God's Holy Land is conditioned by the demands of Torah ethics.

These militant messianists are matched in dogmatic self-assurance by Muslim zealots in the Middle East, as well as by secular nationalist zealots among the Palestinians. These extremists, for whom compromise is sinful and treasonous, need and feed on one another as they prepare for the apocalyptic day of judgment, which they believe will vindicate them.

Between the poles of the secular Left and the religious Right, between Peace Now and Gush Emunim, members of Oz veShalom try to communicate how Jewish tradition should guide public policy in a reborn Jewish commonwealth, one that can fulfill the promise of equal civil rights to non-Jewish citizens, though its prevailing ethos and symbolism are Jewish. We strive to create *shalom* not only between Jew and Arab, Israeli and Palestinian, but between Jew and Jew, so that together we can make the sacrifices necessary to reach a just compromise with the Palestinian people.

Twice I have used the word "sacrifices," a religious concept. It is in assuming this sacrificial task that we Israeli Jews uphold the charge given to us by God in Exodus 19: "For all the earth/land is mine; and you shall be unto me a kingdom of priests and a holy nation." To be a "kingdom of priests" means, in our understanding, to use temporal or state power, as a sovereign community in the land, as a means toward priestly, spiritual, redemptive ends. And what is the essential ministerial role of the priest? It is *to mediate forgiveness through sacrifice*. It is this forgiveness that is the source of real peace, the inner peace of the soul. In our present context, it is not animal bodies which we are asked to sacrifice on the altar. It is the territorial extension of our own fearful, possessive animal bodies and human egos, both of which seek geographic guarantees (especially land unjustly denied us) for our very existence. The priestly task of a religious peace movement is to call both Israelis and Palestinians to suffer the amputation of part of their collective, symbolic bodies and agree to two independent states alongside each other in our common homeland.

Both Israelis and Palestinians must make these sacrifices, by renouncing part of their rightful claims to all the land. And what of Yerushalayim/Al-Quds, the city of Jerusalem? Clearly, the Holy City must be shared. At a minimum, this means that the flags of both nations will have to fly over Jerusalem. Whatever political compromise is negotiated, Yerushalayim/Al-Quds has to be a heterogeneous community witnessing to a pluralistic monotheism — the greatest challenge to any devout believer of any faith, but the only healing path for Jews, Christians, and Muslims in the Holy Land.

Progressive Christians in North America, Europe, and other parts of the world often contribute to, rather than help overcome, the misunderstandings and fears that keep all of us trapped in the conflict over Israel-Palestine. All too readily these Christians identify with the partisan view of understandably grieving and angry Palestinians, who see themselves as innocent victims of greedy, militaristic Zionists. This identification with only one side of the conflict may be due, in part, to imposing liberation theology (of the Exodus model) on the Israeli-Palestinian tragedy. Transferring this perspective from Third World countries to our situation — perceiving Palestinians as the oppressed and Israelis as the oppressor — is historically and spiritually oversimplified and shortsighted. Both the suffering and the power in this case are products of a century-long intercommunal war pitting two oppressed peoples against each other, with legitimate but opposing interests. Not so long ago, the Palestinians were the majority trying to deny the Jews a state.

Some Christians are, perhaps, also influenced by anti-Jewish stereotypes presented in sermons and Sunday school regarding "legalistic," "eye-for-an-eye" Jews, the foils in the gospel story. Too many Christians know of Jews only through the "Old Testament" and christological interpretations of the Hebrew Scriptures. In their perceptions of the Middle East conflict, they might, consciously or unconsciously, think that the Jews abused their power and incurred God's punishment millennia ago when they failed to heed the prophetic warnings, and are now returning as warriors and oppressive rulers.

However tempting it may be to paint a picture of villain-and-victim that fits some model of liberation from oppression, historical and biblical honesty compels us to search more deeply for a way toward justice and reconciliation in the Holy Land. A more appropriate biblical paradigm for the Israeli-Palestinian situation is found in Genesis, in the motif of two brothers fighting over the birthright and the blessing. (Arthur Waskow has developed this theme in his book *Godwrestling*.)

One may gain the upper hand at one moment, but both are weak and sinful and neither can be readily labeled the oppressor.

The sibling-struggle motif runs throughout Genesis from Cain and Abel to Joseph and his brothers, from the second to the twenty-third generation of humanity. Only when Jacob, on this deathbed, is called upon to bless his grandsons Ephraim and Menasheh in the twenty-fourth generation is this rivalry stopped: he gives the two boys a joint blessing. He asks God to "bless the lads; and in them let my name be recalled, and the name of my fathers Abraham and Isaac; and let them grow into a multitude in the midst of the earth" (48:16). Jacob does this while crossing his arms, symbolizing an equal portion of the blessing to the first- and second-born. Joseph protests, trying to correct what he considers his father's mistake. The patriarch persists, because he knows (through prophetic insight, as well as the painful lessons of his own life) what he must do. He can see into the future and knows what will become of both tribes, but that is a matter separate from the blessing. Moreover, he goes on to say, "By thee shall Israel bless, saying, 'God make thee as Ephraim and Menasheh.'" And that is precisely how Jewish fathers like myself bless their sons at the Sabbath table every Friday night, invoking as role models these two relatively minor biblical figures rather than heroic personalities like Moses, David, Solomon, or Samson.

The basic message is this: You are equally beloved and deserving of blessing, in my eyes and in God's; so don't fall victim to insecure egos, jealousies, and conflict. The blessing is meant to be shared, not fought over; otherwise everyone suffers.

The conflict over the land of Israel-Palestine is a struggle to be blessed as the first-born, the rightful heir to the land and its bounties. All the arguments about who was there first (with archaeology often used in a self-serving way) or which people constitutes a "true nation," entitled to self-determination, are pointless. Both Jews and Palestinians have experienced oppression; both are struggling to secure their own welfare and "liberation" in the narrow, nationalistic sense, often against each other. The challenge is to broaden the vision of liberation to include *both* peoples together, so they can share the birthright and the blessing, which are from God. This requires moving beyond self-righteousness and a myopia of both perception and moral judgment. The current tragic impasse can be overcome only through mutual recognition, "re-cognizing" the other, not as an immutable enemy but as a potential sibling and partner in the common struggle for liberation based on a just compromise.

Modern-day Israelis and Palestinians have not yet learned to share the Abrahamic legacy and blessing, the blessing that promises "through you *all* the families of the earth shall be blessed." Three thousand years after Isaac and Ishmael, we are still trying to heal the sibling rivalry. Jacob and Esau were reconciled, but Isaac and Ishmael are still yearning for that reconciling embrace of kisses and tears. The biblical text describes an emotional reconciliation between Jacob and Esau following Jacob's long exile and his dread over the prospect of a vengeful, bloody reunion. Later rabbinic tradition contains a categorical declaration that "Esau hates Jacob," painting him as an archetypal anti-Semite (despite the biblical rapprochement). By the Middle Ages, "Esau" had come to symbolize the church and Christianity, while "Ishmael," the prototypical Arab, had come to represent the other Abrahamic offshoot, Islam. In this century, a redemptive vision of fraternal peace, transcending theological divisions, was delineated by Rabbi Avraham Yitzhak Kook (1865–1935), the first Ashkenazi chief rabbi in Palestine under the British Mandate. Writing from Jaffa in 1918, Rabbi Kook prophesied: "The brotherly love of Esau and Jacob, of Isaac and Ishmael, will assert itself above all the confusion that the evil brought on by our bodily nature has engendered. It will overcome them and transform them to eternal light and compassion."

Postscript, June 1991

In the aftermath of the Gulf War, diplomats are busy contriving formulas that might bring Israelis and Arabs together. Even if they succeed in getting the parties to the negotiating table, I have serious doubts about the likely results.

To focus on land, security, or the Jewish and Palestinian "right to self-determination" is to miss a critical factor underlying Arab-Israeli relations. Before concessions on territory or political control can be considered, deeper soul searching is needed on the level of self-image and moral perception. This entails a readiness to admit the harm done to the other side and to demonstrate repentance for that behavior. This is a challenge that diplomacy tends to ignore — which may be why all the Middle East peace plans over the years have come to naught.

Peace activists, especially when motivated by religious or moral convictions, must speak to our emotions — especially fear, anger, and grief. A "prophetic" stance makes a moral indictment of collective sins, whereas a "priestly" approach to peace making seeks to mediate forgiveness through sacrifice.

In the ancient Temple in Jerusalem, animal bodies were offered up as expiation for the sins caused by our animal nature. Now it is the territorial extension of our own bodies we are asked to sacrifice. Both Israelis and Palestinians are called to suffer amputation of part of their collective, symbolic bodies and agree to two independent states alongside each other in their common homeland. Too often "Israel" and "Palestine" are viewed as mutually exclusive. The inability to make space in one's heart for the other collective identity creates the necessity to deny its existence on the map.

The hardest and most essential sacrifice demanded for genuine peace is that of one's self-image as the innocent victim at the hands of a cruel enemy. If we can be led to see the contribution of our own people to the conflict, moral dualism can give way to a fairer assessment of responsibility for the tragedy.

Imagine how cathartic it would be if public figures in Israel said words like these:

We Jews returned to the Land of Israel because we wanted to be masters of our own destiny. But you Palestinians saw us as foreign invaders instead of as children of the land coming home from forced exile. You demonized us and enlisted your Arab allies in the battle to 'liberate' Palestine.

In defending ourselves and our own interests, we projected onto you the demonic stereotypes that we carried home with us. We saw you as intent on genocide, something fresh in our memories. Our traumatic history and the intensity of the conflict prevented us from seeing that we were, and still are, a threat to you.

The violence you waged against unarmed Jews has caused us great pain and anger, which we cannot simply wish away. Yet despite these strong feelings, we can empathize with you enough to understand and forgive your resistance to our homecoming.

We hope you can forgive us for our violence against you, and for our failure to acknowledge our share of responsibility for keeping so many of you in exile from the land. Now let us together transform this painful legacy into a hopeful future, by agreeing to partition the land into two states for the two peoples who claim it and love it.

Palestinians need to hear such language from Israelis. So long as Palestinian nationalism is burdened by anti-Zionism, it will not be able to develop its full creative potential. Similarly, for Israeli Jews to avoid having their Zionist ethos become only a double negative (i.e., anti-anti-Semitism), they need to hear Palestinians speak to them in words like these:

We Palestinians were the majority in Palestine when the Zionist movement began settling the land with European Jews. We resisted what you call the 'ingathering of the exiles,' since it meant the loss of our land and our political rights to people who were not even born here.

Looking back with greater compassion for your people's experience of persecution, and appreciating more your historic ties to the land, we can understand that you saw yourselves fighting a war of survival in a cruel world that never made you feel at home. This does not excuse the injustices we suffered, including the loss of our homes and fields and orchards in 1948, or the indignities and harsh repression under occupation since 1967. Yet we can forgive you for your self-interested policies, and for the same nationalist excesses that we, too, have been guilty of.

We hope you can forgive us for evoking the traumatic fears that haunted you throughout history. Beyond the arguments over whose claims are more valid, let us transcend the antagonism of the past and affirm mutual recognition of our respective national identities. Let us agree to divide and share the land so that both peoples can live in freedom and dignity.

This is not the kind of language that most politicians speak. Even religious leaders refrain from expressing this sort of confessional truth. But if individuals on both sides could encourage their leaders to speak in this way, the hurts and grievances might recede in the process of mutual forgiveness — from which can come the true inner peace and security that everyone longs for.

Salman Natour

Salman Natour is a Palestinian Israeli Druze (a sect of Islam) who was born in Daliat-al-Carmel near Haifa in 1949. He finished high school in Haifa and studied for a B.A. in general philosophy in Jerusalem and Haifa. For twenty years he worked as an Arabic journalist, an editor of culture and art sections.

Salman has published eleven books in Arabic, including one novel, short fiction and satiric articles. "The Wedding in Heaven" will appear in his new book, *Walking on the Wind*, to be published in Arabic by the Jaffa Research Center, composed entirely of impressions of meetings with residents of Beit Shean concerning the Palestinian question, the occupation, and the relations between Oriental Jews and Arabs.

Active for twenty years in peace organizations, in 1982 Salman established the Solidarity Committee with the residents of the Golan Heights. Because of this activity, he was put under house arrest for six months. Salman is a member of the board of Israeli and Palestinian Artists Against the Occupation.

The Wedding in Heaven

Salman Natour

And she went under the wedding canopy alone, and the commander commanded to "bury her in silence," and in silence she was buried.

And maybe there, somewhere up above, the heavens are clearer, and blood is not spilled, and there are no Jews and no Arabs.

And maybe there, somewhere up above, only the angels dance, and, beneath the wedding canopy and the crown of flowers in the city of brides, there are two in white dresses, one from Nablus [in the West Bank — ed.] and one from Beit Shean [within the Green line — ed.]. And who knows what they are saying and what they are dreaming. And here, under the dark heavens, two mothers, about sixty years old, one from Nablus and one from Beit Shean, do not stop crying, and do not stop dreaming about the two brides who left behind only a white dress, and maybe a scrapbook and maybe, maybe, one hair, and much pain and many pictures. And here, my dear, is the tale of the wedding in heaven, two brides whom I never met but each has a mother, about sixty years old, and both of them I did meet. And the mothers asked, Why?, and maybe you will say that this is an Oriental cry, romantic suffering, that both this one from Nablus and this one from Beit Shean were stricken: Why? A few days before the wedding? And all this happened in the year after Sabra and Shatila.

Whose mourning is this?

Of no one other than that mother, dressed in black and her agony breaks her heart, and between silences, a sigh bursts forth and the mourning is all her lot.

Translated from Hebrew by Judith Green

"In my dream I saw her, a bride in a white dress.... I didn't dream I would see her dumb, like a vegetable, and when I kissed her forehead, she was cold like ice and she was, and she no longer is."

How does an Arab mother cry who lost her daughter?

How does a Jewish mother cry who also lost her daughter?

No one sees this crying, and those with their fingers on the trigger or those who give the order or those who simply abuse our mothers and theirs — they don't hear it. Ours — we, on the mothers' side; and theirs — they are giving the commands. Or ours, we who are on this side of the Line, and theirs, over there in Beit Shean; and everywhere the border is muddled, since pain has no border, nor does love, and you are a human being, you fall asleep, get up. This was the cry I heard.

July 1983, yet another casual announcement on the radio: "A young woman was killed in Nablus. The army is investigating."

Alham abu Zarour. Not quite a young woman, but a twenty-one-year-old girl. Her eyes were brown, her hair black and her skin was the color of wheat; a student at An Najah University.

"Do they kill children?"

She asked her mother, when she was four and it was June 1967, at the sight of the tanks and armed soldiers in the streets of her city — and she stuck close to her mother's side. And she grew and grew until that day, one week before her wedding to her cousin Bassam.

She traveled to Jerusalem with her mother to invite relatives to the wedding, and she returned with her mother from Jerusalem as early as possible, so that she could get to the seamstress who was making her bridal dress. And her mother said: "Let's go on Palestine Road," the main street in the city center, and the girl insisted on taking a shortcut by crossing the square. And there, exactly there, a gray Peugeot van was stopped, and a Jewish settler fired off a round of bullets, and Alham fell, covered in her own blood.

And in the middle of the night, only in the middle of the night, was her burial permitted. Seven men accompanied her last journey. They carried her on their shoulders, and her soft body swayed in a bare stretcher. And there were no songs nor strains of music, and her eyes were closed and didn't see the light of the moon; there was only the slow walk toward pain and death, and eyes that cried. Prayer was not allowed, and the voice of the *muezzin* was not heard, nor the ringing bells of the churches. And she, Alham, went alone to her wedding canopy, to the dwelling of girls her age. In her white dress, and two heavy braids, and the smile of a twenty-one-year-old girl. All around were armed soldiers, and the commander who commanded stiffly, "Bury in silence," and in silence she was buried.

And in that same house in the center of the city she left her mother, about sixty years old, lying on her bed in a small room, and around her were three children. One carried in his hand a picture of Alham, and the two others just stared, and the wrinkled mother asked: "Why did they take her from me?" And she grabbed the picture, and she kissed it and wiped her tears with a red kerchief and more than pain separated her, the terrible pain of her daughter's departure, a week before her wedding. "May she have a wedding in heaven, and white angels will dance around her, there, somewhere, in the heavens above," the mother murmured and buried her head in her bosom. And we all cried in the small room, and the two children just stared.... And on the radio they announced that the army was investigating, and they said on the radio that the weather would be hot and dry, humid along the coastal plain. And there was silence.

*   *   *   *   *

Our body must get along with their body.
Esther had a good soul.
Why did they kill her?

Maybe somebody continued to investigate, but from then on I didn't hear anything about Alham, I didn't meet with her mother, and I don't know if she is still in the small room. I published her story and the picture of the girl in the white dress one week after her death, and I took it with me to Beit Shean....

Esther Ohana. How does a Jewish mother cry who lost her daughter one week before her wedding? This is what I asked myself all the way to her house, in the Eliayahu neighborhood, in Beit Shean. She had also been a girl of twenty-one, she also lost her life one year after Sabra and Shatila, and she was also on her way to Jerusalem to invite relatives and friends, with her beloved Yaakov. She also took a shortcut and went through Hebron, where Arab youths threw a rock, and the rock struck her in the head, and she fell in the arms of her beloved, and she breathed out her soul in the hospital. She wanted to study law..."and she had a good soul."

So then, two girls, two others. A small bit of reality, almost matching, one reality to the other reality and, without going into details, to match and to bring nearer: I am sitting on the sofa, in a small room, opposite a woman about sixty years old, and beside her is a picture of a pretty girl, twenty-one years old. At her side is a five-year old granddaughter and they named her Esther too, and on the table is a tape recorder which doesn't cease recording pain and grief. And the mother stirs the teapot and the tea leaves float and sink as, in my memory, the pictures float and sink of the same meeting, under the same circumstances, seven years before in Nablus. It is hard for me to ask Mrs. Mas'ouda Ohana, "Tell me about your daughter Esther! Where was she born and where did she study, and do you hate Arabs, Mrs. Ohana? Actually, do you hate me? I, who am sitting here with you at home, drinking tea with *sheba* [absinthe], and speaking to you about pain and suffering and peace and stones, bullets, Israelis and Palestinians?"

"She had a good soul, an intelligent girl, she studied in Kfar Saba. Everyone loved her. She was an actress in the school, and the principal said to me 'Esther will be a better actress than Hannah Meron.' And she took pity on the old people, she would caress them on the bus. I raised her, she had a good soul toward everyone.... One month before they killed her, she said to me: 'Mother, I have a feeling that I will die.' I said to her: 'What are you talking about?' I thought that maybe she had argued with her boyfriend. I said to her: 'No my dear, you'll live for one hundred and twenty years.' I didn't think at all about death and I bought her the dress, and on that very Shabbat, before Tu b'Shvat, in 1983, I handed out the invitations to her wedding. And she traveled to her boyfriend in Beersheva, and the two of them traveled to Jerusalem. And they took a shortcut, and she shortened her life...."

Mrs. Mas'ouda Ohana spoke quickly, and brought out newspaper clippings and pictures, and said that Yaakov Ahimeir made a television film. And one day, at two in the morning, the telephone rang and they asked her to go to New York to the United Nations to be a witness to the fact that stones kill. And she went and took with her the jar with the fatal stones that killed her daughter. That was during the first days of the Intifada...and "they came from all over the world and asked me about my daughter and they saw the stones that the doctor had given me on the day they killed my daughter. It was in the jar; and the doctor said to me, 'Take it as a souvenir,' and I put it in my bag and I didn't know what was in the jar. After a month, my bag stank, I opened it and saw the stones that they took out of her head, with pieces of brain and flesh, and my husband said we should bury them and I said we should leave them for a souvenir. When it hurts me, I smell the stones. And all the world saw the stones, in the United Nations with our Ambassador, Netanyahu, and they asked me how a stone could kill.... I said, 'Here, look.... Didn't David kill Goliath with a stone?"

Esther, the granddaughter, who sat and listened to her grandmother's words, took the picture of her aunt off the shelf and put it on the table. When she tried to play with the small tape recorder I had put on the table between the tea cups, her grandmother said, "No, *mamale*, don't play with it...." And the girl looked for something else to play with and her grandmother continued to talk about the charming girl whom they killed, a week before her wedding, and whom everyone loved. "Children aren't property, they aren't furniture or a car. Our government isn't strong; the army caught the people who killed my daughter and the judge gave them ten years in prison. I didn't accept this. The next day I went on a hunger strike, beside the prime minister's house. Under it I dehydrated and they took me with an infusion to the hospital. For days and nights I was on a hunger strike. Nothing helped. It hurt me, I said I would take revenge, if I had the strength, because my daughter didn't do anything. One day I sat in front of the television and I saw that they exchanged two of them for our prisoners. Days and nights I didn't sleep. What is this? They welcomed them home with rice, and all we have is a piece of marble. What can I tell my people? What good did it do? Nothing at all. There isn't any rule, no government. We were in a lot of demonstrations with the Thamam family and a Yemenite woman, and an Iraqi woman.... I asked for the death sentence, but it didn't help. I destroyed myself...I don't go to demonstrations any more...."

Mrs. Ohana, you appeared in a lot of demonstrations, with politicians and Kahane. Don't you think they were cashing in on your daughter's blood and your grief?

"If there was a death sentence, there wouldn't be exchanges. The PLO said to them, don't point guns at the Jews, just stones...Molotov cocktails, and bombs. They put them in jail and they just keep on.... They do whatever they want. If there were a death sentence, they wouldn't exchange prisoners. There isn't any state where they free a man who killed a girl like my daughter.... There isn't any state where that happens, only in Israel, because we're suckers. But the demonstrations didn't help. I'm tired and sick, and I can't keep it up; nothing will help my daughter...."

Mrs. Ohana, did you ever meet an Arab mother?

"No...if I see an Arab I start shaking. If I had the strength...."

Do you hate all Arabs?

"Yes. Sure. They killed my daughter.... I raised her for twenty-one years and they killed her...."

Why are the Arabs who didn't do anything guilty?

"An Arab is an Arab. For generations they have hated Jews. If you would tell them that they are free to kill Jews, you would see what they would do. They come here to sweep and the children see them in the park and they start trembling...they are all shaking, like they ate something sour."

Mrs. Ohana, they only want a state on the West Bank and Gaza!

"They have twenty-four states. We have one. Can't they live there?"

They want to live in their own state. Then we can all live in peace and neither Jews nor Arabs will be killed.

"O.K., O.K., I'll tell you. Look, we made peace with Egypt. What happened this week? They killed Jews in a bus. Why did they go to Egypt, scientists, doctors, and important people? It's not easy. Do you see what they did? Even the bus driver joined in."

But Mrs. Ohana, the Egyptians condemned it and so did the PLO!

"An Arab is an Arab, we can't have any negotiations with Arabs. They hate Jews. I was born in Casablanca. The Arabs loved the Jewish girls, they married them.... We need an iron hand, we need a few good

Jews in the government, like Sharon and Kahane, and they would have an iron hand."

What would they do?

"If they throw stones in a village, they need to destroy the village."

Mrs. Ohana, do you agree that it is wrong for one nation to rule over another nation by force? Look, the Turks and the British were here, and they used an iron hand, where are they now?

"As long as we have the army, may God help them, and a strong government...there's nothing to be afraid of."

But how long can you rule by force? You aren't thinking about the future or about your children. You are a mother and you know what a mother's feelings are who has lost a child. How can we continue like this?

"I am also thinking about my children. As a mother, I am right. I don't want them to go to war. I don't want other parents to be in my situation. I want peace, as a mother."

Mrs. Ohana, today the whole world is saying to the government, "What do you want from the territories? Take care of your own small state, and give the rest to the Arabs. Let their government take care of them. What do you want this headache for?"

"The government gave in to the Egyptians, but if they are close to the border, it brings the danger closer. You are asking me, as a mother? I don't want anybody else to be in my situation. But the Arabs, you give them a finger, and they want the whole hand. Don't you remember the katyushas?"

But we are talking about peace. When there is peace, there won't be any katyushas.

"No peace is going to help. Take the example of Egypt."

It's not enough to make peace with the Egyptians. It must be also with Jordan, with Syria, and with the Palestinians. It's like you and your neighbors: you don't hurt them and they don't hurt you. Everyone gives in a bit and everyone lives together, with dignity and peace.

"The Jews are always the good ones. They give the Arabs national insurance benefits, they study at the University, they give them electricity, everything.... They have better apartments than we have, everything is next to the house. Go look at Umm-el-Fahm."

In Umm-el-Fahm they are citizens and pay taxes!

"They are citizens and some of them are terrorists. Arabs are Arabs, from my childhood I have heard how they hate Jews. Outside the country we got along with them because there was trust, but here you can eat with them one day, and the next they will kill you."

Mrs. Ohana, what can be done to lessen your pain?

"My pain, even if I were to break my head against the four walls, it wouldn't help. Until two years ago I wore only black. Someone came to me from the Baba Sali's family and said to me, 'Mrs. Ohana, enough. Change your clothes, your daughter won't return....' I lost my daughter. I'm not like an Arab woman who breeds twenty children. If I had twenty, I would donate one to avenge the blood of his sister. The Jewish woman raises one. She gives her everything, but the Arab has twenty, and she says to them, 'Go throw stones....' They threw a stone on my daughter, a week before her marriage. They killed her."

Mrs. Ohana, in 1983, I met a Palestinian mother in Nablus who also had a twenty-one-year-old daughter, and she was also killed one week before her wedding. She hadn't bought her white dress yet, and a Jewish settler killed her, he shot at her and ran away, and he wasn't brought to trial. When I sit with you I am reminded of that mother and her daughter.... She was pretty, look at her picture, she danced on the day of her engagement.... I talked with her mother. She was a pretty girl, wasn't she?

"Look, it's hard both for Jews and Arabs...."

Mrs. Ohana, I don't want to talk politics, but motherhood. I understand your pain, and also the pain of the mother from Nablus....

"Mothers? Look, at first I said that I hate Arabs, but a mother is a mother, it doesn't matter if she's a Jew or an Arab, what she went through, I also went through. Death is death, for Arabs as well as Jews. The mother of an Arab and the mother of a Jew, it's the same thing. She gave birth to her after nine months, and I gave birth to my daughter after nine months. There's nothing else to say, she's a mother and I'm a mother. But they take revenge."

If you, Mrs. Mas'ouda Ohana, and that woman from Nablus, the mother of Alham abu Zarour, were given the chance to tell the politicians what to do, what would you tell them, all the leaders in Israel and in the Arab states and in the PLO?

"I have nothing to say. It won't help. Listen to something interesting. During the time when my daughter died, there were some Arabs here, working on the road, here, next to my house. I don't blame everybody. One of them came to me and asked for water, it was summer in Beit Shean. What is summer here? A sauna, a real sauna. And I saw him come to my house and I said, 'Why should I give you water? They killed my daughter.' But afterward I thought, 'Should I let a human being dry up, next to my house?' Water belongs to God, and I gave him water. The next day he came again to ask for water, and I gave him. I said to him, 'If you don't have any water, come and get some.' And I would prepare bottles and give them to them. What? Should I let them dry up next to my house? They are human beings, aren't they? And water belongs to God, doesn't it? But if there were a Jew who killed an Arab girl, and Jews were to come and ask for water from the Arabs, would they give it to him? They would give him poison. They don't stand by their word. We are a people who gives in."

Mrs. Ohana, I can see that you have a good heart. How can we live in peace in spite of everything? I want to make sure that my children and yours will live in peace. What do we need to do? Hasn't enough blood been shed?

"I have grandchildren, I don't want what happened to my daughter to happen to them. We want to live in peace with the Arabs. When we were in Casablanca, we lived in a big house, and an Arab family lived next to us. We grew up together, the Arabs would bring us *arak* to drink, and we drank. They ate our food, but we didn't eat theirs. Only pita or an egg. I am thinking about my children and my grandchildren. Of course I am thinking...."

If you were to meet the mother from Nablus, would you sit together? When I listen to you, I am reminded of her words, the same sorrow, the same pain. Why can't your voice and hers be heard for the sake of peace? Why shouldn't you meet and be heard as bereaved mothers, a voice crying out for peace?

"We both have the same love for the girl. The same story, nine months, nine months. Just as I raised my daughter, she raised her daughter. Her daughter is missed at home, and my daughter is missed in my home, the same feeling. But what can we do? It isn't up to us. It is up to our body and their body."

What do you mean, "body?"

"The government, our government and theirs...the big ones. Our body is the government, Shamir, and the Arabs' body is, for example, the PLO. They need to get along together, and Shamir will sit with the PLO and their government, and there will be negotiations and there will be peace. What we contributed, we contributed. The children that are gone cannot be returned. The heartbreak of the Jewish mothers and the Arab mothers. We have the same love. On a holiday, I leave one empty chair for her. Everything depends on the body; if the leaders get along, we have to accept it.... But the problem is that everyone is looking out for his own interests.... They are worried about their jobs, their dollars; they are not worried about the community, there's nothing to be done about it.... What does a member of the Knesset do? He talks for ten minutes and gets a salary for it. I was destroyed, did anyone help me?"

And what are those two girls doing, somewhere up above?

"The two of them, Alham and Esther, in white dresses and a flower in their hair, and silk gloves. And one approaches the other and whispers something in her ear and steps backward, and the dance continues. And strains of music come from above, and the lights are always changing, now red, and now purple, and now green, and everything flickers, and the dance continues. And this is what we called a wedding in heaven, and the two girls don't stop the dance, and they never look down, they don't see us, we who live from our own pain. And in their world everything is white as snow, everything flows like a calm stream, everything continues without end. And there is no empty space and there is no time, and there is no force which can stop this divine dance, because there, up above, everything flows toward eternity and there is no end to dreams, no end, and there is no end to the life of death. And we, here, have closed ourselves in and drawn borders, and within our own borders we shed our blood."

Chaya Weisgal-Amir

Chaya Weisgal-Amir was born in New York and went to Israel to join a kibbutz soon after the establishment of Israel. She has been involved in political activities for Arab-Jewish rapprochement since the 1950s, and in movements against the occupation since the 1967 war. She works with the Women's Organization for Women Political Prisoners, a group which monitors prison conditions and attempts to provide legal, political, and humanitarian assistance for women prisoners of the Intifada; and with the Workers Hotline, a group which assists Palestinian workers in Israel who have been deprived of their basic rights.

Chaya, who lives in Tel Aviv, holds a B.A. and M.A. from Tel Aviv University in poetics and semiotics. She works as an editor, translator, and free-lance writer. She is married, has four sons and eight grandchildren.

Prisoners and the Intifada

Chaya Weisgal-Amir

Christmas Day 1990

It was supposed to rain yesterday, but it didn't. It wasn't supposed to rain today, but it did. Israel is supposed to be a democracy, but it isn't. Who can you trust?

The headlines on this morning's news broadcast were about prisoners. The news is always about prisoners. Prisoners being taken, prisoners being released, prisoners being harassed, prisoners being killed, prisoners going swimming, prisoners being deported, prisoners being supported. Today's headlined prisoners were seven in number, four of one kind and three of another. The four, among them a teacher and a lawyer, were going to be deported. The three, among them people found guilty of murder in cold blood, conspiracy, and violence, were going to be released. The four will never be tried, merely deported. The three have been tried, sentenced to life imprisonment, and released after less than seven years. The four are Palestinians. The three are fine, upright, Jewish boys, cold-blooded murderers perhaps, fanatic perhaps, dangerous perhaps, but look at it this way, through the prism of Israeli democracy: The three were only doing what many other fine, upright Israelis would do (in fact do do, but in uniform). They were shooting to kill, maim, and otherwise injure Palestinians out of the noblest of all possible sentiments — the national good. The four Palestinians, on the other hand, again through the prism of Israeli democracy, may not have done anything for which they can be taken to court. But they have inspired others to behave out of the basest of all possible sentiments — the national good. Theirs, not ours.

The three Israeli prisoners being released were sentenced, as noted, to life imprisonment for entering a theological seminary in Hebron and gunning down Palestinian students at random. Three dead, many injured. It was nothing personal, really, and there was no reason for anyone to take it personally. It was a selfless, rational/national impulse. They performed a number of other selfless deeds, such as booby-trapping Arab buses, shooting the legs off the mayor of Nablus, and attempting to destroy the most sacred of Muslim holy places in Jerusalem. Their sentence of life imprisonment shocked Israeli public opinion at the time, because when a Jew murders an Arab it is not really murder and should not be so perceived. That's why they are the kind of prisoners who are sometimes taken to the beach to go swimming. Happily, our president, Chaim Herzog, an honorable man, believes that the quality of mercy should drop as sugared popcorn, blessing him that gives and him that takes. He reduced their sentence three times; first from life to twenty-four years, then to fifteen, finally to ten. And don't they deserve some time off for good behavior?

A week before Christmas our prison headlines read: "Seventy Thousand Palestinians Arrested since the Beginning of the Intifada." The good news was from the Chief Army Prosecutor Amnon Strashnov. Herzog, no doubt, was disturbed by the news, and the vision of prisoners pushing one another to get a breath of air in the overcrowded prisons may have kept him up at night. Since he is a religious man and here it was smack between Chanukah and Christmas, a gesture to Muslims was in place. He could reduce the crowding by getting some of the Jewish boys out.

Seventy thousand Palestinian prisoners — that's quite a number.

I remember an apocalyptic dream I had soon after the 1967 war. The members of my family were sitting at home and outside. Wherever we turned, we saw barbed wire. Everything but my home and family was enclosed within its prickly compass. In my waking moments, I was well aware of the fact that the longer the occupation continued, the larger the prison facilities would have to become until, perhaps, they would indeed impinge upon my field of vision. This has come to pass.

It is a common enough platitude to say that we are all prisoners of the Intifada, Israelis and Palestinians alike; and it may even be true in certain ways. But one cannot mention the moral or metaphorical — or even physical — imprisonment suffered by the good Israeli in the same breath with the abject humiliation and brutality suffered by the Palestinian prisoner. The good Israeli, the indignant Israeli, the politically active and totally committed Israeli, and even the conscientious objectors among us, are able to take time off from the Intifada, for our jobs, our studies, our families. We can take our kids to the beach or our friends to a pub. We can take in a good movie occasionally; listen to the opera, if we're so inclined; or go abroad, if we can afford it. True, the Intifada is always there, hanging over us ominously, agonizingly. But it still lets us breathe even if, at times, we feel ourselves being suffocated, metaphorically.

My use of this particular metaphor is not gratuitous. The Palestinian prisoner cannot breathe because a jute sack dipped in excrement has been placed over his or her head during interrogation. Or because canisters of tear gas have exploded in the schoolyard prior to arrest. Or because a rubber, or plastic, or even real — as opposed to imaginary? — bullet has penetrated his or her skull and imprisonment has become superfluous. The difference, one must admit, is significant.

The number of Palestinian prisoners today is hard to pinpoint. Some sources estimate it at twenty thousand, some at thirty to forty thousand. There are also degrees of imprisonment, from curfew, to home or town arrest, to administrative detention, to life. A Palestinian may be free to go from his home to the market but not free to go to work. He may be free to go to work but not free to go abroad.

Most prisoners are men. Many are children and youths between the ages of twelve and eighteen. Some are women, perhaps a hundred of them, some of them pregnant, some of them nursing mothers or mothers of small children. A very large number are administrative detainees, that is, people arrested and held for six months or a year, or more, without any charges being pressed against them. This is lawful because men and women make laws for other men and women and there is apparently no limit to the inventiveness of the human mind. It is also convenient: no evidence need be submitted to a judge. There are numerous other conveniences in the Israeli science of "prisonology." But I do insist on stressing that Israel did not invent this particular discipline and is certainly not alone in practicing it. We are simply adept, as a people, at acquiring useful national skills.

It is convenient, for example, to imprison many Palestinians — though certainly not all — in Israel and not in the territories, although the practice is contrary to international law. This makes it difficult — and recently, with the closing of the territories for various periods of time, impossible — for their families and lawyers to visit them. Very often reports of arrest or detention are withheld, denied, or distorted. An inaccurate report of arrest can send families and lawyers scurrying from one end of the country to the other, seeking confirmation. And even if lawyer, father or mother, sister or brother, son or daughter, husband or wife know exactly where their client or relative is being held, and have the time and the money and the physical stamina to undertake the trip, there are even more convenient regulations in our inventory. Visits are not always allowed, even if they are scheduled. In Hasharon Prison, for example, where most of the women and 25 percent of the minors are held, the monthly or bimonthly visiting hour may be canceled after the visitors have traveled two or three hours to get there. Why? There are always good reasons. Two of the girls were caught singing in their cells. Or one of the women threw her food out without touching it. Or called a guard a dirty pig — after he had made sexually insinuating remarks. Collective punishment is the rule and canceling visits or prohibiting them for months at a time is too common to be noteworthy. How often have visiting privileges been canceled because an imprisoned mother tried to touch her child during a visit when everybody knows that the wire mesh is there to prevent such transgressions against Israel's security.

And because Israel is egalitarian in many ways, what goes for the family visits goes, frequently, for the lawyers. They are kept waiting for hours on end and finally dismissed without ever seeing their clients. They are told that their client is ill or not there or that they don't have the proper identification or that they are public nuisances or agents of the PLO.

There is no point in expatiating here on the quality of life in the prisons, the lack of heating in the winter, the heat in the summer, the lack of minimal facilities for washing, the indifference to prisoners' health, the often inedible food, the blatant discrimination between Jewish and Palestinian prisoners. Nor is there any point in expatiating on pre-imprisonment procedures: the interrogations accompanied by the infliction of various forms of "reasonable pressure" (as permitted by a high court ruling) — from humiliation and insult, through slapping and beating, to sexual threats, torture, and unexplained demise. The quality of prison life in Israel and the Occupied Territories is no different from that in any nondemocratic country where discrimination against certain parts of the population is the norm.

*   *   *   *   *

Fortunately, although we may not be able to change the system, we are still able to speak out against it, to monitor it, to help those inside in small ways. There are a number of organizations in Israel that make it their business to keep the subject of the maltreatment of political prisoners in the public view. The Association for Civil Rights in Israel is one of them. The Committee Against Torture is another. There is a group which monitors the conditions of juvenile prisoners of the Intifada, children between the ages of twelve and eighteen. And there is the Women's Organization for Political Prisoners (WOFPP), which deals primarily with women prisoners. It was through working with this last group that I gained my insights into the system.

They informed me, shortly after the beginning of the Intifada, that a Palestinian friend of mine had been imprisoned on suspicion of keeping seditious materials in her house. (According to the law, any leaflet calling for an end to the occupation is considered inimical to the security of Israel and, ipso facto, seditious.) She was held in a Tel Aviv detention center for more than three months, after which she was released without charges being pressed. During the time she was in prison, her mother came to visit her with her two tiny children, a girl of three and a baby boy. The mother, a woman of over sixty who had traveled three hours to make the visit, was told that either she *or* the children could go in. The mother could not leave the children alone outside nor was there any way that the two children could possibly go in by themselves. My friend saw neither her mother nor her children that day.

I was impressed by this sophisticated form of cruelty and was to learn in my work with the WOFPP that the prison authorities were able to come up with ideas like this at the drop of any reasonable request.

Israel didn't invent the brutality prevalent in its prison system. We merely learned its uses and by so doing turned the Golden Rule on its head. No longer is it "Do unto others as you would have them do unto you," but it has become "Do unto others as others have done unto you."

Roni
Ben-Efrat

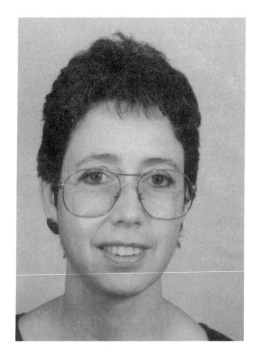

Roni Ben-Efrat's par-
ents came to Israel from
England in 1950 out of
Zionist motives. They were
among the founders of
kibbutz Kfar Hanassi in
the upper Galilee, but left
the kibbutz shortly there-
after to found an agricultural
village, Kfar Mordechai.
Roni was born there in
1952 and led a very calm
and beautiful childhood.
An intensive reader, she formed a general humanist view on life, in an
environment that was not especially political.

At the age of fifteen, a year after the occupation began, Roni began
to be critical of its continuation, a view which isolated her from her
peers. She was not enthusiastic about going into the army and delayed
her army service by entering a teachers course. She received her
teaching diploma, and simultaneously finished a B.A. at Hebrew
University in history and Bible. During this time she also married and
gave birth to two children, which secured her exemption from the army.

Becoming increasingly politicized, Roni writes that she "rejected
Zionism as an essentially racist, colonialist ideology which seeks not
simply to colonize the Arab inhabitants of what was Palestine, but to
uproot them." After five years of teaching, she was fired for refusing to
wear a pin saying "I am a Zionist," that all teachers and students were
obliged to wear. A year-long struggle with the Ministry of Education over
this resulted in being allowed to teach again, but she lost interest in the
profession and began working as a full-time activist and journalist for
the Nitzotz collective.

The Lebanon War deepened her commitment to the struggle for
justice and her critique of the Israeli government's continuing attempts
to do away with the Palestinians by military means. Together with other
Nitzotz friends, Roni started learning Arabic, "a skill unfortunately not
many peace activists share." She considers Arabic "an essential tool to

understand and communicate with the Palestinian people, their politics and culture, which strengthens our bonds and solidarity with their cause and ending the occupation." Of equal concern to her is the elimination of racism towards Arabs in Israel and the creation of a democratic state for all citizens of Israel on the basis of a two-state solution.

Being a Jewish Opposition During the Intifada

Roni Ben-Efrat

Being a Jewish leftist activist in Israel was never a very great threat. Even organizations considered to be extremely radical by the establishment were never considered a threat. Although we were frequently subjected to harassment, such as being blacklisted and denied jobs, or unpleasant delays and searches at the airport, in general the authorities always treated us as "part of the family," albeit black sheep.

The outbreak of the Intifada lent events a new dimension at a dizzying pace. Within the peace movement, new tones were beginning to be heard regarding active refusal to perform military service in the Occupied Territories. Jewish intellectuals began speaking about forms of civil disobedience and refusal to collaborate with the occupation in even broader aspects — economic, social, and more. From solidarity with the Palestinians in the territories the atmosphere changed to support for the Intifada. Among the Arabs in Israel there were the Peace Day demonstrations on December 21, 1987 (a general strike in solidarity with the Intifada), that were identical to the confrontations one might have witnessed in the territories, for example in Nablus or Gaza.

In 1986, prior to this, our organization, Nitzotz ("spark"), had formed a new Jewish-Arab editorial board in addition to the group which up to then had published its Hebrew-language publication, *Derech HaNitzotz*. The two journals, Hebrew and Arabic, were published alternately each week and rapidly became an indispensable source of information, describing and documenting the developments in the Occupied Territories — the building of the popular organizations on one hand, and the occupation's repression on the other. The Arabic-language publication, whose target public was the Arab community inside Israel, rapidly gained fifteen hundred subscriptions in dozens of Arab villages and towns, and its overall distribution was over three thousand copies. With the outbreak of the Intifada it became known as the "Intifada newspaper;" and we worked around the clock in order to accurately document the number of victims and to tell the story of the Palestinian Uprising.

The day I first began feeling that I was being treated as an opposition was the day a somber clerk from the Ministry of Interior appeared at our office at Koresh Street 14 with a letter to be delivered in person. It was an order from Eli Suissa, the Jerusalem District Commissioner of the Ministry, canceling the license of our publications in Hebrew and Arabic, *Derech HaNitzotz* and *Tariq a-Sharara*, charging that they were linked to the Democratic Front for the Liberation of Palestine. During the following months our entire group would undergo much worse and bitter experiences. However, Eli Suissa's letter clarified for me for the first time, that the authorities had decided to deal with us by means that had, up to then, been preserved for Palestinians only. The closure of a Hebrew-language paper by administrative order was an unknown precedent to the Israeli public and naturally aroused a storm among journalists and liberals in Israel. Although the storm began over the Hebrew publication, it was undoubtedly the Arabic paper that they were after. Our group, which stood behind both papers, was unwilling to save its Hebrew publication at the cost of losing the Arabic.

The authorities gave us a strong indication of what we were to expect in the future. On February 16, 1988, two days before the paper was closed down, the editor of the Arabic edition, Ribhi Aruri, was arrested. He was interrogated under harsh conditions. After twenty-one days of interrogation, when no evidence was found against him and a judge ordered him released, the minister of defense decided to detain him administratively and he spent six months in Jnaid prison and Ansar III detention camp. Aruri said that the questions he had been asked during his interrogation all concerned the Jewish editors of the paper. Aruri was expected to supply the authorities with information incriminating the Nitzotz editors.

Some six weeks passed before the next move. In the meantime, although our paper was closed, we continued to publish under different names and formats. We called one of our publications *In Spite of It*. This edition sold to the last copy. Our persistence in publishing placed us directly in the range of the Security Services (the Shin Bet). On April 15, Yakov Ben-Efrat (my former husband) was arrested and on April 23, I was arrested at Lod airport while on my way to an antifascist conference in Italy. Three more of my comrades were arrested after me, one after the other: Michal Schwartz, Hadas Lahav, and Assaf Adiv. Each week there was another arrest. The Shin Bet wanted to create a psychosis of uncertainty, terror, and fear.

In the course of the detentions, the authorities had us taste the flavor of opposition. For the first time we became intimately familiar with what we had previously termed the "kingdom of darkness," which had belonged to Palestinians alone, and which we had written about but had not known ourselves. This was our trial of fire.

Through collaboration between the Prime Minister's office (which is in charge of the Shin Bet) and the Ministry of Justice, undemocratic laws and restrictions that had previously been used only against Arabs were employed against us. The press was prohibited from publicizing the charges against us and all court sessions at which our detentions were extended were secret. We were not allowed to meet our lawyers for fifteen days. During the entire period there was a diabolic campaign against us, in which the Shin Bet was free to leak rumors and hints. When the editors of the daily newspapers protested against the cloak of secrecy around the affair, the head of the Shin Bet held a meeting with the Editor's Committee (a body composed of the editors of the daily papers, established in the 1960s, who are privy to classified information their papers are prohibited from printing). In exchange for their silence the head of the Shin Bet told them the nature of the charges against us: meeting with a foreign agent (a Palestinian leader) and membership in a hostile organization (the Democratic Front for the Liberation of Palestine — DFLP). The charge sheet was based upon the confessions of three of us in detention, confessions which were all recanted immediately after the interrogations ended.

During the entire period, the Shin Bet was free to use a massive array of pressures to force us to confess to those charges. The Shin Bet formed a special team of eight interrogators who were brought especially for the duration of our interrogations to the interrogation center in Petah Tikva. The interrogation center is annexed to the police station in the city but is totally autonomous. This is the Shin Bet's uncontested kingdom. The police, which acts as a rubber stamp for all of the Shin Bet's acts of torture, plays at best the role of a go-between between the Shin Bet and the courts. It was the former which recorded the confessions dictated earlier by the Shin Bet interrogators. The police is not even permitted to care for the maintenance of the cells; from fixing clogged pipes to changing a light bulb, everything has to go through the Shin Bet.

The Shin Bet intended to "rehabilitate its undermined image" by means of the Nitzotz case; at least that is what it announced to us five detainees. In reality things did not work out that way. In spite of the cloak of secrecy and the prohibition on meetings with lawyers, facts about the methods of interrogation began to leak out. Once it was about the systematic blowing of smoke rings at the breasts of one of the women among us; then about the beating of a Palestinian detainee as psychological pressure in order to extract confessions from the Jewish detainees; humiliation; the use of lies concerning the condition of our children; the use of intimate information regarding our private lives in an attempt to break us down; sleep deprivation; placing one of us in an unnatural position for a lengthy period; the use of forged notes; and so on.

In mid-June Professor Yehuda Bauer, researcher of the Holocaust, opened a debate in *Ha'aretz* daily. The article he wrote was a response to the disclosures of our comrade Hadas Lahav, who was interviewed by Israeli television and press on the day she was released without charges against her. Bauer's article was entitled "Shin Bet Interrogators — How Do You Sleep?"

In the article he attacked the courts' willingness to accept confessions extracted by means of humiliation and torture, even if the latter was not physical; he attacked the police for covering up the *Shin Bet*'s deeds and also accused himself: "As long as Palestinians were treated in this manner we were silent. It was outside our herd-society. Our conscience was silent, sleeping in sweet slumber. Now it touches home, 'one of ours.' "He accused the Shin Bet and treated it as no Israeli Zionist had ever treated it before:

> There remains the plain fact that the eight interrogators who tortured Hadas Lahav — and this was not denied — walk among us, mingle with us. Their children go to school with our children, their wives shop at the same supermarket. I have no doubt that they are good husbands, wonderful fathers, and great sons to their parents; if they have them. They treat cats and dogs nicely and tend to the garden. On Saturdays they swim with us at the same beach or pray with us at the same synagogue. But until it is denied and if it is not denied, people who act thus are defined as the scum of the earth; and I hope it is denied. If not — let them and their deeds be ostracized.[1]

Professor Bauer, who cannot be suspected of being a leftist by any means, chose to stand on our side in the confrontation between us and the Security Services. And he admitted that the Shin Bet had decided to employ against us norms which he had accepted, although not happily, in regard to Palestinians. This was the straw which broke the camel's back. The public debate concerning the manner in which the Nitzotz members should be treated grew deeper.

The next issue on the agenda concerned the courts and the question of whether or not to release us on bail. Here, as well, we were treading virgin ground and discovered that the rulings were a barometer of two tendencies in Israeli society, and expressed the prevailing attitude towards us. The first ruling by District Judge Ben-Zimra stated that, save for Yakov Ben-Efrat, defendant no. 1, the three other defendants including me should be released on bail. He stated that it was not proven that the defendants would endanger the public nor was it established that their actions had caused any harm to the public. Ben-Zimra also addressed the fact that two of the defendants were mothers. Of course, Ben-Zimra's ruling, on the eve of the trial, was a hard blow to the prestige of the Shin Bet, which had attempted to incite the public against us and to portray us as a dangerous espionage ring.

The Shin Bet appealed to the Supreme Court through the prosecution and the appeal was passed to Judge Barak, a judge who enjoyed prestige as "Israeli law's wunderkind," having set several very important legal precedents. His personality combines liberalism with a tough security-mindedness.

While ruling on our issue Barak chose to reveal his security-mindedness in a manner which bordered on hysteria. In an unprecedented, severe ruling he stated that we would not be released on bail because we had "lent our hands to uprooting the state's body and soul." His ruling stunned not only intellectuals, who issued a petition denouncing the ruling, but also well-known jurists such as Professor Ruth Gabizon, who published a stinging article in the Lawyers Association magazine rejecting Barak's ruling:

> The judge's concept of severity arouses wonder: the court invites us to make most dangerous, and not at all obvious, analogies. There is no doubt that joining an organization, even if it is a terrorist organization, in order to publish a newspaper and organize politically, for an ideologically marginal group with no connection to violence, is very far from "uprooting the state's body and soul." And these are still in the sphere of *political activity*, in contrast to *violent action*, which harms people's bodies and lives (emphasis added).

Gabizon went on to criticize the discrimination drawn by Judge Barak between the violent actions of the members of the Jewish terrorist underground and the Nitzotz detainees:

> We did not hear such severe statements regarding the "uprooting of the state's body and soul" in regard to the violent actions of the Jewish underground defendants, and there were those who openly supported them and considered their ideological motives a mitigating factor.[2]

Lastly, Gabizon expressed the manner in which a large sector of intellectuals in Israel viewed the charges against the Nitzotz members. "In my eyes," she said, "it is not at all obvious that openly preaching for the use of *violence against the innocent* in the name of Jewish self-defense is less severe than the *ideological* joining of a Palestinian organization. In the conditions of this country, the former is, in my view, overwhelmingly more dangerous." That was the controversial atmosphere in which our trial was conducted.

In October we presented another request for release on bail which was reviewed by District Judge Zvi Tal, who was also the head of the team of three judges presiding over our trial. Judge Tal ruled even more strongly than Judge Ben-Zimra previously that all four of us should be released on bail and placed under house arrest. He claimed that if there had been membership (in the DFLP) at all, it was nominal membership, and relied on Judge Barak's ruling, stating that he saw nowhere in the ruling any claim that we would constitute a security risk if released. This was an additional slap in the face to Barak's ruling, which was universally termed draconian in conclusion and emotional by nature. The Shin Bet once again appealed to the Supreme Court. This time the case landed with Judge Shlomo Levine. In a dry ruling Levine canceled the ruling of Judge Tal and stated that we would remain in detention until sentencing. This chapter was extremely important to us when we analyzed the mood of the Israeli public. There is no doubt that the statements of Judges Ben-Zimra and Tal and attorney Gabizon were far-reaching and expressed a departure from the past demonization of the PLO and anything connected to it.

After four months, in January 1989, we decided to end the trial by plea bargaining, eliminating the severe charge of contact with a foreign agent, but leaving the charge of membership in a hostile organization. The sentences proposed by the plea bargain were adopted by the judges. I was released the day the trial ended, having served nine months in prison; Michal Schwartz and Assaf Adiv were sentenced to eighteen months imprisonment, which they served in full. Yakov Ben-Efrat was released on October 14, 1990, after serving the maximum term of thirty months imprisonment, twelve of them in solitary confinement.

The Shin Bet, the police, and the courts were one arena in which we conducted a stubborn battle for our political positions and our right to operate as a legal opposition. Another battle, different yet no less fascinating, concerned our demand to be imprisoned among the Palestinian political prisoners. We did not estimate what a bomb we were to throw into the world of racist concepts ruling Israeli society. The ever-so-comfortable division in Israeli prisons, in which a security prisoner was synonymous with Palestinian, was being challenged. What was to be done with a solid group of four Jewish prisoners who stated relentlessly that they wished to be imprisoned with Palestinian prisoners?

The Prisons Service jumped from one pretext to another and ran around in circles simply in order not to admit its reliance on racist norms as the reason for its refusal to respond to our demand. The first step was an unprecedented campaign of incitement which took place in Neve Tirza, the only women's prison at the time, against the "traitors." Upon our arrival there we met with a violent reception by the prisoners, who had received a green light to assault us. We learned that the prison officers had encouraged the hostility towards us, both by exaggerating the charges against us, and by calling us "Arab lovers" and "Jew haters." The riot in prison at our arrival became uncontrollable, and on the first night we were placed in a room with Palestinian prisoners in order to protect our lives. This idyll did not last long. By the following morning, with the prison in a state of emergency and under a veritable curfew, we were transferred to the separation wing and isolated from all prisoners — Jewish criminals and Arab security prisoners. The prison authorities chose to define us as "needing protection," an extraordinary type of prisoner, deserving isolation and punishment. A short time after we were placed in isolation, the prison authorities also chose to define Yakov Ben-Efrat and Assaf Adiv as "needing protection," although they were not attacked by any prisoners whatsoever.

On July 18, Nelson Mandela's birthday, we decided to embark on a five-day hunger strike, demanding to be removed from isolation and to be placed among the political prisoners. Once again we transferred the ball into the court of Israeli public opinion and placed on the agenda a question which had not been previously addressed by the public. The Prisons Service squirmed. Enlightened public opinion denounced the inhuman treatment we received. The prison authorities were accused of punishing us doubly. News of our hunger strike spread to all security prisons where, from that time, prisoners followed our struggle to be imprisoned among them and participated (at least in Kfar Yonah, where the men were imprisoned) in all the future hunger strikes we held.

When criticism of the Prisons Service grew, its directors suggested transferring us to wings where "privileged" criminal prisoners were held. We rejected the proposal. The Shin Bet, in the meantime, continued to pull the strings. None of the Nitzotz prisoners earned parole for good behavior or leave from prison. Representatives of the Shin Bet, who participated in all the discussions concerning parole, described us as a security risk, even six months before we were due for release.

Why did the prison authorities refuse to grant our demand? Because, responded M.K. (Knesset Member) Shulamit Aloni, who visited us in prison during our hunger strike, "You have hit the primitive and racist tribal instincts of the establishment and it will not forgive you for doing that." The authorities never agreed to reveal the simple and crude truth behind their refusal to allow us to be imprisoned among the political prisoners — the undeclared policy of apartheid.

Now, almost three years later, Israeli society is undergoing a dangerous process of fascistization. The refusal of the Israeli government to recognize reality and read the new political map drawn up by the outbreak of the Intifada is dragging the entire Middle East to the edge of a volcano. The open cries of "death to the Arabs," "Hebrew labor," and "transfer" will become stronger as long as the Palestinian-Israeli conflict remains unsolved. These deepening contradictions create difficulties for the peace movement and isolate it. On the other hand, there is no doubt that they increase the necessity for us to fight for a fundamental solution of the problem and for the democratic nature of this state.

The authorities have denied us the possibility of creating direct contact with the masses by means of our publications in Hebrew and Arabic. However, there has not yet been a movement which desired to struggle for democratic change and which has found a way to circumvent the restrictions imposed against it. Our views are currently expressed from broad and numerous podiums, in Hebrew, Arabic, and English. We are struggling for a political and social change in the framework of all movements in the peace camp: the women's movement, Women for Women Political Prisoners; the movement of reserve-duty soldiers who refuse to serve in the Occupied Territories, Yesh Gvul; the peace movement publication *Challenge*. We issue a bimonthly newsletter on violations of the freedom of expression and repression of journalists, as well as a newsletter in Arabic; and are involved in all the struggles for equality of the Arab Israeli population. We published, in February 1991, a booklet in Arabic dealing with the Gulf War. It looks critically at the Arab population in Israel vis-à-vis the Intifada. A second Arabic publication is in process concerning the latest wave of land confiscations from Arabs in Israel.

The principle which guides us is the unification of the existing political forces, Jewish and Arab, around a realistic program of action which will solve the Palestinian issue through the establishment of an independent Palestinian state, headed by the PLO, in the territories occupied since 1967.

Notes

1. Yehuda Bauer, "Shin Bet Interrogators — How Do You Sleep?" in *Ha'aretz*, June 12, 1988.

2. Ruth Gabizon, *Halishka* (magazine of the Lawyers Association), July 1988.

Rela Mazali

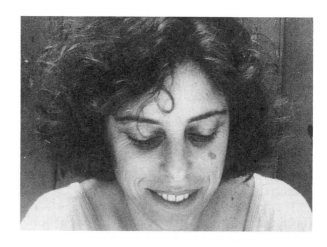

Born in 1948, at Kibbutz Ma'ayan Baruch in the Upper Galilee, Rela Mazali spent most of her childhood in Tel Aviv and Kansas City. She studied philosophy and comparative literature at Tel Aviv University, where she received her master's degree. She is married and the mother of three children.

A soldier serving in the Galilee during the Six Day War, Rela emerged from the war with a sense of waste and horror, contrasting sharply with the general feeling of euphoria. This alienated, angry attitude appears in her novel *WhaNever a Novel* (Kerem Publishing, 1987), in which four women's views on the Yom Kippur war in which their partners are fighting break a deep-set Israeli taboo on voicing objections to war, and on questioning its necessity and importance. They also overstep the taboo on openly allowing personal fear to play a legitimate part in one's opinions.

Rela was active for over a year in the Liberated Territory group which published alternative editorials in the press, ending with the first public statement against the war in Lebanon. Later, in The 21st Year movement, opposing the occupation, she specialized in work with youth. At present Rela is working with the Testimonies group on a documentary film about Israeli soldiers who have served in the Occupied Territories. She is also working on her second novel, translations, and several educational projects.

Given a Continuing Immoral Occupation and a Probable Unnecessary War

Rela Mazali

The seminal axis of my political sensitivity is my motherhood. Simultaneous with, and ever since, the birth of each of my three children — especially my two sons — I have felt forced to supply a serious, detailed, and practical answer to the question, "What, in the world, is worth the death of my child?" This fact of my life is at the core of my compulsion — and it's a compulsion — to political activism.

It is typical of Israeli cultural consensus that I feel obliged to apologize for the pathos of my opening. Maybe it's the pathos inherent in every part of our lives, down to the most mundane, that causes Israelis to prefer shoulder shrugging and lopsided smiles as the accepted terms on which to meet loaded emotions. A confessed participant in this ethos, I still see it as a central component of the harmful Israeli machismo that chooses to play down fearsome and highly painful questions. The alternative to phrasing questions as accurately as possible, attempting a truthful answer and taking the action this would necessarily entail, is one which may lead to impossible or unbearable personal contradictions. It also risks making yourself laughable, which is somehow felt to be worse than the risk of getting yourself killed. So this course is consistently evaded by most people, aside from political activists on the one hand and politicians on the other, both of whose formulations aren't usually taken personally or, in other words, seriously.

But I won't apologize. I'll go on with what it means to me to live in this country today. Motherhood, though never easy or comfortably intuitive for me, has undoubtedly proved the most powerful and unrelenting tie I have experienced. The force of the feelings it involves becomes, through a transitive relation, the force of my emotions on political issues, which necessarily affect the lives of my children. The fact of having your son go to the army and risk his life is one that is born along with every Jewish baby boy in this country. Daughters, although they also serve in the army, are rarely involved in combat situations. It is a fact that has remained constant for the duration of the country's existence, though most young mothers take the temporary escape route of believing that peace will have come by the time their son enlists.

My attitude towards this constant fact is, of itself, a political position. Do I believe there is no choice? Do I accept my sons' risk as justified because it is part of my country's fight for life, which we would willingly exchange for peace given a practical chance? Or do I think the word "security" is being misused, and the country's state misrepresented? Do I see the threat to my children as deriving from tenets and beliefs that do not really concern the life or death of this country, and which, as such, produce policies that I take to be unnecessary and immoral? Can I face the prospect of having my sons fight and possibly lose their lives or health, or parts of their soul (as many seemingly uninjured sons do today in the Intifada) for the sake of policies that I find both unnecessary and immoral? To what extent do I continue to see this country as *mine*, when it persists in implementing such policies? And when the time comes for my sons to carry them out? Then what? Do I still want any part of it? If so, if I still want to be part and see it as mine, what should I do about the laws and instructions which serve to carry out the immoral policies (for instance, mobilization laws governing reserve military duty)? Uphold them and protest? Violate them in protest? How far am I capable of biding by a decision on the last question, with everything this implies? How far am I able, or do I wish, to determine my growing sons' choices on these matters?

And then again, if I opt for leaving, to what extent do I still believe, as we were all brought up to, that the only place where I, born a Jew, can really live freely and equally is in this country. In other words, to what extent do I go on believing that living here is the only really feasible alternative open to me and my children? But there are so many Israelis, all over, apparently doing no less okay than I. So, to what degree is my decision to go on living here a freely made choice, resulting from the deep and intricate ties and support systems that I've built and with which I feel comfortable? And what is the weight of these parts of my life relative to risking my sons' lives?

It is through these basic questions that the underlying infrastructure of my beliefs and values (humanism, equal rights, etc.) is mapped onto concrete political positions and views about the actual events taking place around me. The mechanism is a highly selfish one, although guided by a definite morality. Its point of departure is the well-being of my children and myself. It examines options, policies, and deeds (my own and my government's) in terms of their effect on us.

But it is just this personal handle that makes the attitude I'm describing universally applicable (and shared in practice). In 1980, East German writer Christa Wolf asked concerning the situation then of Europe:

> Do we have a chance? How can I rely on the experts who have led us to this desperate pass? Armed with nothing but the intractable desire to allow my children and grandchildren to live, I conclude that the sensible course may be the one that holds out absolutely no hope: unilateral disarmament.... This is wishful thinking, you say? So, is it completely misguided to want to think and to have a say about the life and death of many, perhaps all future generations?
>
> The atomic threat, if it has brought us to the brink of annihilation, must then have brought us to the brink of silence too, to the brink of endurance, to the brink of reserve about our fear and anxiety, and our true opinions.[1]

It is the very immediate threat of my children coming to harm that brings me to the brink of my reserve about my true opinions, elementary and basic though they may seem — naive and unrealistic though they may be called, especially by those who have led me here. Christa Wolf also argued for active criticism:

> To prevent wars, people must criticize, in their own country, the abuses that occur in their own country. The role taboos play in the preparation for war. The number of shameful secrets keeps growing incessantly, boundlessly. How meaningless all censorship taboos become, and how meaningless the consequences for overstepping them, when your life is in danger.[2]

And I might add, your moral soul too. Except that when your life and soul are in danger, the question of efficacy becomes cardinal too. There is a constant, enormous sense of smallness, of impotence. Does it really help to criticize? Even if it does, will it help enough fast enough? Isn't it more rational to get my family out of here before my oldest son has to enlist? To criticize from safety across the ocean, in hopes of making a difference to what I'll undoubtedly go on feeling involved in, while keeping our lives and health intact? Why do I stay? Why should I hope? Do I hope? Or am I just succumbing to a form of fatalism? And then: would the fact of having tried to make a difference really stay me if my son were killed or disabled? I don't kid myself. I don't think it would. I would know I was to blame, at least partly, for knowing and having had a choice, and not leaving. How to bear the (even partial) blame for the senseless death of your child? But then again, would it really help any if I believed it wasn't senseless? Can anything help? The belief that I had no choice? Do I believe that? Still, if I do stay, I can't not try.

My present feeling is one of constant debate with myself. Why do I stay? What do I hope? Really, realistically hope? (Or, is that perhaps a contradiction?) Am I wrong in making this decision to stay? Am I making a decision or just letting myself put one off? And given the present state of my decision, what can I do that will have some effect? Most of my close friends are preoccupied with the same questions, although many of them stop short before the last point, and make no commitment to political activism.

Which raises the question of the actual options for political activism open to people who think this way. How can I (at least try to) make a difference? A practical answer should involve a look at the cluster of organizations through which my political views could be amplified, given a form that makes them more forceful than the incidental views of an unknown, individual woman. But I don't intend to sketch an anatomy or analysis of what's commonly called the Israeli peace camp, or the Left. What is pertinent to my story is that the options these organizations presently offer for political action are extremely limited, frustrating, and disappointing. They are not cohesive, well-formed, or actively recruiting groups to which I'm invited to add my voice, time, and money. Real activism here today (as opposed to occasional attendance at demonstrations) involves, to a large extent, making your own way, finding both the means of expression and the partners. This fact contributes disproportionately to the sense of alienation and sometimes desperation, which already exists in the face of Israeli reality today.

And this, while it's so much simpler and so seductive to just go on living my personal life. As most people around me are doing. The atrocious manifestations of my country's immoral policies are almost nowhere to be seen here. To know about them, you have to want to very much. They are not on the TV screen; they're not on the radio. Most of the major newspapers print very few items on what goes on beyond the Green Line. We've accustomed ourselves to what's been coined "invisible Arabs," who build, and pick fruit, and clean up our cities around us, while we habitually look through them. The goings-on in the Occupied Territories are, for the most part, as invisible as the Arabs they concern. Just getting the information on what's happening is a form of activism.

For me, however, the deduction is still inescapable. If I disbelieve any chance — even the slightest — of making a difference, of inching towards a reversal of the present state — that of an immoral occupation and probable unnecessary war — then I have no reason to stay and every pressing reason to leave. I should get out as fast as I can. If I don't, I must have some reason, hope, some deep-set belief in the possibility that I can budge things. In the value of trying, which it is then my responsibility — particularly to my children — to do as best I can. In other words, protest in some form is my last claim to rationality. My only means of offering some justification for a choice which I nonetheless recognize as largely irrational; to live in my country.

Notes

1. Christa Wolf, *Cassandra: A Novel and Four Essays* (London: Virago Press, 1984) pp. 229–30.
2. Ibid., pp. 258–9.

Amos Gvirtz

Amos Gvirtz was born and continues to live at Kibbutz Shefayim. He became a pacifist as a result of a long moral process which began in his teens. He is an active member of the Israeli peace camp, especially through War Resisters International and the International Fellowship of Reconciliation. Amos is one of the founders of Palestinians and Israelis for Nonviolence, and also of the relatively new Committee for a Change in the Taxation Policy in Gaza. In 1989 he spent a month on a U.S. tour about nonviolence and Israeli-Palestinian peace with Nafez Assailey of the Palestinian Center for the Study of Non-Violence.

Peace: A Necessary Condition

Amos Gvirtz

It often happens that, under pressure of activity and events, the objectives of an institution may change. We witness the establishment of an institution whose function is to provide solutions to various problems; with the passage of time, the existence of the institution itself becomes more important than the providing of answers to these problems. Therefore, it is worthwhile and necessary to ask why and to what end we are doing what we are doing.

Faced with the reality in Israel and the region, it is proper that we ask for what reason Zionism was conceived. Zionism, as I understand it, developed to provide an answer to the existential problems of the Jewish people, who lived as a minority in every country in which they resided, subject to the good or ill will of the majority. Anti-Semitism and persecution forced them to flee from some countries to others which varied in their willingness to accommodate Jews. Worse than everything before was the Holocaust, in which six million Jews, whose only crime was to have been born as such, were slaughtered.

When I review my relationship to Zionism, I am confronted with certain questions: Does Zionism meet the demand of safeguarding the existence of the Jews; is it viable in moral terms; and does it really guarantee the independence of the Jewish people?

Translated from Hebrew by Howard Shippin.

This article appeared in the Summer 1991 issue of *Reconciliation International*, the magazine of the International Fellowship of Reconciliation.

When Jewish immigration began at the end of the nineteenth century, Israel-Palestine was populated mainly by Palestinian Arabs. To a large extent Jewish settlement was accomplished by the displacement of the Palestinians. It is against this background that the conflict between the two peoples was born, growing more acute with the passage of time. The establishment of the State of Israel caused most of the Palestinians within its borders to lose their houses and lands and become refugees. Thus a situation unfolded in which, by its solution to the Jewish problem, the Zionist Movement created the problem of the Palestinians. This is where Zionism fails to answer those questions most important to me when I assess my relationship to it. As a result of the realization of the Zionist ideal, another people suffered the same kind of mistreatment as the Jews in the Diaspora. They lost, and continue to lose, their homes, lands, and human rights, simply because they were born Palestinian. This moral failure results in the inability to provide a proper answer to the existential question.

The situation of total war between Israel and her neighbors, and the arms race, which has brought weapons of mass destruction to our region, places in constant danger the very existence of Israel and the lives of her citizens. In such a situation, I seriously doubt that we are doing a service to those Jews who come to settle in Israel. In no other place in the world outside the Middle East is there such an explicit intention to injure and destroy us because we are Jews. Consequently, the State of Israel today stands ready to annihilate millions of people under the threat that others are poised to do the same to her — and to test the phrase, "I shall die with the Philistines." This leads me to the conclusion that the Zionist Movement has failed both morally and existentially.

Because of this security situation we have developed a high degree of economic, military, and political dependence on the United States, which means that the independence of Israel as a state is to a large extent illusory. Again, as in the Diaspora, we are collectively subject to the good or ill will of others. This dependence contributes to a parasitic mentality: a constant stream of money unearned by our labor allows us to live at a standard far beyond our means.

Today, when I observe Israel's behavior on the issue of Soviet Jews, I have serious questions about my country's intentions. The government of Israel and the Jewish Agency are making every effort to pressure the nations of the world to close their doors to Soviet Jews, thereby forcing them to come to Israel — destination by decree. Is Israel truly concerned for their welfare, or does the state see in Soviet Jews a means of strengthening itself? Soviet Jews have escaped from a regime which believed it knew their needs better than they did. We know the outcome of this type of thinking. Now, Israel is acting towards them in the same manner: "We know that only Zionism is good for you, and therefore we will decide for you where you should live." Thus, instead of Israel as an instrument for the solution of the Jewish problem, Jews become an instrument to strengthen the state.

The only possibility I see of providing real answers to the above questions is for us to build a peace which encompasses a just solution to the Palestinian problem and that demonstrates to other Arab states that Israel has no territorial ambitions. Only with such a peace will Israel become a center which attracts Jews, who simply desire to live in security and not to suffer from anti-Semitism or hatred. It seems to me possible to arrive at such a situation, if Israel would return all of the territories which it conquered in 1967 and agree to the establishment of a Palestinian state at her side.

And now we come to the major difficulty: How to arrive at such a solution when a large proportion of the Israeli people are against it? The extremists among us are likely to immerse Israel in civil war in order to prevent such a solution. There are two possible ways to arrive at this solution without the danger of civil war. One way is external coercion applied by the United States and other countries. A second way is a nonviolent Palestinian struggle in conjunction with increasing nonviolent support from Israelis opposed to the occupation. The resulting process of nonviolent escalation could transform Israeli public opinion and bring in its wake the hoped-for change.

Most opponents of territorial compromise fear that Israel's security would suffer if the Occupied Territories were returned. Acts of Palestinian terror reinforce this fear and confirm the standing of the nationalistic elements in Israeli society which oppose the creation of a Palestinian state. Although terrorism cannot endanger, only disturb the existence of Israel, it does strengthen the opposition to a compromise with the Palestinians. The deportation of Mubarak Awad (founder of the Palestinian Center for the Study of Non-Violence in East Jerusalem) illustrates this point. His deportation was demanded by extremist settlers in the West Bank; they petitioned the High Court with a plea against the government. Why should the settlers, who are after all the first to suffer from terrorism, support the deportation of a man who favored nonviolent struggle as a substitute for violence? When one witnesses the rise in support for the extreme nationalist movements, the additional government assistance to settlements, and the heavy-handedness in dealing with the Palestinians that follows every act of terrorism, one can see why a nonviolent Palestinian struggle so threatens them. If acts of terrorism towards Israelis stopped, the settlers stand to lose a primary motivator in their practical and emotional legitimacy, which is fed by sentiments like fear, injury, anger, and vengeance.

I don't want to be misunderstood at this point. Palestinians have been hurt by Israelis to a much greater extent than Israelis have been hurt by Palestinians. They lost their homes and their land, and were made refugees. The Israeli government continues to expropriate their land and systematically oppress them, and the number of Palestinians killed and wounded is incomparably higher than the number of Israelis. Still, Israeli propaganda persists in depicting Palestinians as terrorists who are out to destroy the state of Israel. And most Israelis continue to view themselves as the victims of Palestinian terrorism. Only a nonviolent Palestinian struggle has the chance of changing Israeli public opinion and counteracting the deep-seated resistance to coming to terms with both the Palestinians and the Arab world. It would also have a profound effect on Western public opinion, as Israel was established, and to a great degree exists, by virtue of its moral claim vis-à-vis the Christian world. This fact makes both Israel and the West acutely sensitive to the moral claims of others upon the Jewish state, claims that would be heightened by a nonviolent Palestinian struggle.

Nonviolence is a means of struggle which reduces those sentiments that feed extremism and thus makes it easier for the adversary to consider the humanity and needs of the other side. The process of nonviolent escalation could create a situation in which extreme nationalists would lose their support within Israel, thereby reducing the danger of civil war and paving the way for the only just solution to the conflict: the return of the territories captured in 1967 and the establishment of a Palestinian state alongside Israel.

Gila Svirsky

Gila Svirsky was born and brought up in New Jersey, took a B.A. in philosophy at Brandeis University, and an M.A. in communications at Hebrew University. She has lived in Israel since 1966. Until August 1991, she was the director of the New Israel Fund (NIF), which she left in order to pursue her writing. The NIF funds activities in the areas of human rights, religious freedom, women's issues, Jewish-Arab cooperation, and social justice. Gila is also an activist with Women in Black, who have been conducting Friday afternoon vigils for peace for three years.

Zionist Reasons for Being Anti-Occupation

Gila Svirsky

This essay was written in October 1990, before the Gulf War broke out, but in the atmosphere of crisis that preceded it.

Itzhak Perlman is performing tonight in Jerusalem with the Israel Philharmonic conducted by Zubin Mehta. I couldn't get tickets. Sold out. Amazing, the rarefied heights of culture while gearing up for war. I wonder what Saigon was like in the sixties.

These are complex and scary days for us in Israel. My daughter Denna went on a camping trip with her youth movement last week. Before they left, the parents were told what shelter the children would be led to, should war break out before the trip was over (and should they have enough time to reach the shelter). My friend Etti wouldn't allow her son Alon to join the trip, because she wanted him near home when the war broke out. On second thought, I can understand why the concert hall tonight is sold out.

Occupation has become a marginal issue during these days of the Gulf crisis, and it gets harder and harder to explain why the occupation is wrong. Some people believe that Saddam Hussein's invasion of Kuwait and threats against Israel — and the PLO's support of him — have something to do with justifying Israel's occupation of the West Bank and the Gaza Strip. The connection is spurious, of course. But it is harder, in this war-terrorized atmosphere, to explain that.

I usually talk about the occupation with Jews in one of two ways. In one, I explain how it is in the security interest of Israel to get rid of the territories, with over a million and a half Palestinians — all haters of

Israel and the Jewish regime, and, in short, not healthy to have in one's country. In the other, I plead for an end to the corruption of the Jewish soul in Israel.

I am not happy about using the first argument — the security claim. First, because it is based on a racist view of demography ("they multiply so fast — do you want to live in a country with an Arab majority?") And, second, because it assumes hostility toward the Palestinian people, and I do not feel that hostility. Ever since the Intifada, I have met and become (yes) friends with a sufficient number of peace-loving, nonviolent, rational, and kind-hearted Palestinians to convince me that the fifth column argument may be effective, but it is based on an assumption that I do not wish to promote. Becoming friends with Palestinians is not knee-jerk liberalism; it is just being human and open to decency.

I feel much more conviction about the latter argument — that occupation corrupts. Corrupt it has. In today's Israel, racism has achieved legitimacy, whether in public discourse about "transfer" of Palestinians or in public beatings of innocent Arabs caught near the scene of other violence. The government-sanctioned discrimination, abrogation of basic human rights, and a policy of beatings and oppression in the territories has turned the stomachs of many of our young men. Keeping such pictures out of the media has enabled Israelis to believe that the brutality doesn't exist, except as "deviations." Nothing could be further from the truth.

Today's paper carried more testimony to this effect: Career Officer Nir Keinan, after serving several tours of duty in the territories and being awarded a medal for heroism, was today convicted in military court for refusing to serve there once more. He is the 125th soldier to so refuse and be willing to pay the high price for refusal. Are these soldiers witnessing something that we civilians do not see? Obviously so. These young men are not sacrificing careers, good names, and clean records for some abstract principle of justice. They simply cannot bear to go back and continue to do what they have done before.

The litany of violations of basic human rights in the territories does not need repeating here. And I would be willing to concede that this occupation is more "enlightened" than that of any other country. Even if this claim were true (and there is good evidence that it is not), it is not persuasive. Our occupation has been sufficiently brutal, ugly, and unjust for me to want to end it, and I don't care if there were worse occupations in history. It's the soul of my nation that this occupation is corroding.

I would like to state that I come to this view not as a "universalist" or an anti-Zionist. Quite the opposite is true. Many of my left-wing friends were surprised when I began talking lately about feeling more and more comfortable with the Zionist label. For the past few years I had kept a low Zionist profile, flirting with ideologies of "post-Zionism" and even "non-Zionism." Some friends almost succeeded in convincing me that all forms of nationalism are equally evil and should be erased from the world.

However, the anti-Semitism sweeping Europe and the Soviet Union was an important lesson for me. So many people seem to take a perverse pleasure in hating and persecuting us. Although hard to explain, this phenomenon is unfortunately not the figment of anyone's imagination. I think you have to be blind or suicidal not to admit that there are important, rational reasons to preserve a state which will be a safe haven for Jews everywhere. This is — or should be — the basis of nationalism: the nation as a safe haven, not an expression of chauvinistic aggression.

But everybody deserves a safe haven, not only Jews. The Armenians should have a place of their own, where prejudice and antagonism can no longer hurt them. The Basques should have their own place, where they can feel safe from the hostility of their non-Basque neighbors. The Palestinians should have their own home, where no one — not Israelis and not other Arabs — can close their schools or subject them to taxation without representation, or detain them indefinitely in prisons for no stated reason and without standing trial. And, of course, we Jews should have our own place.

But we cannot claim the right to a safe and secure home at the expense of another people. That is indefensible morally, and even leads to a loss of our security in the long run, as the displaced people respond. Thus, I find myself feeling more Zionist than I have felt in years, and more respectful of the point of a Jewish state. And therefore, also respectful of the point of a Palestinian state.

I am part of the large movement of women for peace in Israel and an active member of Women in Black. As attacks on us from the Right become more virulent, I wonder if it is because the Right feels threatened that our position is taking hold. Are Israelis more ready to compromise than ever before? I don't think so. Surely not given the Gulf crisis. On the other hand, I believe that right-wing Israel does feel the growing impatience of the big powers with Israel's unwillingness to compromise. I think that the Right — justifiably — is worried about pressure from the United States, Europe, and the Soviet Union. Just when peace seems to be settling in here and there — east and west — nobody wants the Middle East to be the source of a world crisis. World criticism of Israel grows in volume, even among allies. It's no wonder that right-wing criticism of Women in Black has gone from strident to hysterical. We look like we're about to sell Israel out to world pressure.

Saying "No" to occupation is not only the moral thing to do, but it is also the safer position to take strategically. Not for racist arguments, but because it is safer to be in a state of peace than a state of war. This is a very simple premise, and one that some Israelis are finally beginning to appreciate.

But tonight, instead of going to hear Itzhak Perlman, I will stay home and put the finishing touches on my two shelters — one for conventional and the other for unconventional warfare. The instructions are, if both types of warfare break out at once, to go to the regular shelter. My mind tries to grasp the horror of what is going on here. It does not bear thinking about. I would rather listen to some good music as I apply insulating tape around the windows.

Shmuel Amir

Dr. Shmuel Amir is an agricultural research scientist who has been active in peace and left-wing movements since the fifties. Born in Berlin, he was educated in Israeli schools and at the Hebrew University. He was one of the founders of the Peace and Security Movement in 1967 and was among the initiators of the Dai appeal during the Gulf War. Shmuel lives in Tel Aviv with his wife Chaya Weisgal-Amir. They have four sons and eight grandchildren.

After the Gulf War

Shmuel Amir

The Israeli peace movement, from the radical left to the liberal center, has to take a hard look at the "new" situation. Is it really new? What has changed? What in fact is to be done?

One must examine the situation in the wake of the Gulf War on the micro and the macro levels. With regard to the first, very little, thank God, has changed. Radical lawyers and journalists, civil rights activists, prison monitoring groups, humanitarian aid groups, among others, are continuing their daily (and even nightly) Sisyphian efforts to keep the public aware, lessen the brutality and suffering inflicted on the Palestinians, and — above all — make a dent in the consciousness of the self- satisfied and almost inert Israeli public.

On the macro level, we have the paradoxical situation that nothing has changed in the global arena as a result of the Gulf War, whereas everything has changed — for the worse — in the mainstream Israeli peace movement. There has been a retreat to pre-Intifada positions and a reinforcement of the ideological constraints which have always made most of the Zionist peace movement an ideologically lame duck. I wish to examine here the macro paradox in both its aspects and discuss the prospects for radical ideological change within the given situation.

*   *   *   *   *

The Gulf War is over. The modern Hitler on the Tigris and Euphrates has been defeated. The clean, remote-control, surgical strike operation has ended, albeit with a bang, not a whimper. The one hundred to two hundred thousand Iraqis (will we ever learn the exact number, and who really cares?) lie buried in the sand or under the rubble of houses and shelters in Baghdad and other Iraqi cities.

True, it will be difficult to cite any heroic feats of the U.S. army in combat. Images resembling the assault on Normandy or raising the flag in Iwo Jima will be conspicuously absent. The only valid comparison that comes to mind is the occupation of Panama or Grenada. But never mind the missing glory: it was a complete victory. The Middle East (for the moment at least), lies prostrate before the victors. If war is the continuation of politics, no obstacles should now stand in the way of implementing the widely proclaimed "new world order," promised before the great campaign.

True, one cannot complain of any lack of diplomatic activity. The red carpets at Ben Gurion airport are rolled out and back. Baker and Cheney and other dignitaries are coming and going. Even the President of the United States sends a message from time to time. Alas, there is an inverse relation between all this activity accompanied by mountains of media commentary on the "peace process" and any concrete proposals for settling the Israeli-Palestinian-Arab conflict.

Again as before, the discussion is about procedure. Will it be an "international," a "regional," or a "direct-meeting" conference? Is the conference to be convened only for the opening, or again half a year later? Who will be the participants among the Arab countries and who will represent the Palestinians? But before the reader gets bogged down in the maze of all this diplomatic mumbo jumbo, it might be useful to remind ourselves of the basic U.S. pronouncements and activities from the very beginning of this round.

Before James Baker even arrived in Israel, he declared that "the U.S. will not force any peace solution on any Middle East country," and that "a forced American solution is the worst thing that Washington can do" (Ha'aretz 3/4/91). Such a declaration, coming a few days after the massacre in Iraq gives even hypocrisy a bad name. But more important, Israel is the one party interested in the status quo and will not budge without U.S. pressure. Now Israeli policy makers know the limits of the new game. More assurances from Baker followed: "No talks with the PLO," "looking for an alternative Palestinian leadership," and further assurances that negotiations will not lead ultimately to a Palestinian state (Ha'aretz 4/10/91).

More outspoken than the State Department, National Security Adviser Brent Scowcroft told Bush to "stop activity on the Israeli-Arab conflict" and that "furthering peace solutions in the Middle East should be abandoned" (Ha'aretz 4/26/91). A month later Dick Cheney arrived and backed up his first pronouncement that "the U.S. is committed to the security of Israel and its military advantage" with a few gifts: "The U.S. will finance 72% of the 'Chetz' missile project, and will provide fifteen additional F-15 airplanes," he said, blatantly adding that this in no way contradicts Bush's new "disarmament" plan (Yediot Aharonot 5/31/91). And if there still remains any misunderstanding as to the aim of this plan, he elaborated to Israeli Defense Minister Moshe Arens that the plan would deal only with conventional weapons (*Ha'aretz* 5/31/91). Not surprisingly, William Quandt (formerly of the National Security Council on Middle East Affairs and presently of the Brookings Institution) is quoted in *Ha'aretz* (5/30/91) as saying that the Bush initiative would practically leave Israel as the sole country in the Middle East in possession of nuclear weapons, giving Israel a great advantage over her neighbors. Meanwhile the Institute for Strategic Studies in London estimates that Israel has one hundred nuclear warheads. So much for the new U.S. "Peace Plan," "Disarmament Initiatives," and the "New World Order."

Whatever the aims of the U.S. in the region, an Israeli withdrawal from the Occupied Territories, which is the first and basic precondition for peace, will not be the result. As such, it can only be — as from 1967 onward — more of the same.

I still remember when, in the aftermath of the 1967 War, we founded the Movement for Peace and Security, which stood for the return of the Occupied Territories. The first appeal was signed by an overwhelming number of distinguished university professors. We were all convinced that the occupation could not last, that world opinion, the superpowers, and peace forces inside Israel, would compel the government to retreat to its pre-1967 borders. That was twenty-four years ago.

The secret of Israel's "success" in maintaining control of the Occupied Territories has been the unfailing support — financially, militarily and diplomatically — of the United States. Otherwise the maintenance of the status quo would have been utterly impossible. True, the United States has endorsed UN resolution 242, has come out against the annexation of Arab East Jerusalem, against Jewish settlements in the Occupied Territories, and lately even against settling Soviet Jewish immigrants there. Baker has gone so far as to describe the establishment of new settlements at each of his visits as "obstacles to peace." But the United States has also pronounced, loud and clear, during all these years that it is opposed to:

1. The establishment of a Palestinian state alongside Israel.
2. The recognition of the PLO as the legitimate representative of the Palestinian people.

American statements can therefore be divided into two sets. The first set of statements can be ignored, trampled upon, circumvented, and disregarded. They reflect "differences of opinion between longstanding friends" as frequently noted by Shamir and Arens. The best description as to the significance of this kind of statement appeared last year in a piece by Thomas Friedman of the *New York Times*: "If Mr. Shamir's government builds more settlements in the Occupied Territories it will likely receive $3 billion in aid from

Washington, and if it doesn't build more settlements it will [also] receive $3 billion in aid" (6/17/90).

The second set of statements are of a very different nature and are adhered to by both governments. They are based on maintaining Israel's military supremacy and the status quo for as long as possible. Many observers ascribe American support of Israel to the power and influence of the Jewish community in the U.S. — to the American Israel Public Affairs Committee (AIPAC) and other Jewish organizations. The U.S. government has done very little to dispel that impression, giving the appearance that it is merely responding to broad democratic pressure in carrying out its policy in our region. This is an exaggeration, to say the least. Basically the United States is pursuing its own interests. Does anyone really think that Kuwaiti or Saudi lobbies were needed to initiate the Gulf War?

The power attributed to the Jewish organizations vis-à-vis U.S. policy is due to the agreement between them. The extent of their real power can only be tested if and when a substantial difference emerges between Israeli and U.S. interests. Then we will discover if the tail really wags the dog — or the other way around.

Another argument frequently offered in defense of U.S. policy vis-à-vis Israel is that the U.S. cannot force the Israeli government to change. In this case it would be well to remember Israel's retreat from the Sinai under pressure from President Eisenhower (and Bulganin), coming only a short while after Ben Gurion's speech about the "third kingdom of Israel." The second retreat from Sinai, as a result of the Camp David Accords, was also under U.S. pressure. Few people remember the evacuation of the Yamit region with its flourishing agricultural settlements, carried out by none other than the minister of defense at the time — Ariel Sharon. Clearly the U.S. can, considering Israel's complete dependence on it, easily force Israel to retreat from the Occupied Territories — if it so desires. The Gulf War is, of course, the latest example of a lack of scruples when imperial interests are threatened. The image of the benign giant who cannot force his will on others has always been a fiction. So to explain U.S. support for Israel: It is in the interests of U.S. global and Middle Eastern strategy to maintain a strong, loyal, and dependable ally in a very unstable region, a region of vital interest in terms of global economic strategy and the control of oil.

But, does all this still hold true in the aftermath of the Gulf War? Some observers point out that in the Gulf War Israel was not needed. On the contrary, it was requested to keep a low profile. Others argue that now the U.S. really "owes one" to its staunch Arab supporters: Egypt and Saudi Arabia, among others. Perhaps another weighty argument is that Israel has lost its strategic function vis-à-vis the Soviet Union and the Cold War imperative for containment.

Although there might be some truth in all these arguments, it seems that, in fact, the opposite is true. In the overall summary in the wake of the war, Israel has become an even more important asset. In pursuing its global policy long before the Gulf War, the U.S. discovered that its main adversary in the Third World was indigenous national movements that resent and oppose foreign domination. The long-term effects of the Gulf War will only deepen America's collision with the national movements in the area. The U.S. press reported widely how the Arab man-in-the-street supported even Saddam Hussein against U.S. intervention, because for a short while he became the symbol of pent-up national grievances and aspirations let loose. Sadly, the defeat of a tyrannical regime became also, for a short while at least, the defeat of justified legitimate demands of these national movements (e.g., "linkage" between the Iraqi occupation of Kuwait, and the Israeli occupation; that the demands for withdrawal and the respect for national rights be uniformly applied). U.S. domination most certainly is not a recipe for tranquility in the region. It augurs rather, instability, turbulence, and active resistance to it. In this situation Israel's supporting role becomes even more attractive. Since the fall of the Shah in Iran, there has been no power in the region which by its military muscle, its popular support, and longstanding conflict with all the Arab countries, is better suited to be a "loyal and dependable" ally of the U.S. All present Arab allies lack popular support to a greater or lesser degree, especially when it comes to alliance with the U.S. The struggle against the Arab national movements is exactly where American and Israeli policies coincide. This is also the tragedy of Israeli occupation, contributing to the cycle of dependence on the U.S. — as we became more of a "strategic asset," we also became more dependent.

It seems that the grand design of the present "peace process" is to bring Syria into the U.S. fold. This would entail returning at least a part of the Golan Heights. Here a comparison with the Camp David Accords comes to mind. Egypt came back to the U.S. fold for the return of all Egyptian territories occupied by Israel since the 1967 War. Israel was compensated by being given a free hand towards Lebanon and the Palestinians ("autonomy" was never taken seriously by Israel). The Lebanon War was the logical outcome. Today, compensation for returning at least a part of the Golan Heights would be peace with Syria and perhaps peace agreements with Saudi Arabia and other Arab countries. This would look like fair payment to the Arab countries which supported the United States in the Gulf War. It can also be presented to the public as an evenhanded peace plan in the same way that Camp David was presented and partly accepted in Europe and elsewhere. In short, it would lend respectability to U.S. domination of the Middle East.

The Palestinians in this updated version of the Camp David Accords would again be promised a limited autonomy. That is, they would be left in the lurch. A Palestinian state is not in the cards because in the eyes of U.S. policymakers it would be a stronghold of Arab nationalism — exactly what the Americans want to avoid. If Baker can persuade the Syrians to agree to the above mentioned deal, some cajoling and pressure on Israel will still be needed (as during the Camp David negotiations). But the final outcome is quite clear: if the Americans so desire, Israel will have to submit. Yet, this submission will leave Israel still in charge of the occupied Palestinian land. The limit to which the Americans are ready to push Israel, as in Camp David, is again a limited autonomy — on paper. So much for the "windows of opportunity."

No Israeli government, whether Likud or Labor, will act in open defiance of U.S. policy. Israel is too dependent for that. Consider that the annual grant by the United States is $1.8 billion in military aid and $1.2 billion in economic aid. Israel is now asking the U.S. for large guarantees for immigrant absorption loans. There can be no doubt that Israel's economic dependence could be used as a most powerful lever by U.S. policy makers *if they chose to*. Nor can there be any doubt that any Israeli government could or would withstand such pressure. The United States comes out officially against settlements in the territories, but indirectly it is helping to pay for them. The $3 billion grant amounts to nearly 20 percent of the annual Israeli budget! There are no official figures on the costs of the occupation — estimates range between $1 and $3 billion. But clearly Israel's precarious economic situation would make it difficult to build new settlements without U.S. aid.

Having said this, one should not stretch the economic argument too far. Some in Israel argue that Israel is on the losing end in its economic relation with America, notably the economist Esther Alexander. For example, she argues that Israel is repaying about $4 billion in debts against U.S. grants of about $3 billion, of which more than half is payment on interest. It is "not the United States which supports Israel, but Israel which supports the United States" (*The Might of Equality in the Economy*, 1990). This argument may be true in the long run, but in the short run the U.S. economic lever is as strong as ever.

The Likud and Labor basically agree on the concept of Israel as strategic asset. The more one moves to the right, however, the more emphasis on the importance and low price of this asset for the U.S. As such an asset, Israel has great leeway in its policies vis-à-vis the United States; the extent of this leeway is the main political argument between the Likud and Labor. It loomed large during the negotiations with Baker in 1989 over the "Shamir-Rabin" plan. Rabin and Peres tended to accept Baker's demands; Shamir refused. Baker did not press and the negotiations were suspended. Indirectly he helped Shamir oust Labor and form the present fully right-wing government.

But even the Likud is forced to recognize the limits of their leeway. They did not annex the Occupied Territories when Menachim Begin formed the first Likud government in 1977, despite the fact that "Greater Israel" is a basic tenet of Likud ideology. They chose the relatively more pragmatic Moshe Arens over the ideological Ariel Sharon as Minister of Defense. In the Gulf War, they yielded to U.S. demands not to retaliate against the Iraqi SCUD attacks and to keep a "low profile" — and this despite considerable public pressure even from the Left! Under real pressure Shamir, like Begin, will yield.

For its part, the Israeli peace movement is not an homogeneous entity. On the one hand, there is the pragmatic, consensual, and larger movement of Peace Now. On the other hand, there is the radical peace movement. Peace Now represents the Zionist Left in Israel, and is supported by Ratz (Citizens Rights list), Mapam, Shinui, and by Labor party doves. This section of the peace movement has a considerable following among the intelligentsia. Mass support during its most successful campaigns has come from the kibbutz movement, professionals and young people. It has no strong roots among Oriental Jews, Arabs, or working-class people.

During the Gulf War Peace Now, in the wider sense, collapsed. It came out in full support of the war, calling it a "just war." It supported the government in its policy of restraint. In the words of one Knesset Member (M.K.), Peace Now was ready to "embrace" Shamir. M.K.s Yossi Sarid (Ratz) and Yair Tzaban (Mapam) called for convening the Knesset Foreign Affairs and Security Committee in order to reach a full understanding between the parties and express complete national unity. Several M.K.s repented having opposed the 1981 bombing of the Iraqi atomic reactor by the Begin government. Peace Now supporters, for the most part, could have changed their movement's name to "War Now" or "Peace Between Wars."

Amos Oz and A.B. Yehoshua, the foremost intellectuals of the Zionist Left, raged against peace demonstrators abroad. They called on them to stop demonstrating and support the war. Oz explained that he was not a pacifist but a peacenik; that there are wars which are not only justified but holy; and that the Western world thinks that the Jews' place is on the cross. A.B. Yehoshua said, "The problem with the peace movements is that they are suspicious of the interests of America in the region." When asked about the possibility that Israel would use nuclear weapons against Iraq, he answered: "If the choice is a second Auschwitz, then there is no choice!" (*Hadashot*, 2/2/91).

The dismal behavior of the Zionist Left should surprise no serious observers. They have always been an integral part of the establishment, self-declared "true Zionists" and "better patriots." Their patriotic credentials stem from their mass following in the kibbutz movement and from the many officers among them. Since its founding (and even before) Israel's main ideology was formed by its conflict with the Arabs. Had the establishment of Peace Now been based on the pursuit of universal values and equality between Arabs and Jews rather than on consensual Jewish ethnocentricism, they might have been able to muster the moral and intellectual courage to withstand the nationalistic onslaught during this war.

Not that their positions were radical before the war. They never came out for withdrawal from *all* occupied lands, including Arab East Jerusalem. Only under the impact of the Intifada and the 1988 Palestine National Council resolution in Algiers did they endorse negotiations with the PLO and approach an endorsement of the two-state solution.

It is a serious setback that in the wake of the Gulf War the majority of this peace camp has retreated from the explicit to the implicit. Instead of "two states," it is now (again) "self-determination." Instead of talks "with the PLO" it is now "Palestinian representatives," etc. M.K. Tzaban already speaks of a "Palestinian-Jordanian" representation for the Palestinians.

The main reason for this retreat during the Gulf War is the Zionist Left's unfailing support for U.S. policies in the region. They supported the Schultz plan in 1988; the Baker-Shamir-Rabin plan in 1989; they welcomed the American victory in the Gulf; and are now waiting for the U.S. to impose a "new world order" in our region. The State Department — with or without two states and the PLO — was and is their hope. For twenty-four years of occupation they have clung like a tenacious lover to an old flame, hoping that eventually their love-hope will be requited: the U.S. will get Israel out of the territories and peace will descend on the region. Hope springs eternal.

Their abiding belief in the United States shows how alienated the Zionist Left and liberals are from the rest of the Left and peace movements around the world. How alienated they are especially from national liberation movements in general, and the Palestine Liberation Movement in particular. The struggle against U.S. aid and dependence in the Third World is completely unintelligible to them. Imperialism is a dirty word and passé.

The struggle for conventional and nuclear disarmament is beyond them: "In our region the situation is different." The Palestinian state, if it comes into being, must be demilitarized. Israel will still need "defensible borders," a euphemism for "border adjustments," which is a euphemism for keeping some of the occupied lands. Official Israeli discourse, which sees the United States as the lodestar of democracy and freedom and the defender of Israel, is their model.

Peace Now never pretended to be radical, and largely refused cooperation with the radical peace movement. It never let Israeli Arabs join (although lately some of its more radical rank and file have coopted Arab members in the north of the country). It shunned the issue of nuclear weapons production in Israel like the plague. It resisted the call against army service in the occupied lands.

And yet within the confines of the national consensus, Peace Now initiated and carried out radical and imaginative activities. They organized mass demonstrations and protests, parliamentary activity and public discussions. They provided valuable information on the oppression of the population in the territories (B'Tselem was founded by Ratz M.K. Dede Zucker). They demonstrate at the groundbreaking of almost every new settlement in the occupied lands. And we should not forget that Emil Gruenzweig, murdered by extremists while demonstrating against the occupation, was a member of Peace Now.

The radical peace movement is composed of the (Arab-Jewish) Hadash-Democratic Front for Peace and Equality, which includes the Communist party; the Progressive List for Peace (Arab); and the Arab Democratic party. Hadash has three M.K.s, the others, one each. There are a number of smaller left-socialist groups, active mainly in the Jewish sector of the population. They all support a two-state solution, recognition of the PLO as the sole and legitimate representative of the Palestinians, and full equality for Israeli Arabs. And there are various nonpolitical groups, mainly but not exclusively Jewish, the best known of which is probably Yesh Gvul. Other organizations include Women in Black, Dai L'Kibush (End the Occupation), the Women's Organization for Political Prisoners, Workers' Hotline, the Committee Against Torture, and various professional groups of doctors, lawyers, writers, and university people.

During the Gulf War an ad hoc umbrella movement, Dai ("enough"), was founded and collected several hundred signatures for press statements which condemned the United States for unleashing the war, while also condemning Saddam Hussein for invading Kuwait. It stated that both Bush and Saddam were motivated by a lust for power and oil, and called for a cease-fire supervised by the United Nations.

The great problem of the Israeli peace movement is that the larger, mainstream movement has no clear aims, and the smaller, more radical movement has no mass following. The reason is quite clear: one works within the official discourse, whether one calls it state ideology, Zionism, Israeli ideology, or whatever; the other is outside it. One must therefore ask if it is true that to change popular politics one has to change the popular ideological perspective as well?

There is certainly some truth in this. It is difficult for people who are part and parcel of official Israeli discourse to understand the aspirations of the Palestinians. In developing empathy for the Palestinians one has to know their history, and in order to know their history one has to confront one's own history. This for the Israeli is as bitter as gall. What would remain of the Israeli ethos?

We have to remember that ideological discourse changes much more slowly than political concepts. Many "good Zionists" are members of Yesh Gvul and chose to sit in prison rather than compromise their conscience. Still there is a difference between "ideological" (non-Zionist) and "pragmatic" (Zionist) peaceniks. A real political and/or ideological breakthrough can only follow a change in the real situation. Old political concepts will decline only when the necessity for peace becomes abundantly clear to broad sectors of people. Nobody is totally blind. Poll after poll show that long before any basic ideological or political upheaval has occurred from the impact of the Intifada and growing international isolation, half of the Israelis are ready to give up the territories. But their reasons are purely pragmatic. They will not see it as urgent as long as the United States continues to support Israel. And so again, the Israeli peace movement is being stymied by the actions of the United States.

As stated above, it is in the power of the United States to force Israel out of the territories if, as in 1956 and 1978, it so desires. But as also stated above, this is not in the present interests of the U.S. A change in U.S. policy will not result from pleading with the U.S. to change its policy or trying to "enlighten" American policy makers as to what their real interests are. And certainly not by acting as the self-appointed defenders of U.S. policy in Israel — as much of the Israeli peace movement does. This is exactly the trap which the radical peace movement should avoid.

U.S. policy will only change when it becomes untenable because of a changing situation: from popular struggles in the area against external domination; growing competition with Europe; growing condemnation of the occupation around the world; a tenacious struggle by the Israeli and U.S. peace movements; and of course the continued civil struggle in the Occupied Territories — the Intifada.

The task is to articulate a consistent peace policy based on opposition to America's imperial plans as they affect our country. We must oppose the plans that deny representation and statehood to the Palestinians and thus doom Israel to perpetual war; that force colossal and impoverishing new arms deals on the area. The peace movement must oppose so-called U.S. military and economic aid, which in fact makes the recipient more and more dependent. It must strive for solidarity between Israel and Palestinian peace forces.

Perhaps it is appropriate to plead for greater coordination and cooperation between the peace movements in Israel and the U.S. in working out joint (but flexible) peace strategies, based on our common aims and divergent situations. Fighting against U.S. policy in the Middle East is certainly a task we share. Emphasis should also be placed on the many areas of American-Israeli cooperation which militate against peace in the region and around the world, such as the shady arms deals from the Iran-Contra scandals to the collusion of the Mossad (the Israeli Secret Service) and the CIA.

After the Gulf War it may seem that nothing can stand in the way of the U.S.'s imperial power. But this is not so. Again and again in this century we have seen how the imperial powers are forced to retreat under the impact of popular movements fighting against oppression and subjugation. The Middle East will be no exception. The vision of a peaceful Middle East where Israel and Palestine act in friendly cooperation will prove stronger than any momentary setbacks.

Stanley Cohen

Stanley Cohen grew up in South Africa, where he was active in the Zionist youth movement and, as a student, in the anti-apartheid movement. He and his wife Ruth left in 1963 for Britain. There he completed his Ph.D. in Sociology and started an academic career. He taught at various universities, including Durham and Essex, where he was professor of sociology from 1973 to 1979. Stanley did research and wrote several books on criminological theory, juvenile delinquency, prisons, and social control, among other topics. He was active in prison abolition and civil liberties groups, and in developing the "critical criminology" movement in Britain and Europe.

In 1979, Stanley and Ruth took their two daughters to Jerusalem for his sabbatical year at the Hebrew University. He writes, "Through the usual combination of reasons that guide one's life — personal, political, impulsive, impenetrable — we decided to stay on in Israel." Since 1980, he has been professor of criminology at the Hebrew University.

"At first, I thought that the natural home for my vaguely radical politics was Peace Now," he says. "Looking back, I'm amazed how many myths about Israeli society I had absorbed, how ignorant I was about what was happening. My involvement in the Committee for Solidarity with Bir Zeit and then — most dramatically — the outbreak of the Lebanon War, opened my eyes to the restrictions and compromises of Israeli 'liberalism.' I moved from the mainstream to the marginal, alienated section of the peace movement. I was active in various free-floating groupings working against the occupation and for the two-state solution, such as Dai L'Kibush (End the Occupation) and the magazine *Israleft.*

By the second year of the Intifada, many of these groups had broken up. "I began to move — partly out of the despair recorded in my article, but more out of a sense that this work was important — into the human rights movement." Stanley was one of the founders of the Public Committee Against Torture in Israel and, with Daphna Golan, wrote a report on the subject of torture for B'Tselem. His main work now is with the Public Committee and on the subject of settler violence. He is also writing a book, which is a more theoretical reflection about denial and passivity.

Resuming the Struggle

Stanley Cohen

> Estragon: *Nothing to be done.*
>
> Vladimir: *I'm beginning to come round to that opinion.*
> *All my life I've tried to put it from me,*
> *saying, Vladimir, be reasonable,*
> *you haven't yet tried everything.*
> *And I resumed the struggle.*
>
> —Samuel Beckett, *Waiting For Godot*

The bitter truth is this: if we look just at the balance of forces in Israeli society, there are no prospects in sight that the occupation will end or that a Palestinian state will be established. Nowhere on the political horizon is there anything even resembling a just response to the Palestinian cause. Yes, "End the Occupation" still appears on our pamphlets, posters, buttons, and T-shirts, but this is little more than a religious incantation, like "Make Love, Not War." Even those in the peace movement whose moral unease and liberal sentiments are real enough, share in the depths of their heart the same kabbalistic dream as the rest of Israeli society: you wake up one morning and behold, the Palestinians are not there anymore.

The despair that I want to convey in these few pages is not yet Estragon's "Nothing to be done," but it is getting close to this. It derives not from any standard political analysis of the forces lined up against us — whether religious nationalism, racism, fear, or the cynical power of the United States. No doubt this is the crucial analysis to make. I want to talk rather about my increasing sense of the weakness of our "own" people. It is not so much that many are unwilling to pay the price of their conviction; it is that they have not recognized that a price has to be paid.

Before listing some forms of this political weakness, let me make a comparison which is natural to me, but will no doubt sound unfair, even shocking, to people from the U.S., particularly American Jews who think of themselves as democrats or liberals. The comparison is with South Africa. And I don't mean the conventional questions: Are these both different types of colonial or settler societies? Does Zionism aspire to be a form of apartheid or care if it results in that? Will Israel replace South Africa as a pariah state? I mean rather the moral comparison — which tells me that the situation of Palestinians under occupation is now worse than that of Blacks in South Africa. And the intuitive comparison — that there is more hope in South Africa, an inexorable movement in the direction of justice, than here in Israel.

Johannesburg, February 1990

On February 10 1990, I left my father's apartment in Johannesburg and drove to the airport to return home to Jerusalem. The news came on the car radio: Nelson Mandela would be released the next day.

This had been an extraordinary few weeks back in the country I had left in 1963. I had watched the live broadcast of President de Klerk's speech — with its promises of negotiation, an end to "the season of violence," the release of political prisoners, the legalization of the African National Congress (ANC) and other organizations banned for thirty years. I had heard the foreign minister — in an urbane "Nightline" discussion with an ANC leader — use the phrase "my Black brothers." Mandela, the terrorist, the violent revolutionary, the communist, the anti-Christ — in prison for all the twenty-seven years that I had been away — was now "Mr. Mandela," the figure of compromise, peace, and reconciliation.

All of this was like a hallucination, a Dali film where the once solid objects dissolve in front of your eyes. Not just the changes themselves, but the reaction of most of the whites to these imminent changes. I don't mean the predictable reactions of the white conservatives on the one side, or the mass democratic movement on the other, but of the "nonpolitical" whites in the middle. To be sure, there was deep apprehension, mixed (curiously) with an unrealistic sense that the old privileges will more or less continue. But above all, there was a sense of resignation. These people talked of "historical inevitability" with a faith that no Marxist retains. It had happened in Eastern Europe (everyone I spoke with referred to this); the winds of change had finally blown here.

None of this, of course, had happened suddenly. Looking back for at least a decade, all the ground had been laid. In the siege economy of the eighties, economic sanctions began to bite and the Afrikaner ruling class divided into pragmatists and fundamentalists. The mega-companies that control the economy were already producing blueprints for a post-apartheid society. By the middle of the decade, the fine regulations of petty apartheid were being relaxed and the culture of racism undermined from within. Grand apartheid (denial of democratic rights, gross inequality) remained in place, as it still is. But in the arts and literature, the universities, parts of the printed media, and in everyday relationships, people seemed to be acting as if apartheid had already ended. It was like an imaginary rehearsal for the performance that now opened.

Of course all is not over. There is a long bitter period of violence and turmoil ahead: from the one side, the counterrevolution, from the other, the awesome depths of Black frustration. But no one can have any doubt about the outcome. It is a matter of passing massive obstacles rather than going back or taking another path.

Why am I writing here about South Africa? As I returned from Johannesburg to the Israel where I had lived for ten years, I could not escape the comparison. My biography forces it on me. In 1963, I had moved from South Africa to England. In the eighteen years I lived there, South Africa appeared as a grotesque moral anomaly. There might be other very bad places in the world, but nowhere else were there the special horrors of legal, institutionalized racism. From the smug contours of English life, it was easy to be morally righteous.

Now, however, I was returning not to England, but to an Israel that had been an occupying military force for twenty years, two of them spent in the brutal suppression of the Palestinian Uprising. I knew that the level of state violence to which Palestinians were exposed — shootings, beatings, deportations, curfews, tear gas, collective punishment, torture, administrative detention — was, person for person, more intense than that suffered by Blacks in South Africa.

Jerusalem, May 1991

Yes, I know that the history is different, the conflict is different, and the solution is different. The movement for social justice in South Africa is aimed (and always has been) at coexistence in a democratic, multiracial society. The "peace movement" here, at best, looks towards an uneasy separation from the "enemy:" the two-state solution. But my existential comparison remains. On the one hand, a wholly closed and rigid society, a pariah state for generations — now forced to open up, to become pragmatic, to enter the international moral community; in deep conflict but knowing that only one direction is possible. On the other hand, a society becoming more closed, locked in fundamentalist delusions, full of doom and with a government and majority of the population profoundly antidemocratic and unwilling to even visualize any pragmatic solution acceptable to the international consensus. The truth is that no one today, Israeli or Palestinian, can make any certain prediction of the future — except that in the absence of a mutually agreed target, things will get worse.

Nearly three years ago I wrote in *Tikkun* (September 1988) about the sense of denial here, the refusal to change, the psychotic way in which most people were shutting out reality. For the vast bulk of the Jewish population, the simple realization that came to South African whites a few years ago has not arrived: that the party is over. This sort of change in consciousness (simply: how people look at Palestinians as human beings) will, of course, follow from a political solution. For this, we will have to wait for another version of the grand political and economic juncture that brought about change in South Africa. In political — as in personal — life, we continue as we are because the price of staying the same is less than the price of changing.

There, on the tip of the African continent, the price for staying the same finally started becoming too high. And this brought about a change of heart. While the political economy of apartheid fell apart, there was a genuine transformation among Afrikaner intellectuals as their moral ground slipped from under them. Here, there is no such crisis — neither economic (as long as the United States signs the checks for absorbing the Soviet and Ethiopian immigration and for policing the Palestinians), nor military nor moral. Israelis are not yet paying any costs for maintaining the occupation or suppressing the Intifada. It has now become obvious that the dependency on the U.S. — some $13 million *a day* in aid — is wholly unconditional on how Israel behaves. A perfect dependency — because it depends on nothing.

As for internal moral ground, this is a society where shame cannot be mobilized. Nothing, not the steady exposures of gross human rights violations, not the current news about hunger in the Gaza Strip, can make enough people angry enough. Indeed, hearts have hardened. The Palestinians' behavior during the Gulf crisis, each brutal knifing in the streets, each "collaborator" killing, removes them further from a shared moral community. The whole society is becoming brutalized. The particularly subtle Israeli form of racism towards "Arabs" has become more pronounced (believe me, those of us who grew up in South Africa can smell this better than most).

So, we wait — either, like Beckett's tramps, doing nothing or else struggling a little. We have little idea what to do. It is natural (though wrong) to complain that we have "tried everything." Increasingly marginalized from our own society by our quixotic adherence to universalistic, rather than particularistic values, we feel besieged. In fact, however, the curious paradox of Israeli society is that despite the overall ideological closure, the formal contours of democracy — for

Israeli Jews, at least — remain intact. We can operate with a freedom unknown to liberals in South Africa twenty years ago.

Under these conditions, the political battles that we can fight lie on the terrain of legitimation: the struggle to define what the social order is and what it should be. As intellectuals, professionals, and academics, we are in the business of generating knowledge and moral meanings. If both our knowledge (what the occupation is doing to the Palestinians and to us) and our moral message (that this is an evil to be ended) are clear, then certain forms of political action should logically follow. Israeli liberals however (the peace movement, democrats, the opposition), are simply not taking the actions which they are still quite free to take and would be appropriate to their cognitive knowledge and moral sense.

I am not trying to be "more radical than thou." I am not talking about taking to the barricades, placing yourself between soldiers and Palestinians, going on hunger strikes, or any other form of resistance which deliberately breaks the law. I understand the barriers to these actions for us all (described well by Daphna Golan in her article in this book). All I want to ask (yes, I know, the question is a little disingenuous) is why people are not acting in the right way — "right" in the logical and moral senses.

Let me list three areas where this question appears.

Finding Some Distance

Way back in the sixties, a political style developed among Western liberals and radicals (though not in Israel, where the "sixties" did not happen) in which concepts like "integrity" and "legitimacy" became important. An ideological discourse emerged — shared by the civil rights, student and antiwar movements, the gay movement, and then, most explicitly, the women's movement — in which the boundaries, between personal and political life became deliberately blurred. This style is now much discredited and indeed many critics of the supposed "failure" of the cultural politics of the sixties blame this for the subsequent political reaction and retreat into the personal. Whatever its actual political effectiveness though, those of us who shared this vision cannot forget it.

In this context, the concern for "integrity" means trying to follow your political ideology and moral sensitivity into your everyday life. If you are against racism you don't tell racist jokes; if, as a man, you "support" feminism, you behave appropriately to women; if you think that a war is immoral, you don't fight it. In a world of impossible contradictions, you at least try to find a little consistency. The concern with "legitimacy" means being careful not to cooperate — however passively — with institutions and practices that give a gloss of acceptability to the unacceptable. You try not to work in or take money from corrupt institutions; you are sensitive about your journal, television station, or university being used to make the immoral into the socially respectable.

Both these concerns call for taking a little distance, for a self-conscious attempt to remember that your very presence — your lack of reaction — may be a form of collusion. By drawing attention to your position, you take the opportunity to remind those in power that they cannot take your cooperation for granted. These are small, symbolic matters: things that most of us, most of the time, pass by without noticing. And your protest might be entirely ineffectual. But, as Foucault has taught us, each tiny "microsystem of power" is simultaneously a point of resistance. This is where we can work: not just by privately thinking oppositional thoughts, but by making a public gesture of disobedience.

Let me give a few examples where not only are these opportunities not taken, but where the liberal Israeli community actually colludes in the unacceptable. The area I know best is academic life. A political science professor appears in his uniform (as an intelligence officer) at an interrogation center in Gaza to "request" the cooperation of Palestinian detainees in his research on attitudes to the Intifada. A Faculty of Law invites the minister of justice to give the speech at the annual graduation ceremony. The universities regularly invite generals and defense ministers to conferences about "national security." The Israeli Society of Criminology invites the minister of police to open its annual conference. The army attorney-general teaches a course in a law school. The Hebrew University each year invites staff who are going on sabbatical to attend a "briefing" by the Foreign Office. In May 1991, the Faculty of Arts at the Hebrew University elects as its dean, Professor Menachem Milson who in 1982 to 1983, as head of the Civil Administration of the Occupied Territories, was responsible for closing down Bir Zeit University and banning books.

And so on. What all these examples have in common is a lack of concern, a refusal to find some distance. Note that I am not arguing against the liberal principle of academic freedom. On the contrary, I believe that in the best of all possible worlds, the university should be a terrain of free inquiry wholly sheltered from political or any other practical considerations. It is precisely because each of these examples is such a shocking violation of this principle, that the integrity and legitimacy of the liberal university is at stake. I am not saying that my university colleagues do not have the "right" to these decisions; of course they do. They invoked the principle of academic freedom — and this is as it should be. I am not questioning the right of the people involved, but their moral judgment. In each case, the decisions were discretionary: they did not have to be made. Why should the minister of the police — responsible only a few months earlier for the Temple Mount massacre — be invited today to a university?

Or take the medical profession. Allegations have been circulating for some time — currently documented in a campaign by the Public Committee Against Torture in Israel and a research report by B'Tselem — of medical involvement in the ill- treatment and possible torture of detainees. Doctors attached to military, police, or prison service detention centers check detainees before, during, and after interrogation. Other doctors in casualty wards of regular Israeli hospitals have treated Palestinian detainees for injuries inflicted during interrogation. Silence about all this is totally prohibited by all codes of medical ethics. No one reports, no one is reported, no one blows the whistle.

Here is another well-publicized case. A pregnant nineteen-year-old Palestinian woman, suspected of a security offense, was taken by prison guards from her cell to the Meir Hospital in Kfar Saba when it looked as if she was about to give birth. Throughout the entire time that she was in labor in the hospital, both her hands were manacled by handcuffs to the sides of her bed. The prison authorities insisted that they had merely acted "according to regulations," but apologized for the "lack of sensitivity" the guards had displayed. The head of the gynecological department said that he couldn't be expected to know of everything that went on in his department. Unlike the prison authorities, he did not even apologize. He has not been disciplined; he has not been expelled from the Israeli Medical Association.

The moral fabric is woven out of countless acts of commission and omission. It is impossible to remain pure or consistent. I am not looking for the private and self-indulgent moral gesture. On the contrary, the worst self-indulgence is exercised by people who see, know, disapprove — and then say nothing. What is needed is to convert the knowledge and moral judgment into some collective, organized, political reaction.

Serving in the Army

All the spheres of social life — the university, the professions, arts, literature, mass media — in which some distance is called for, are utterly insignificant compared with the army. This is too obvious to even argue: no army, no occupation.

By far the most powerful weapon in the struggle against the occupation, is selective refusal to serve in the territories. Whether you choose this weapon or not remains the litmus test of political commitment in Israeli society. This is not just because of the physical dependence on the army to maintain the occupation, but because of the deep interdependence between what is going on in Israeli civic society and in the territories. Concepts like "colonialism," "settlements," and even the word "occupation" itself, mask this dependence. The army is the interface. This is not a conscript army drawn from the underclass, into a Foreign Legion sent from the empire to distant lands. At every level — compulsory military service, symbolic meaning, socialization — the civic and the military intersect. The strongest political and moral force against the occupation thus comes from Yesh Gvul, the support group for soldiers who selectively refuse to serve in the territories.

Much has been written about this subject, both about the movement's "success" (over 150 reservists sent to prison for refusing to serve, perhaps a thousand others quietly allocated to other duties) and "failure" in not becoming a mass movement. In any event, for Peace Now activists to demonstrate against the odd temporary housing on the West Bank or a new settlement of twenty families can have little meaning when the same demonstrators are, day after day, serving in the army which maintains the occupation. And they supply not just the simple soldiers patrolling the alleys of the refugee camps or the *casbah* of Nablus. This is merely the convenient iconography of the occupation, the visible image that can be shown on prime-time television. The occupation is also invisible: the social workers and psychologists who staff the mental health services; the doctors who do their military service in the prisons and detention centers; the lawyers who sit in the military attorney general's office or act as defenders, prosecutors and judges in the military "justice" system. Without these functions, the occupation loses its institutional legitimacy.

The most powerful political weapon, therefore, is not being used. There are of course, rational arguments, which can't be easily dismissed, for refraining from using this weapon. One is that by staying in the army, you can do some good — or at least prevent some bad. If those with moral scruples disobey, then the army would be entirely run by the must unscrupulous. The other argument is that the "nonpolitical" character of the army must be preserved at any cost. If the "Left" refuses, this will create a dangerous precedent by politicizing military policy. So that when the crunch comes — the forced evacuation of settlements — then the Right will feel free to refuse.

These arguments are important, but both rest on an appeal to hypothetical situations, as against the very real evils that are preventable by refusing to serve today. No one can prove that the conscience of isolated liberals working within the system is a more effective moral force than mass refusal — either refusal to serve altogether or to obey an evil order. And the notion that right wing forces are only waiting for the peace movement to act before they make the army into their own political tool is not credible.

But there are other reasons this powerful weapon goes unused. We are talking here not just of rational argument, but a deep taboo. To refuse to serve is to place yourself outside the *Gvul*, outside the boundary of the national consensus. And so the personal price is high.

Waiting for the Americans

My bleak opening sentence about the prospects of ending the occupation was based on a reading of the internal Israeli scene only. As everyone understands — from the far left to the far right — the real source of change lies in the international arena, notably in the nature of United States foreign policy interests. "American pressure" has now become the most banal of political clichés here (even more of a cliché than the "peace process"). Will the indulgent rich uncle — out of a combination of strategic interest, sentimental support for the "only democracy in the Middle East," residual Holocaust guilt, and pressure from the Jewish lobby (choose your theory) — continue to pay the bill, however crazily the niece continues to behave?

This now is the national parlor game. Like Sovietologists used to scrutinize the nuances of every communication from the Kremlin, so every State Department utterance is examined and debated. Did Ms. Tutweiler say that the settlement policy was condemned as "the major" or "a major" or merely a "significant" obstacle to peace? So, the "Left" hope and the Right fear that one day, the sign will come. (Most people couldn't care either way — except for the blocked Jerusalem streets due to yet another visit from Mr. Baker.)

My subject here is not the objective chances of any such external pressure. To assess this, you need the sort of head (which I don't have) that can make sense of U.S. foreign and domestic policy, security interests, electoral considerations, the global power balance...etc. My mere intuition detects no sign that the same U.S. foreign policy which for two decades has so resolutely blocked any just solution for the Palestinians is now about to change. The balance of interests between maintaining a client mercenary state and recognizing Palestinian rights should be obvious. The current Baker circus has proved that there is apparently no limit to U.S. tolerance of Israeli provocation and intransigence.

Nor is my subject here the objective chances that even if pressure comes, the government will respond realistically. To go back to the South African comparison, there indeed as the external pressure increased (economic sanctions, disinvestment, isolation, sport and cultural boycotts), the elite fragmented, the fundamentalists became marginalized, and the pragmatists took control. I simply cannot see this happening here yet. It would be a great mistake to underestimate the power of national-religious ideological commitment. And even if given the choice between two commitments — absorbing the Soviet immigrants or settling the Land of Israel — the present government would choose the settlements, that is, the occupation.

These hypothetical futures, however, are not my subject. I am more concerned (bewildered, rather) by something very strange in the way the "waiting for the Americans" truism appears among Israeli liberal and peace forces. Let us examine it again. This should be a three-part syllogism: number one, "we want the occupation to end;" number two, "the only way it will end is through American pressure." Now, if one and two are correct, surely number three follows: "we are doing everything we can to bring about this American pressure."

But this doesn't follow. These same forces refuse to say anything that even hints of a desire for U.S. pressure, let alone actively requesting this pressure. The slightest mention of United Nations protection, economic sanctions, boycotts, cutting off aid or making aid contingent (as it should be by U.S. law) on Israel's human rights record, is taboo. Any explicit attempt to call for sanctions or even cutting aid, is bitterly resisted. At times I think that this taboo is even deeper than the one against selective army refusal.

I confess that of each of my three examples of the gap between sentiment and action, I find this one the most puzzling. It is easy enough to understand the long historical distrust (shared by all sectors of Israeli society) of outside pressure: the hostility to the United Nations, the lack of trust in the "goyim," the spirit of self-reliance. And it is easy to understand the current right-wing fear of external pressure: this will lead to an international conference, which will lead to negotiations, which will lead to concessions, which will lead.... There is no limit to the Right's hysteria that this process might even begin. (For Tehiya party Member of Knesset Geula Cohen, even a regional conference is a dangerous trap, which she publicly compared with the lines outside the gas chambers at Maidanek concentration camp, where the victims naively believed that they were entering showers.)

But why should members of the organized peace movement who are supposedly in favor of a negotiated settlement and who know that some pressure is needed, buy into any of this hysteria? If they really know that real economic pressure is necessary (though not inevitable), why not give the little bit of encouragement needed to bring this nearer? All they have to do is express mild public support for the quite legitimate idea that aid should be conditional on human rights performance. Or to call on the Jewish community in the U.S. to be more selective about where their money will be sent. Can "Bypass the UJA (United Jewish Appeal)" really be such a dangerous, revolutionary slogan?[1]

Some coherent and rational (although in *my* view incoherent) objections can be found against military refusal. Here, the objections make no sense. The main argument, as I understand it, is that if aid is actually cut, the Right would become more intransigent and all United States influence would be lost. This is to assume, however, that the Right needs a reason to become even more intransigent and that current U.S. influence is benevolent.

Nor — unlike army refusal — is there any real price to be paid for calling for outside pressure. The only price is to be criticized for being "disloyal." The fear is that you will be discredited if you are seen to call on outside intervention or pressure. But the society is already so polarized that the peace forces can hardly be much more marginalized and discredited. Even a group of dovish Knesset members who went on a speaking tour of the United States just after the Gulf War were widely branded as "traitors," "informers," or "self-hating Jews." (Israel must be the only country in the world where people drawing attention to human rights violations are called *informers*.)

I can only conclude that some of this stigma has rubbed off. The inhibition is internal and ideological rather than logical. Somewhere, there lies the notion that although it makes perfect sense to sit quietly and hope that the Americans will move, it is unpatriotic to do anything about this hope. Thoughts do not get translated into appropriate acts.

This gap is, of course, common to all three of my examples — and poses the classic question of political psychology. In Stanley Milgram's famous experiment on obedience, the question was not simply why people obeyed orders (to inflict harm on others), but why did they obey while convinced that what they were doing was wrong. Many protested even while they obeyed, sweating as they pushed the "electric shock" button. As Milgram wrote: "Between thoughts, words, and the critical step of disobeying a malevolent authority lies another ingredient, the capacity for transforming beliefs into actions."

This is the crucial missing ingredient here. Even if people get satisfaction from feeling that they are on the right side (shooting and crying rather than just shooting) it doesn't matter. Milgram again, about his reluctant subjects: "What they failed to realize is that subjective feelings are largely irrelevant to the moral issue at hand so long as they are not transformed into action." His non-laboratory example is relevant: the "intellectual resistance" in occupied Europe, in which people by a twist of thought felt that they had defied the invader.

What has to be explained in Israel today is why good people are too obedient to authority to translate their values into action.

*   *   *   *   *

"Well? What do we do?" asks Vladimir. "Don't do anything. It's safer," replies Estragon. And Vladimir gets the point: "Let's wait and see what he says." So we all find ourselves waiting and seeing. The State Department is the unlikely and ever absent Godot.

But in the meantime, "What do we do?" Few of us really believe — or want to believe — that nothing can be done. So the old mixture: demonstrations, petitions, human rights work, the occasional gesture of defiance, the endless whining (of which this article is an example) about why others are not doing more. I do not want to sound righteous or intolerant about forms of political commitment other than those I favor. There are thousands of committed people in the mainstream peace movement, in the parliamentary opposition, working in different ways that might turn out more effective. My point rather is that both styles — moral protest and responsible opposition — seem to have reached their active peak. New people are not being drawn into the struggle. As the Intifada becomes routinized — a mere continuation of the occupation and not the dramatic break it was — and the full anticlimax of the Gulf War is absorbed, so mobilization becomes more difficult. How can we expect more activism when the Palestinians themselves are driven back to waiting and seeing?

The deterioration in the post-Gulf War period cannot be observed in the usual visible dramas of violence. The latent message to the Palestinians behind the current wave of "liberalization" in the Occupied Territories — easing the searches on the bridges from Jordan, making noises about re-opening the universities, talking about improvements in the "quality of life" — is not that these are temporary measures pending a settlement, but that "this is all you're going to get." Together with Sharon's building policy, aimed at eroding what was left of the Green Line, there is an increasing Israeli self-confidence and sense of permanence. We are here to stay; and now we know for sure, that the only force in the world capable of imposing a solution, the United States, has no intention of doing so.

I remain an optimist, however, in the sense that Beckett is. It is precisely because the landscape is so bleak, the prospects of success so poor, that we resume the struggle. It has never seemed to me a very good idea to look for success, effects, or results, nor to join struggles that will be won anyway. We oppose the occupation because we have to. In the meantime, things do change: South Africa, East Germany, even Albania. How far behind can we be?

Note

1. The United Jewish Appeal is a national Jewish organization founded in 1939 as a channel for American Jewish and other philanthropic, welfare, and political monetary assistance to Israel.

About the
Resource Center for Nonviolence

The Resource Center for Nonviolence in Santa Cruz, California, offers a wide-ranging educational program in the history, theory, methodology, and current practice of nonviolence as a force for personal and social change.

Beginning with a reverence for all life, nonviolence is a practical and vital approach to life's situations, from personal, everyday events to global conflicts. While nonviolence acts as a social force bonding people in cooperation, it also forges non-cooperation with, and resistance to, violent and oppressive social relations. Nonviolence attempts to engage those in conflict in cooperative discovery of solutions that meet the needs of all.

Nonviolence is rooted in the conviction that a peaceful and just society cannot be created by violent or unjust methods. Violence creates new forms of oppression and begets further violence. Instead stategies for change must employ concerted political action aimed at both changing institutions and changing attitudes.

The Resource Center provides settings for both structured and informal discussion and learning in many dimensions of nonviolence, including an internship program of a month or longer, weekend workshops, two-week nonviolence trainings for organizers, study groups and summer workcamps. The staff is available to speak and to lead discussions or workshops. Individuals especially knowledgeable or with extraordinary experiences in nonviolence are occasionally invited to Santa Cruz as residents. The Center also has a large library on Gandhi and nonviolence, a literature service and bookstore, and a periodic newsletter.

APPENDIX:
Israeli Organizations Working for Peace and Justice

Protest

Ad Kan (This Far...)
Department of Sociology, Tel Aviv University
Tel: (3)749-639 (h)
Contact Person: Professor Moshe Shokeid
  Tel Aviv University faculty group formed in early 1988 to organize teach-ins, symposia, and demonstrations against the occupation and related policies. Maintains contact with Palestinian academics and lawyers in the territories.

Committee of Israeli and Palestinian Artists Against the Occupation
P.O. Box 6370, Haifa
  Among other things, has a letter-writing campaign to end judicial proceedings against Shafik Habib, a Palestinian-Israeli poet who made history as the first Israeli to be arrested for the contents of a book of poems.

Drawn with permission from "Palestine and The Other Israel," Alternative Directory of progressive groups and institutions in Israel and the Occupied Territories, published by the Alternative Information Center, compiled by Ingrid Gassner and Maxine Nunn.

(Note: this listing does not include Palestinian groups in the occupied West Bank, but does include Israeli sponsored organizations in East Jerusalem.)

Kav Adom—Red Line/Jews and Arabs Against the Occupation
   P.O. Box 207, Nahariya
   Tel: (4)854-691
   Contact Person: Anneke Kelner, Kibbutz Shomrat, Western Galilee
      Western Galilee-based, began with four-day march from the northwest
      corner of Israel to Jerusalem. Visits West Bank villages with food,
      clothing, and medical aid; and public appearances at kibbutzim,
      villages, and schools. Espouses negotiations with PLO and two-state
      solution. Works in conjunction with the Council of Heads of Arab Local
      Authorities.

Peace Now
   42 Montefiore St., P.O. Box 6733, Tel Aviv 61066
   Tel: (3)293-064 Fax: (3)203-286

   6 Lloyd George St., P.O. Box 8159, Jerusalem91081
   Tel: (2)664-716 Fax: (2)631-750
   Contact Persons: Janet Aviad, Ronny Kaufman

Americans for Peace Now
   27 W. 20th Street 9th floor
   New York, NY 10011
   Tel: (212) 645-6262
   Contact Person: Jonathan Jacoby
      Besides its well-publicized mass rallies and "peace days," in October
      1991 PN filed a suit against the government challenging the legality of
      the settlements. Branches have been researching and organizing smaller
      demonstrations against new settlements; solidarity visits (e.g., to the
      village of Nahalin on the first anniversary of the massacre there).

Human and Civil Rights

Association for Civil Rights in Israel (ACRI)
   Nat'l Hdqtrs: P.O. Box 8273, Jerusalem 91082
   Contact person: President: Justice Shimon Agranot
   Vice President: Haim Podok
   Tel: Jerusalem: (2)638-385 or 617-727 Fax: (2)630-487
   Tel Aviv: (3)663-162/3
   Haifa: (4)348-217
   Beersheva: (57)39094
      Advocacy for civil rights in Israel and the Occupied Territories. Recent
      achievements include pressing successfully for forty-eight hours' notice
      of house demolitions, to enable removal of goods and possibility of High
      Court appeal. Haifa and Beersheva branches do solidarity and
      fact-finding visits to the northern West Bank and Gaza Strip,
      respectively; Beersheva group also does weekly court watching in Gaza.

Association of Israeli & Palestinian Physicians for Human Rights
P.O. Box 10235, Tel Aviv 61101
9 Gordon St., Tel Aviv 63458
Contact Person: Dr. Ruhama Marton
Tel: (3)524-1828

Israeli and Palestinian (from the Occupied Territories) physicians working together to improve the medical conditions in the Occupied Territories, protect Palestinian medical personnel from harassment, build clinics, etc. Brought medicines to territories during wartime curfew, Israeli members have treated patients at Palestinian clinics. Produces bimonthly and annual reports.

B'Tselem—Israeli Information Center for Human Rights in the Occupied Territories
18 Keren Hayesod, Jerusalem 92149
Contact person: Daphna Golan, Research Director
Tel: (2)667-271/4

Maintains daily contact with Palestinian and Israeli information sources; publishes monthly and special-topic (Hebrew and English) reports widely quoted in Israeli press, including on human rights in the Occupied Territories during the Gulf crisis, torture during Security Services (Shabak) interrogation of Palestinian detainees. Shared 1990 Carter-Menil Human Rights Award (with Al Haq). Assisted in its work by a lobby of ten Knesset members from various parties.

Hamoked—Hotline/Center for the Defense of the Individual
2 Abu Obeidah St., East Jerusalem
Contact person: Dalia Kerstein
Tel: (2)283-555

Independent center assisting Palestinian victims of violence (e.g., by police, army, settlers etc.) and furnishing information to ACRI. Donations pay legal fees, publish quarterly newsletter, annual reports (English and Hebrew).

Public Committee Against Torture in Israel
P.O. Box 8588, Jerusalem 91083
Tel: (2)630-073
Contact Person: Stanley Cohen

Founded in 1990 by lawyers, psychiatrists, and other professionals; fights the use of torture as a means of interrogation by uncovering and publicizing facts to press for its abolition. Worked with B'Tselem on report of torture during interrogation of Palestinian political prisoners.

Women

Isha l'Isha—Haifa Women's Center
88 Arlozorov St., Haifa
Tel: (4)664-949
> Extensive program of feminist and general women's support activities; sponsors activities devoted to Palestinian-Jewish women's dialogue, cultural exchange, and feminist analysis.

Reshet—Women's Network for the Advancement of Peace
P.O. Box 9668, Jerusalem 91090
Tel: (2)410-002
Contact Person: Kochi Gamliely
> Grew out of Brussels meetings of Israeli and Palestinian women (1989). Attempts to bring broad political spectrum of Israeli women—mainly mainstream—into contact with leaders and grassroots of Palestinian Women's Committees, through visits to projects in West Bank and Gaza, and inviting Palestinian women to speak with women's groups in Israel.

Shani—Israeli Women Against the Occupation
P.O. Box 9091, Jerusalem 91090
Tel: (2)619-870
Contact Person: Ruth Cohen
> Founded in 1988, makes solidarity visits to Palestinian camps and villages, brings Palestinian women to speak to audiences of Israeli women, conducts discussion and study groups, prepared booklet of questions/answers aimed at Israelis with doubts about feasibility of two- state solution and negotiation with the PLO (English and Hebrew).

Tandi—Movement of Democratic Women in Israel
P.O. Box 29501, Tel Aviv
Tel: (3)292-792 or (3)695-4020
Contact Person: Yafa Gavish
> Founded in 1948, local branch of the World Federation of Democratic Women; Jewish and Palestinian Israeli women working together for peace and equal rights for women and children.

Women and Peace Movement (aka Women and Peace Coalition)
P.O. Box 61128, Jerusalem 91060
Tel: (2)240-188 (h)
Contact Person: Yvonne Deutsch
> Participants from Palestinian Israeli, Jewish, and mixed women's organizations working together with "independent" women to end the occupation and other forms of oppression. Sponsors annual Women's Peace Conference, and other topical conferences and marches.

Women in Black
P.O. Box 61128, Jerusalem 91060
Tel: (2)255-984
Contact: Chaya Shalom

P.O. Box 65190, Tel Aviv 61651
Tel: (3)523-8653
Contact: Dita Bitterman

P.O. Box 3610, Haifa
Tel: (4)664-949
Contact: Hannah Safran
Women's silent vigil each Friday afternoon 1:00 to 2:00 P.M., in over thirty locations throughout Israel (and several in Europe and North America), demanding an end to the occupation. Started within weeks of the outbreak of the Intifada (1987). Gathers in Jerusalem in "France Square" beside the Kings Hotel, and in Tel Aviv, near the Northern Train Station.

Women's Organization for Women Political Prisoners (WOFPP)
P.O. Box 8537, Jerusalem 91083
Tel: (2)241-159
Contact: Tikva Parnass

P.O. Box 31811, Tel Aviv 61381
Tel: (3)227-124 Fax: (3)528-6050
Contact: Chava Keller or Chaya Weisgal-Amir
Assists Palestinian women prisoners in finding lawyers, covering legal expenses, etc.; pursues information for prisoners' families, bring clothes and other necessities to prison, tracks location and/or transfer of prisoners, visits after release, publicizes conditions. Semiannual report. Jerusalem and Tel Aviv groups function separately. Tel Aviv group publishes newsletter in Hebrew, English, or Spanish.

Palestinian Israeli

Association of the 40
Hantki 9, Haifa
Tel: (4)257-474 Fax: (4) 348-878
Defending and publicizing the plight of over one hundred (originally forty) Arab villages in the Galilee, "unrecognized" by the Israeli government, and therefore subject to arbitrary house demolition and lack basic infrastructural support.

Association for the Support and Defense of Bedouin Rights
P.O. Box 5212, Hativat Hanegev St., Beersheva
Tel: (57)31-687 (o); (8)229-401 (h)
Contact: Nuri El-Okbi
Organization of Bedouin with participation of Jewish supporters, defending Bedouin rights (e.g., land) in the Negev, and working to raise cultural, social, health, educational, and housing standards.

Committee for the Defense of Arab Lands

Kufr Yasif

Tel: (4)962-360; (4)666-648

Contacts: Rev. Shehadeh Shehadeh (Director); Saliba Khamis (Secretary)
Struggles against further confiscation of Arab lands in Israel.

Druze Initiative Committee

Yarka Village, 24967

Tel: (4)961-393

Contact: Jamal Muadi
Calls for an end to conscription of Israel's Druze (a sect of Islam) citizens,
and defends imprisoned Druze military refusers. Makes solidarity visits
to the Occupied Territories.

Al Raabitah—League of Jaffa Arabs

P.O. Box 41087, Jaffa 68171

73 Yeffet St., Jaffa

Tel: (3)812-290; (3)821-351 (h)

Contact: Nahleh Shaker
Organizes annual International Volunteer Work Camps, where Israeli
Jews and Arabs and (mostly) Europeans join local residents in this effort
at "constructive protest," e.g., they protested the municipality's neglect
of the Jaffa Arab community by constructing roads, improving play and
kindergarten facilities, cleaning streets, etc. Lobbies for the rights of
Jaffa's Arab community.

Militarism and War Resistance

Hashministim—High School Group

P.O. Box 33847, Tel Aviv 61338
Young people who in their final year of high school informed the
minister of defense of their unwillingness to serve in the Occupied
Territories. Active since 1989, organizing meetings for youth, holding
protests, collecting signatures to send to the Defense Ministry, and
supporting those currently in prison for refusal.

International Movement of Conscientious Objectors

P.O Box 28058, Tel Aviv-Jaffa 61280

Tel: (3)372-252

Contact: Toma Shik
Founded in 1945, this pacifist organization offers counseling and other
support to Israelis seeking exemption from military service. Local
section of War Resisters International.

Yesh Gvul ("There is a Border/Limit")
P.O. Box 6953, Jerusalem 91068
Tel: (2)250-271
Contact: Ishai Menuchin

Tel Aviv: (3)513-1472

Friends of Yesh Gvul
1678 Shattuck Ave., P.O.B. 6
Berkeley, CA 94709

> Begun during the Lebanon War, now has petition signed by some 600 reservists who refused to "take part in suppressing the uprising in the territories." To date, some 200 have been imprisoned; others refused service, but were reassigned within the Green Line. Offers moral support for selective refusers and potential refusers, holds public forums, demonstrations of solidarity with imprisoned refusers and more. Published soldier's pocket handbook to "know your rights."

Coexistence

Israeli Council for Israeli-Palestinian Peace (ICIPP)
P.O. Box 956, Tel Aviv 61008
Tel: (3)556-5804
Contact: Adam Keller

> First Israeli Zionist organization to meet with PLO (1976), advocates negotiations with the PLO and a two-state solution. Organizes non-academic forums and public statements. Publishes *The Other Israel* (see publications below).

Re'ut—Friendship
Arara Village
Tel: (6)351-384
Contact: Mohammed Milhem (Arabic or Hebrew)

Tel Aviv: Mordechai Yarkoni (3)338-249 or Omaima (3)541-5438 (English, Arabic, or Hebrew)

> Palestinian-Jewish youth movement undertaking to promote respect, understanding, and defense of civil rights of all Israeli citizens.

Shutafut/Partnership
P.O. Box 9577, Haifa 31095
Tel: (4)641-805
Contact: Nabila Espanioli

> Israeli Jews and Palestinians; activities include bringing food to children in Gaza Strip refugee camps, solidarity visits, club for Palestinian and Jewish children of Haifa. Plays a central role in broad coalition of peace groups in Haifa area.

Oriental Jews

Committee for Israeli-Palestinian Dialogue
P.O. Box 20373, Tel Aviv 61204
Tel: (3)752-0212 (h); (3)266-244
Contact: Latif Dori
> Believing that Oriental Israelis can serve as a bridge between the Arab world and Israeli society, promotes Israeli-Palestinian dialogue; participated in group of Israelis that met with PLO representatives in Hungary in 1987.

Hamizrach el Hashalom—East for Peace
P.O.Box 29094 Jerusalem
Tel: (2)719-710
Contact: Shlomo Elbaz
> Founded in 1982 to challenge the stereotype of the Oriental Jew as a warlike hater of Arabs. Works for social equality between Eastern and Western Israelis, and for Israel's integration into the Middle East via recognition of its inherent by Eastern nature.

Neighborhood Coalition for Social Justice and Peace
House 22, Moshav Beit Za'it, 90815
Tel: (2)340-188
Contact: David Ish Shalom
> Neighborhood activists very active in issues of social justice for Orientals and interdependence with the struggle for a negotiated peace with the Palestinians. Conducted a hunger strike at 1988 government-forming process, during which they visited the (largely Oriental) Shas Party spiritual leader, Rabbi Ovadia Yosef, calling upon him to be consistent with his earlier statements extolling peace as the highest value, and to withdraw his support from the Likud "war government."

Tidua (Alternative Popular Institute—"Conscientization")
Nahalat Binyamin 33A, Tel Aviv
Tel: (3)624-849
Contact: Elana Sugbecker
> Founded in 1987, main program is adult courses on social and political issues. Operating on a shoe-string budget, five such courses have been given to date. Also organizes an Oriental Women's Group, who have met monthly since 1990, discussing such topics as feminism and the situation of the Oriental woman.

Yated ("Tent Stake")
P.O. Box 559, Kiryat Ata 28000
Tel: (4)448-182 Fax: (4)441-112
Contact: David Hammou
> Founded in the late seventies to fight inequality, promote Mizrachi social position, and contribute to peace with the Arab environment. Publishes *Iton Aher* (Hebrew only), dedicated to showing Israel's "other face," the one that does not appear in the established media.

Religious Jews

Oz veShalom/Netivot Shalom
P.O. Box 4433, Jerusalem 91043

Tel: (2)610-712 (o)

Contact: Yehezkel Landau
> Religious peace activists working since 1975 for a political solution. Support division of the land, despite Orthodox beliefs in biblical claims. Public forums, occasional demonstrations, newsletter available in English.

Rabbis for Human Rights (formerly Rabbinic Human Rights Watch)
P.O. Box 32225, Jerusalem

Tel: (2)255-175 Fax: (2)245-591

Contacts: Rabbi David Forman, Rabbi Ehud Bandel
> Orthodox, Conservative, Reform, and Reconstructionist rabbis speak out against human rights abuses against Palestinians, making condolence visits to victims of settler violence, countering inaccurate information with personal witness testimony.

Clergy for Peace
P.O. Box 8343, Jerusalem 91083

Tel: (2)630-073

Contact: Rabbi Jeremy Milgrom
> Muslim, Christian, and Jewish clergy engaging in dialogue and other activities to promote mutual understanding.

Miscellaneous Specialized Groups

Council for Peace and Security
56 Ein Kerem D, Jerusalem

Contact: Moshe Amirav, Director
> Generals and other high-ranking reserve and retired officers publically taking the position that the occupation is destructive to Israeli security.

Imut—Israeli Mental Health Workers for the Promotion of Peace
P.O. Box 23864, Jerusalem

Tel: (2)722-758

Contact: Dr. Shafiq Masalha
> Israelis and Palestinians (mostly but not exclusively Israeli citizens) working together against the occupation; conferences on subjects such as Psychological Barriers to Peace.

Parents Against Moral Erosion
19 Kfar Etzion, Jerusalem
Tel: (2)732-936 or (2)733-831 (Tamar)
Contact: Hillel Bardin
> Published December 1989 ad signed by over four hundred parents of sons and daughters serving or soon to serve in the IDF, concerned for "their humanity and their moral and mental strength." Decrying the placement of young soldiers in impossible situations, they call for immediate negotiations for peace.

The 21st Year
P.O. Box 24099, Jerusalem
Tel: (2)724-619
Contact: Hanan Hever
> Mainly educators and professionals in other social disciplines, founded in twenty-first year of occupation, engaging mostly in educational activities.

Project-Oriented Groups

Committee for a Change in the Taxation Policy in Gaza
Kibbutz Shefayim
Tel: (52)523-261
Contact: Amos Gvirtz

c/o Shatil, 33 Ramban St., Jerusalem
Tel: (2)634-079
Contact: Emily Silverman
> Relatively new, broad group working in coordination with Palestinian individuals and Gaza professional unions to raise money for school supplies, raise Israeli consciousness of the existence and causes of financial hardship in Gaza, and to press for a more rational taxation policy.

Committee for the Defense of Children Under Occupation
P.O. Box 44984, Haifa 31448
Tel: (4)521-134 (Haifa) and (6)503-688 (tel/fax in Jenin)
Contact: Arna Mer
> Along with its spin-off, "Care and Study," lobbies for end of curfew and re-opening of schools, weekly visits to various towns in the Occupied Territories, especially the West Bank town of Jenin and a neighboring refugee camp "with learning materials and instruments for self-expression;" established a library and game room for children at the camp.

Israel/Palestine Center for Research and Information (IPCRI)
P.O. Box 51358, Jerusalem
Tel: (2)285-210 Fax: (2)289-094
Contact: Gershon Baskin

The Friends of IPCRI
P.O. Box 1120, Long Beach, NY 11565
Tel/fax: (516)431-1909
> Public policy and development think tank investigating problems that will confront Israel and the future state of Palestine in coexistence. Israeli-Palestinian teams research economic aspects of peace agreement, water resources, future of Jerusalem, refugee resettlement, links between Gaza and the West Bank, and more. Documents in English, Hebrew, and Arabic.

Rapproachement—Center for Dialogue and Understanding
3 Avigail St., Jerusalem 93551
Tel: (2)732- 828
Contact: Judith Green or Veronica Cohen (2)713-067
> Jerusalem-Beit Sahour Dialogue Group, going for over three years, now has its own building in Beit Sahour (West Bank) where both sides attempt to understand each other's goals, needs, concerns, and overcome stereotypes, prejudices, and fears. Panel discussions, lectures, and workshops, cultural and sporting events are also held.

Testimonies
Shivtei Yisrael 14b, Herzlia 46500
Tel: (52)501-225
Contact: Rela Mazali
> Group working on a documentary film of Israeli soldiers' testimonies on service in the Occupied Territories during the Intifada.

English Language Publications and Related Services

Alternative Information Center (AIC)
P.O. Box 24278, Jerusalem
Tel: (2)241-159 Fax: (2)253-151
Contacts: Michel Warschawski, Tikva Parnass, Maxine Nunn
> Publishes *News From Within*, on situation in Occupied Territories, and weekly bulletin of translations from the Hebrew press with analytical commentary. Cooperates with demonstrations and solidarity visits; good relations with Palestinians in Israel and in the Occupied Territories.

Derech Hanitzotz/Tariq Isharara ("Way of the Spark")
P.O. Box 1575, Jerusalem
Tel: (2)255-382 Fax: (2)251-614
Contact: Roni Ben-Efrat; Michal Schwartz
> News collective publishes *Challenge* (*Etgar* in Hebrew), bimonthly newsmagazine about the left peace movement, and monthly "Newsletter on Freedom of the Press." Maintains a Fund for Freedom of the Press.

International Center for Peace in the Middle East
P.O. Box 29335, Tel Aviv, 61292

Tel: (3)660-337 Fax: (3)660-340

Contact: Haggith Gor Ziv

> Organizes conferences in Israel and abroad, for Israelis, Palestinians and others; works to influence Knesset members and other influential Israelis towards recognition of Palestinian political rights. The ICPME project, Jewish-Arab Council for Peace Education, prepares materials on peace and democracy education in Hebrew and Arabic, and organizes seminars for teachers, principals, and students. Also publishes *Israel Press Briefs*, excerpts from the Hebrew, Arabic, and English Israeli press.

New Israel Fund
P.O. Box 4156, 33 Ramban, Jerusalem 91041

Tel: (2)634-830

> Major funder of democracy-strengthening organizations in Israel, supports activities for: human rights, religious freedom, women's issues, Jewish-Arab cooperation, and social justice.

New Outlook
9 Gordon St., Tel Aviv 63458

Tel: (3)236-496

Contact: Chaim Shur, Editor

Friends of New Outlook
150 5th Ave., Suite 911, New York, NY 10011

> Opinion and analysis, interviews, and stories from Zionist Left (mainly Mapam, Ratz, Progressive List for Peace), with significant Palestinian input.

The Other Israel
P.O. Box 956, Tel Aviv

Tel/Fax: (3)556-5804

Contact: Adam Keller, Beate Keizer

> Newsletter of the Israeli Council for Israeli-Palestinian Peace; up-to-date information on peace and protest movement with analytical commentary.